IRAN, SAUDI ARABIA AND THE GULF

Iran, Saudi Arabia and the Gulf

Power Politics in Transition 1968–1971

Faisal bin Salman al-Saud

Published in 2003 by I.B. Tauris & Co Ltd
6 Salem Road, London W2 4BU
175 Fifth Avenue, New York NY 10010
www.ibtauris.com

In the United States of America and Canada distributed by
Palgrave Macmillan a division of St. Martin's Press
175 Fifth Avenue, New York NY 10010

Copyright © 2003 Faisal bin Salman al-Saud

The right of Faisal bin Salman al-Saud to be identified as the author of this work has been asserted by the author in accordance with the Copyright, Designs and Patent Act 1988.

All rights reserved. Except for brief quotations in a review, this book, or any part thereof, may not be reproduced, stored in or introduced into a retrieval system, or transmitted, in any form or by any means, electronic, mechanical, photocopying, recording or otherwise, without the prior written permission of the publisher.

ISBN 1 86064 881 9

A full CIP record for this book is available from the British Library
A full CIP record is available from the Library of Congress

Library of Congress Catalog Card Number: available

Typeset in Minion by Hepton Books, Oxford
Printed and bound in Great Britain by MPG Books, Bodmin.

Contents

List of Maps and Tables		vi
Preface		vii
Acknowledgements		xii
1	The Historical Setting	1
2	The 16 January Decision: Britain, the United States and Iran	10
3	From Gunboat Diplomacy to Compromise	29
4	The Nixon Doctrine: Iran and the Gulf	57
5	The Insoluble Disputes	78
6	The Final Year	106
7	Epilogue	125
Notes		130
Bibliography		168
Index		174

List of Maps and Tables

Maps

Map 1	The 1968 Final Offshore Boundary Line Agreed Between Saudi Arabia and Iran	43
Map 2	The Strait of Hormuz	82
Map 3	Abu Musa: 1971 Administrative Line Dividing the Northern (Iranian) and Southern (Sharjah) Sectors	118

Tables

Table 1	Iran, Iraq and Saudi Arabia: Military Manpower	73
Table 2	The Iranian Defence Budget, 1968–1972	74
Table 3	Iranian Defence Expenditure as a Percentage of GNP	74
Table 4	Arms Transfer Agreements and Deliveries under the Foreign Military Sales Programme	75

Preface

Historians often look for events which provide the punctuation marks of history. It can be argued that the British government's decision in 1968 to withdraw forces from the Gulf by 1971 was a turning point of this kind. For reasons of Imperial strategic interest the Gulf was one of the first areas Britain controlled in the Middle East; for domestic political and economic reasons it was the last from which Britain was to depart. The long history of British presence guaranteed the Gulf a prolonged stability unmatched elsewhere in the Middle East, and delayed the rise of historical, political and territorial disputes among countries on both sides of the waterway. At the same time it delayed the development of the small Arab emirates into independent political entities.

The Pax Britannica collapsed in 1968; in the space of four years a viable state had to be carved out of scattered emirates along the Arab coast and borders defined; regional players had to find rules of common coexistence; and the nature of external-regional relations had to be redefined. For the first time in modern history the Gulf was to become an autonomous sub-region in international politics. The manner in which these issues were resolved continues to be, in some cases, a source of instabilities and conflict to the present day.

In the Gulf there was no world power waiting to succeed Britain. The United States was preoccupied with the Vietnam war, and the Soviet Union made no serious attempt to expand its influence in the region beyond Iraq and South Yemen. The USSR took account of the interests of its oil-producing allies, especially Iraq, in maintaining their trade with the West, and America's sensitivity to the potential disruption of energy supplies. Hence, it developed a cautious and largely non-provocative policy aimed at developing long-term economic and political gains in the Gulf region.[1] As a result, Gulf politics 'went local' and reflected the regional balance of power, with Iran as the dominant player.

Existing literature on the subject tends to focus on the role played by external powers, mainly Britain, and treats the period 1968–1971 as the final episode of the British Empire in the Middle East.[2] Works looking at the period from the local powers' perspective remain relatively scarce.[3] The fact is, however, that at a time when British power was in decline the superpowers never established unquestioned dominance or control over the region.[4] In such circumstances, as this book argues, a better understanding of the new Gulf order can be achieved by emphasising local concerns and the degree to which regional powers influenced external powers' Gulf policy in those formative years.

The regional balance of power in the late 1960s and early 1970s calls for a focus on Iran's role. Iran was by far the largest Gulf state. By the late 1960s it had a population of around 26 million, nearly 17 million more than the second largest state, Iraq. From the mid-1960s it had engaged in an extensive military build-up which exceeded those of its nearest regional rivals, Iraq and Saudi Arabia. Iran also had a rapidly growing economy supported from the early 1970s by increasing oil prices. In other words, Iran was, of all the local powers, in the best position to convert its national resources into strong political influence in the region.

Two unique situations developed as a result: first Iran, which since its re-emergence as a centralised state under the Safavids had been surrounded by imperial powers (Russia, the Ottoman Empire and Britain), or by states with substantial territory (Afghanistan and Iraq), for the first time in 1968 had neighbouring countries much smaller in size and possessing a great deal less power. Second, with its increasing military and economic capabilities, Iran was able to look for a security role beyond its territorial boundaries.

This new configuration poses two interrelated questions: first how did Iran handle its regional relations given that it had little experience in direct dealing with lower Gulf Arabs apart from Saudi Arabia? Second, how did Iran influence efforts to reorder the Gulf's political landscape?

From these principle questions this book seeks to clarify how Iran's Gulf policy was conducted and the diplomatic tools used to achieve policy goals, taking into consideration Iran's own interests, the regional environment, and interaction with the international system. It was often said by Iranian officials that Iran's interest in the Gulf was in playing a 'leading role'. The term 'leading role' is elastic and spelt out can mean any of the following: a favourable settlement of territorial disputes, taking over military defence duties, playing a leading diplomatic role, or strongly influencing oil politics.

Thus, Iranian aims will be viewed in the context of an interplay between its ambitions and the regional-international environments. At the regional level Iran was entering unknown political terrain as the Shah's government was unsure of Arab reaction to its Gulf policy. At the international level it is argued here that the US had less influence on Iran than is often believed; rather, Iran applied its traditional policy of playing one world power against the other. In the past such policy was chosen to maximise Iran's territorial integrity. This time the aim was to win support for a long-awaited regional role.

The book begins when the long-standing British order starts to collapse in the second half of the 1960s. Chapter I discusses the factors which led to the British decision to withdraw its forces from east of Suez by 1971 and the international setting at the time of the decision. It stresses the impact of the domestic political and economic factors which changed Britain's international position under Wilson's Labour government. This chapter also pays attention to the American position and the difficulties the Lyndon B. Johnson administration faced in dealing with rising international challenges during the Vietnam war, as a consequence of which the US pressed Britain to maintain its Gulf position and refused to take over its role as guardian of the Gulf. The final section deals with the Iranian position, which changed as a result of three trends: Iran's growing national power; the decline of British power; and America's decision not to succeed Britain.

Chapter 2 focuses on the Iranian reaction to proposals for the future of the Gulf during the first year of British withdrawal. Although Iran had interests in the Gulf the main theme of this chapter is that in 1968 Iran did not have a policy in place to protect those interests. The Iranian government had very little experience in dealing directly with the Gulf Arab rulers, and the Arab reaction to its claims in the Gulf was not fully anticipated. Iran began by taking a hard stance on its immediate territorial claims, mainly Bahrain, and strongly opposed the formation of the proposed Federation of Arab Emirates. However, it gradually modified its position and reached an accommodation with Saudi Arabia, which led to bilateral territorial settlements with the Saudi Kingdom known as the Continental-Shelf Agreement. The historical claim to Bahrain was dropped in January 1969. Long-term questions over regional co-operation and the Iranian claim to the Hormuz islands were left unanswered.

Chapter 3 takes the emphasis to the international level with the advent of the Nixon administration in January 1969. With regard to the Gulf the most significant development of the Nixon years was the announcement of the Nixon doctrine. Its practical implementation in the Gulf, in the form of the 'twin-pillar policy', took the region to the centre of US global strategy. This chapter traces the origins of the twin-pillar policy in the last year of the Johnson presidency, and attempts to describe the considerations which led the Nixon administration to adopt a position strongly in favour of a rapid increase in US arms sales to Iran and an enlargement of Iran's military capability.

Chapter 4 brings the discussion back to the regional level, particularly regional disputes, and takes into consideration the impact of US policy on Iranian behaviour. After Iran dropped its claim to Bahrain, its policy in the Gulf can be analysed by looking at the conflict over the sovereignty of the three Hormuz islands – Greater Tunb, Lesser Tunb and Abu Musa. The focus will be on Iranian policy toward the Arab side and on negotiations with the British government.

Chapter 5, the final chapter, focuses on Iran's decision to occupy the three islands by force a day prior to the formal British withdrawal from the Gulf. The emphasis will be on Iran's diplomatic manoeuvres in preparation for the decision and on assessing its alternative policy options, bearing in mind that at least three factors were working in Iran's favour: Britain was quickly running out of time to broker a settlement and was gradually turning to Iran; Iran-US relations had never been warmer in recent times; consequently the Gulf Arab position was weakened. The result was little opposition from Britain and the US to Iranian troops landing on the three islands, although some Arab states made futile attempts to reverse the Iranian decision.

The subject matter of this study has lead me to focus on sources related to the policy orientations of official decision-makers. The nature of government in Iran during the period left little room for non-governmental institutions to play a significant role in foreign policy-making. Efforts to find a significant role for institutions such as political parties, pressure groups, the media and the bureaucracy proved fruitless.[5] Foreign policy-making was largely centralised in the hands of the Shah and his close associates.

At the time research for this book was completed, sources for the period in Western archives were relatively scarce. Many US government documents are available up to the end of the Johnson presidency, while the Nixon administration documents are mostly classified material. The 30-year declassification rule for

British archives meant that although British government documents were useful in understanding the years leading to the British decision to withdraw, they were not available to me while writing was in progress. However, before taking the book to press I was able to consult Public Record Office documents to the end of 1971. Many of the relevent records, as it emerged, are still closed and those that have been made available do not add substantially to the material already assembled. Where they have thrown additional light on the events of the period I have amended my text and notes.

Declassification rules do not exist for official archives in Iran and other states in the region so the only government documents available to scholars are those made public at the time. A notable exception has been the archives of the Royal Court of Saudi Arabia and the Government of Ras al-Khaimah where I was able to obtain permission to conduct my research.

The limitations of archival sources were surmounted by the fact that many individuals involved in policy making at the time were available for interviews including ex-Iranian government officials now living abroad, former US and British officials, as well as players from the Arab side of the Gulf.

Other useful sources are published personal memoirs and private papers such as Asadollah Alam's *The Shah and I*, and unpublished writings accessible to this author such as Sir Denis Wright's memoirs and his collection of private papers. These sources are supported by public statements made in speeches and journals; attention to the ideas expressed in the semi-official Iranian press of the time has also helped to clarify the Iranian official line of thinking.

Acknowledgements

Over a decade ago, as a final year undergraduate student, I was privileged to meet the late Albert Hourani who encouraged me to continue my studies at Oxford and gave me his wise advice on the various ideas I had for a research project.

That is how this book began its life. I owe a heartfelt debt of gratitude to the many scholars, colleagues and friends who helped me at different stages of my research and writing. Particular thanks go to Avi Shlaim, my first academic supervisor at St Antony's College and later my college supervisor; to Reza Sheikholeslami who supervised my D.Phil; and to Shahram Chubin who read the whole of the draft and provided me with a detailed and indispensable commentary. Paul Dresch, Mamoun Fandy, Gregory Gause and Paul Schofield all read and gave me invaluable help with various parts of the work.

I would also like to thank the statesmen, diplomats, and other eminent figures, all named in the bibliography, who spent many hours patiently answering my questions about the events and personalities of the time. Without them this book could never have been written. Sir Dennis Wright was especially generous with his time, his hospitality and his knowledge of diplomacy in the region during the late 1960s and early 1970s. Sir Dennis allowed me to read and use material from his unpublished memoir, and when my book was complete he went through the whole text with a practised eye, saving me from a number of embarrassing errors.

I should like to place on record my admiration for the staff of the Lyndon B.

Johnson Library who offer an exceptional welcome and superb facilities to scholars and students who use their archive.

The finished thesis was read by Patrick Seale who encouraged me to turn it into a book and provided advice on the intellectual and practical steps that I should take towards publication. Patrick directed me to Anna Enayat, my editor, for whose patient work on the manuscript I am most grateful.

1

The Historical Setting

Iran's long Gulf coast and its trade through the Strait of Hormuz has, from the time of the ancient Persian empires, ensured the continuity of her Gulf interests and meant a desire to play a dominant role in the region. However, the emergence of the first proto-modern territorial state under Shah Isma'il (1499–1524) coincided with external penetration of the Gulf by the Portuguese in 1504, at a time when Persia was in armed conflict with the Ottoman Empire.[1]

Throughout the Safavid period the shahs of Persia made attempts to extend their power into the Gulf. They were largely unsuccessful owing to domestic instability as well as external interventions. One notable exception, however, was the attempt made by Shah Abbas (1571–1629), through an alliance with Britain, which had expanding trade interests in the Gulf, to oust the Portuguese from Hormuz. The Anglo-Persian alliance achieved its goal in 1622 and Persia extended its rule over Hormuz, Bahrain, Qeshm and Bandar Gombrun (later known as Bandar Abbas). Nonetheless, the partial success of Shah Abbas evaporated after the disintegration of the Safavid state which led to an Afghan invasion from the east and Turkish-Russian competition for hegemony in the north.[2]

Nearly a century after the reign of Shah Abbas, Nadir Shah attempted to recoup Persia's Gulf position by setting out to build a large naval force. He succeeded in annexing Bahrain and Muscat. But with his assassination in 1747 and the subsequent collapse of Persia into a state of anarchy that was to last until the rise of Karim Khan Zand a decade later, Persian influence in the Gulf broke down once more.[3] Under the Zand dynasty priority was given to restoring order on the mainland, and Karim Khan did not engage in a policy of confrontation with the Arabs of the Gulf. In that period the Qawasim, rulers of Ras al-Khaimah and Sharjah, extended their control to the port of Lengeh on the Persian shore, and consequently controlled most of the Hormuz islands, mainly the Tunbs and Abu Musa, later claimed by Iran. Meanwhile, the al-Khalifah family established their rule over Bahrain in 1783.

With the rise of the Qajar dynasty in 1796 there was renewed interest in the Gulf, and in the 1840s the Grand Vizier, Hajj Mirza Aghassi, claimed that all of the waters and the islands of the Gulf were Persian.[4] By that time, however, Britain had entered the area.

The British Order

The conventional wisdom is that Great Britain entered Gulf waters to secure its trade routes to India. But Britain's maintenance of naval peace in and outside the Gulf was continually challenged by the 'piratical' Arab tribes led by the Qawasim.[5] The Qawasim were defeated by the East India Company's navy in 1819 and a year later the British Empire signed a naval truce with them and with neighbouring local rulers. In 1823 the first British Residency Agent was appointed in Sharjah, and in 1853 Britain concluded a Perpetual Maritime Peace treaty with the local rulers. From that time, what had been known as the 'Pirate Coast' became the 'Trucial Coast.'[6]

Following the Egyptian drive into Arabia (1816–1818), Britain enhanced its own Gulf position by occupying Aden in 1839.[7] By the late 19th century, the European race for empire was in full swing. With the Ottomans showing renewed interest in the area, and a resurgence of Persian activity (in 1887 Persia forced the Qawasim at Lengeh to return to the southern littoral, annexed the island of Sirri, and threatened to annex the Tunbs[8]), in 1892 Britain consolidated its grip over the Gulf by signing a number of agreements with its Arab rulers. In what came to be known as the 'Exclusive Agreements' the Trucial emirates and Bahrain were prohibited from dealings of any sort with, or ceding territory to, outside powers other than Britain. In exchange they were guaranteed protection against external aggression.[9] Kuwait and Qatar signed similar agreements in 1899 and 1916 respectively. The British continued to exercise unchallenged hegemony in the Gulf throughout the first half of the 20th century and succeeded in keeping the affairs of the lower Gulf separate from developments in the Arabian hinterland.[10] To the British Foreign Office, 'The Gulf states were a special preserve of HMG whose policy toward them rested on a kind of Monroe doctrine.'[11]

The rise of Reza Khan, later Reza Shah Pahlavi, to power in Persia between 1921–1924, and the subsequent strengthening of central government control over Persian territory, was confined in the south to Khuzistan and no attempt was made to challenge Britain's position on the other side of the Gulf. The question of Bahrain was revived by the Pahlavi state, but an attempt to refer the Bahrain and islands disputes to the League of Nations in 1923 met with no success.[12] In 1927 the conclusion of an agreement between Great Britain and Ibn Saud, in which the special treaty relations existing between Britain and Bahrain were acknowledged, drew a protest from the Persian government. A lengthy correspondence ensued in which both the British foreign secretary and his Persian counterpart made reference to various historical documents; but the British denied that they had ever recognised Persian title to the territory while Persia steadfastly maintained its sovereign rights. The issue was eventually dropped and although further notes were exchanged in 1929, 1930 and 1934 their content was confined to brief re-statements of the Persian government position on matters it considered to have infringed the country's sovereignty.[13] The claim to Bahrain was nevertheless kept alive, although it was not actively pursued by Iran until the late 1960s.

The Consequences of the Second World War

In 1942 Anthony Eden wrote, 'I assume that the aim of British policy must be, first, that we should continue to exercise the functions and responsibilities of a world power.'[14] Despite the fact that Britain was economically weakened by the war, and a new bipolar international system was emerging, successive Labour and Conservative governments acted on this same assumption until the end of the 1960s. Thereafter, the Conservative and Labour parties developed differing rationales over the question of maintaining Britain's world power status.

When Britain's rule over India ended, the conventional justification for its presence in the Gulf collapsed. However, new interests had by then emerged. In 1908 oil had been discovered in Iran, and when in 1913 the British navy decided that it should use oil instead of coal the British government purchased a 50 per cent shareholding in the Anglo-Iranian Oil Company and production facilities were expanded.[15] Oil was subsequently discovered in large quantities in Arabia, and by the end of the Second World War the Gulf had become the world's most important source of energy. Britain's economic interests by that time included Iraq Petroleum and Kuwait Petroleum as well as Anglo-Iranian, the companies which produced the bulk of its oil imports.

It was these interests, above all, that led the British foreign secretary Ernest Bevin to declare in 1949 that, 'In peace and war ... the Middle East is an area of cardinal importance to the United Kingdom, second only to the United Kingdom itself.'[16] The impact of Britain's weakened post-war economy was a source of concern to Bevin, but he was equally anxious about the world-wide communist threat.[17] His fear was shared by a number of other decision-makers, including the chiefs-of-staff, who in 1946 argued that if Britain moved out of the Middle East, the Russians would move in.[18]

One of the main challenges to Britain's Middle East policy was the rise of nationalism in the region. Bevin attempted to devise a strategy through which nationalism could be accommodated and British power maintained. He committed Britain to a policy of decolonisation, non-interference and helping moderate Arab countries to achieve socio-economic development, while maintaining both lines of economic exchange to Britain and a British military presence in Egypt, Palestine, Iraq and the Gulf.[19]

In an attempt to accommodate 'moderate' Egyptian nationalists, Britain offered to withdraw from the Canal Zone in 1946. However, with the end of the British mandate in Palestine, that offer was dropped since there seemed no practical alternative to the Suez base.[20] A year later Britain signed a treaty with Iraq allowing RAF squadrons to be stationed on Iraqi territory,[21] and the Gulf remained a secure British enclave.

During the 1950s Britain's military position in the Middle East suffered a setback due to the loss of the Canal Zone base in 1954. Most Canal Zone forces were moved to Cyprus and Libya.[22] As no alternative strategy was in place, Britain was to rely on air power and force mobility in the Mediterranean to maintain order and control in the Middle East. It was not until the Suez crisis that a rethinking of Britain's defence strategy took place.

There is a widespread perception that the Suez crisis marked the end of British dominance in the Middle East. In fact it had the opposite effect on the thinking of many British decision-makers. The outcome of Suez was seen not as a harbinger of inevitable retreat, but as an event that called for a restoration of British power and prestige. Two particular factors influenced Britain's subsequent rethinking: America's increasing role in the Middle East and the inability of British forces to react swiftly to regional crises.

British concern over the growing US role in the Middle East dated back to the early 1940s. Observing the spread of American oil concessions, mainly in Saudi Arabia, and Britain's heavy dependence on Middle East oil, as early as 1944 Sir Winston Churchill told Theodore Roosevelt that, 'There is apprehension in some quarters here that the United States has a desire to deprive us of our oil assets in the Middle East.'[23] The US never attempted to deprive Britain of its oil assets, nor did British apprehension develop into confrontation. Instead a degree of Anglo-American co-operation developed in order to maintain Western oil interests in the region and prevent Soviet penetration and influence.

The 1951–53 Iranian oil crisis was a test of Anglo-American co-operation. When Prime Minister Mossadegh nationalised the Anglo-Iranian Oil company, the Abadan refinery was the largest in the world. In 1945 Iranian oil production had increased from 13 to 18 per cent of the world's total,[24] and by 1950 65 per cent of Britain's oil imports came from the Gulf.[25] After two years of unsuccessful Anglo-Iranian negotiations and a change in leadership in America, the US and Britain agreed on a joint plan, codenamed 'Operation Ajax,' to overthrow Mossadeq. The plan was carried out successfully in August 1953 and the Shah's power was restored. However, the end result was not in Britain's favour. The Anglo-Iranian Oil Company ended up with much-reduced interests in Iran, and the US military and economic role in the country increased. In 1952 the US had no more than 29 military advisors in Iran; by 1956 the number had risen to 400 and the US naval presence in the Gulf was comparable in size to that of Britain.[26] Over the same period America extended as much as 221.9 million dollars in economic assistance to Iran and 84.7 million dollars of military aid.[27]

While its role in Iran was expanding, the US began to take positions on Middle East issues that did not help to support British policy. For example, in 1952 Saudi Arabia sent its forces to take control of the Buraimi Oasis in south east Arabia. Britain claimed that the oasis belonged to Abu Dhabi, an emirate under its protection, and a diplomatic crisis between Saudi Arabia and Britain broke out. Instead of supporting Britain, the US chose to play a mediating role between the two countries.[28] In another striking case, that of Egypt, while Britain believed Gamal Abdul Nasser to be a danger to the West and a protégé of the Soviet Union, the Eisenhower administration was inclined to believe he was his own man.[29]

In 1953 US Secretary of State Dulles introduced the concept of a 'northern tier' to policy thinking on the Middle East, and in 1955 a security pact, known as the Baghdad Pact, was signed by Turkey, Iraq, Iran and Pakistan, with Britain joining in the same year.[30] Although the pact was a US-inspired move, America backed down from committing itself. Furthermore, the US position during the Suez crisis intensified Anglo-American divergence over Middle East issues and helped clarify a distinction between Britain's independent interests and those of America. In 1956, after Nasser's nationalisation of the Suez Canal Company and the tripartite invasion of Suez, the US joined the USSR in efforts to force British, French and Israeli forces out of Suez.[31] The Suez episode not only widened the gap between Britain and the US and damaged British prestige, it also revealed Britain's military limitations in the region. British forces were slow to achieve their military objective, allowing more time for international pressure to force Britain out.[32]

Following the Suez crisis, in 1957 a revolt erupted in Oman when Imam Ghalib bin Ali led a rebellion against the British-supported Sultan of Muscat. The Imam defeated the Sultan's forces in central Oman. On 21 July the Sultan requested British help, and two days later RAF aircraft began operations in Oman. The operation was minor and against poorly equipped forces, but it drew attention to what Britain's Gulf role might be. It was argued that British forces should retain the ability to launch a rapid reaction to local instabilities in order to maintain the territorial status quo. The lesson was that air power and nuclear capability were no substitute for ground troops in the area.[33]

By April 1957 a new strategy had been devised for Britain 'east of Suez.' As Anthony Verrier aptly put it, 'The political essence of the new east of Suez strategy lay neither in its assurance of Britain's Arab friends nor valid veiled warnings to Moscow, but on the requirement to be independent of America without incurring American hostility.'[34] The new strategy was announced in the British government's 1957 defence document known as the Sandys White Paper. To enhance Britain's prestige, the White Paper emphasised that priority should be given to nuclear weapons, while conventional forces were to be smaller, better equipped and more mobile.³⁵ The need for an alternative base to Suez became a persistent question for British defence policy-makers, to which the answer was to develop Aden.

In 1956 an independent command for Britain's Middle East forces was established in Aden.³⁶ Aden was a small airstrip with poor housing facilities, and in 1959 a major development programme to expand facilities was announced. In 1961 a decision was taken to develop 'Little Aden' – an area 20 miles away from the main town – to house 2,500 soldiers and their families. The project was the single largest military construction scheme undertaken by the British government in the post-war period.³⁷ By 1961 Aden became one of three bases in which Britain's east of Suez nuclear weapons could be stationed, along with Cyprus and Singapore.³⁸

The test for the new strategy came in 1961 when Iraq claimed Kuwait and threatened to invade the oil-rich emirate. Although some believe that the possibility of an Iraqi invasion had not been seriously contemplated by London, the Kuwait operation appeared as a test of 'strategic mobility.' Between 30 June and 5 July Britain dispatched 6,500 troops and 45 warships to Kuwait.³⁹ The Iraqis backed down and several months later the British Resident in the Gulf, Sir William Luce, wrote to London, 'British stock in this area has perhaps never stood higher than it did on the morrow of our intervention in Kuwait.' Arguing that Britain was more deeply committed there than at any time since the War, Luce went on to say that, 'The Persian Gulf, thanks to our presence, is an island of comparative stability surrounded by a sea of uncertainty.'⁴⁰

The Iranian Rediscovery of the Gulf

When the Shah regained his role in foreign policy after the ousting of Mossadeq in 1953, his main security concern was, as before, the northern frontier. The Shah saw Iran's security interests as best served through alignment with the US and hence joined the US-proposed Baghdad Pact (later the Central Treaty Organisation, CENTO). The Gulf only began to re-emerge as a source of threat with the 1958 coup in Iraq. Not only did a pillar of CENTO collapse with the coup, which led to a decline in the importance of the security pact throughout the 1960s, but also a revolutionary pan-Arab regime seized power on Iran's borders.

After the Qasim coup, Iraq showed sudden belligerence toward Iran over the question of the Shatt al-Arab, claiming that it had signed the 1937 treaty organising the legal status of the waterway under duress. The issue soon faded but returned to the fore in 1961. Iran's response at the time did not go beyond strongly worded statements[41] and soon after the dispute again died down. However, on the wider Middle East scene, rivalry developed between Iran and Egypt and Iran began to view the threat to its security in the wider context of an Arab threat.

Iran responded to the new situation by quickly recognising Syria after the separation from Egypt in 1961. It then allied itself with Saudi Arabia in an effort to help the Royalists in Yemen against the Egyptian-backed Republicans. When Iran recognised the state of Israel the Egyptian response was to launch a verbal attack on Iran's territorial integrity by claiming Khuzistan, or as Nasser called it Arabistan, as part of the Arab World under Iranian occupation. The ensuing propaganda war continued throughout the 1960s.[42]

One inevitable reaction to the perceived Arab threat was to arouse Iranian national sentiment in support for the country's territorial integrity. Another was to adopt a policy of strengthening its military capacity. At the beginning of the 1960s, however, the Shah was aware of his country's limitations, as reflected in remarks he made in 1959 on his desire to develop a large naval force in the Gulf:

> Of course it is one [sic] our great wishes to strengthen our natural position not only in the Persian Gulf by building up a strong Navy and a large merchant fleet, but also to [see our] flag flying on our ships sailing on all oceans and seas. Iran, once, had a first-class Navy and it is fitting that she should regain her position among maritime nations ... But as I pointed out last summer to operate a single vessel you need well trained personnel as well as large [sic] amount of money. If I remember correctly, the operation of a 1350 or 1500 ton destroyer costs annually some 200 million rials. In everything we do in this respect we must have all these considerations in mind.[43]

In the circumstances Iran seemed more than ever keen to see Britain continue its Gulf role. In conversation with British officials the Shah would frequently stress common Anglo-Iranian interests in the Gulf and the common threat posed by Nasser.[44] The Shah had always reminded western officials that Iran was the only barrier to the expansion of Soviet influence southwards into the Middle East oil area. By the early 1960s the emerging Arab threat was presented as equal to that of the Soviet Union. As one British Embassy telegram put it, 'He [the Shah] does broadly believe that the importance of Iran's role is understood [by the West]. But the reality and inter-connection of the dual threat from north and south is always present in his mind.'[45]

On a number of occasions Britain reassured the Shah that it had no intention of leaving the Gulf.[46] Nevertheless, Iran began to take steps aimed at developing closer ties with the Gulf Arabs. As early as 1959 the Iranian government attempted to cultivate Arab rulers' goodwill through SAVAK (security-police)-arranged visits to Iran. According to British sources, on one such occasion the head of SAVAK, General Bakhtiar, told the Ruler of Dubai, '... that the British connection with the Trucial States would come to an end, by secret Anglo-Iranian agreement, within 15 years, and that he would therefore do well to look to Iran.'[47] In 1962 the Iranian prime minister Ali Amini participated in the Saudi-inspired pan-Islamic conference, visited Mecca and invited the King of Saudi Arabia to visit Iran, along with Saudi *ulema*, in an attempt to bridge religious differences between the two countries.[48] In 1963 a Persian Gulf department was founded in the Iranian Foreign Ministry,[49] and in the same year the Iranian prime minister inaugurated a seminar in Tehran on ways of increasing trade with the Gulf.[50]

To that extent Iran aimed to befriend the Arab Gulf states. However, with the exception of Kuwait, no formal diplomatic relations were established with the shaikhdoms. More importantly, Iran revived its claim to Bahrain which in 1957 had been given a seat in the Iranian Majlis as the country's 14th province. As a result Bahrain was excluded from efforts to encourage trade with the Gulf and from bilateral contacts.[51] Iran also continued to claim sovereignty over the Hormuz islands – Greater Tunb, Lesser Tunb and Abu Musa – which Britain insisted belonged to the Arab side.[52] Nonetheless, Iran made no serious effort to resolve its territorial claims with the Gulf rulers, nor was the issue allowed to bedevil Anglo-Iranian relations as Britain was serving Iranian interests more broadly by maintaining the regional status quo. It was only when Britain decided to depart from the Gulf that these and other issues came to the surface.

2

The 16 January Decision: Britain, the United States and Iran

On Tuesday 16 January 1968 Britain's Labour government announced that there would be a total withdrawal of British forces stationed east of Suez by the end of 1971. The British decision marked the end of more than a century and a half of British dominance in the Gulf and the opening of a new chapter in its history. For the first time in the modern era the Gulf states had to assume responsibility for the security of the area against regional and international threats.

This turn of events raised many questions about the future political order of the Gulf which were to be answered by December 1971. This chapter aims to outline the international context of the period. It focuses on three main questions. Firstly, why did Britain decide to retreat from the Gulf? Secondly, what was Iran's position during the period leading to British withdrawal and what was its reaction to the British decision? Thirdly, what was the United States' role during that period from its position as Britain's closest Western ally, Iran's closest international ally, and the power which could, arguably, have succeeded Britain as the guardian of the Gulf? Above all this chapter seeks to demonstrate how the forces which influenced the actions and reactions of Britain, Iran and the US prior to 1968 – the year of decision – laid the foundations of their policies in the years to come.

Rethinking the Empire

When the Labour Party narrowly won the 1964 general election it inherited an unprecedented balance of payments deficit of 750–800 million pounds and the value of sterling had seesawed dramatically.[1] To deal with the economic situation the new government ruled out politically unpopular decisions such as a devaluation of sterling. In addition to some domestic economic measures,[2] government efforts were focused instead on two remedies: seeking international financial support for sterling, and large cuts in the previous government's defence budget.

These two remedies became inextricably linked as most financial support was to come from the United States. The US had a big stake in Britain maintaining the military capability to play a stabilising role in the oil-rich Gulf. Even more important at the time was the Far East, where the US was involved in Vietnam, and regional instabilities erupted when Indonesian soldiers began infiltrating across the Malaysian frontier in what came to be known as the 'confrontation.'[3] The US hoped that British support for Malaysia would help maintain the regional status quo.[4]

Many British politicians believed that one of the main targets for defence cuts was Britain's overseas commitments. Britain had forces stationed in the Mediterranean, east of Suez (in Aden, the Gulf, Singapore, Malaysia and Hong Kong) and the Caribbean.[5] Prime Minister Harold Wilson admitted that 'Britain's defence forces were overstretched almost to breaking point.'[6] However the debate over defence cuts centred around commitments east of Suez, where the largest number of troops outside Europe were stationed at an annual cost of around £400 million pounds.[7] To Wilson and some senior members of his government, the question of overseas commitments was not merely one of rationalising expenditure. After Ernest Bevin's grand anti-Soviet strategy for post-war Britain and the previous Conservative government's idea of independent 'British interests,' the new Labour government saw Britain's defence policy in the context of a 'world role': As Wilson later argued, '... a majority [in the Labour Party], including myself, were moved more by thoughts of a contribution to international peace-keeping than by considerations of imperial splendour.'[8]

In the twilight of Empire, overseas commitments were seen as helping to maintain Britain's world power status. They would present an image of a loyal ally to Commonwealth partners, earn Britain the right to a pivotal place in NATO and the United Nations, and help strengthen Anglo-American relations. Wilson was therefore glad to see 'the full recognition the United States gave to our unique role as a world peace-keeping power.' In a specific reference to east of Suez, he said, 'I want to make it quite clear that whatever we may do in the field of cost, value for money and stringent review of expenditure, we cannot afford to relinquish our world role.'[9] The regional ramifications of ending Britain's commitments were secondary considerations.

According to one source, the foreign secretary, George Brown, and the Foreign Office staff supported the prime minister's idea of a British world role.[10] Denis Healey, the defence secretary, wrote in his memoirs, 'At the time I myself believed that our contribution to the stability of the Middle East and the Far East was more useful to world peace than our contribution to NATO in Europe.'[11] The advocates of Britain's international role had a majority in the Cabinet,[12] but Philip Darby notes the existence in 1964 of a silent opposition within the ruling party,[13] while the Treasury pressed for defence cuts.[14] Soon after the elections the Treasury presented the government with a detailed paper arguing the case for major reductions in defence spending.[15] When the matter was considered by the Cabinet in November 1964 a provisional decision was taken to reduce the defence budget planned for 1969–1970 from 2,400 million to 2,000 million pounds at constant prices; however, no public announcement was made of the new target and no decision was made regarding commitments.[16]

In the Cabinet George Brown argued:

> We alone can play a stabilising role [in the Middle East] because of the position we hold along the eastern and southern shore of Arabia; it would not be possible for the United States or any other Western Power to take these over from us. The support of our military efforts in the Gulf is one of the main reasons why we need the base at Aden and why the continuing involvement of Nasser in Yemen, with its consequent stepping up of subversion in the South Arabian federation, has caused so much concern.

Brown also stressed a convergence of British and American interests in 'all important respects' and the need to work closely with the United States in the Middle East.[17]

After assuring the US of its intention to play a world role,[18] the British government sent James Callaghan, the new chancellor of the exchequer, to seek support for sterling in Washington and New York. According to Callaghan, New York Federal Reserve officials showed understanding for Britain's difficulties and were concerned that a sterling devaluation might lead to speculative attacks on the dollar in the international money markets. Callaghan recalls that Charlie Coombe, the director of foreign exchange operations at the Federal Reserve, warned banking colleagues on 24 November 1964 that, 'If Britain's reserves run out and [Britain was] forced to devalue, the next step might be an extremely dangerous attack on the dollar.'[19] In coordination with Canada, Japan and eight European central banks, the Federal Reserve assembled a credit package of 3 billion dollars to buy up any sterling that was offered in the market. This move dampened speculation about a devaluation. A similar exercise was repeated in September 1965.[20]

During Anglo-American co-operation on the money market, no explicit links were made between US financial support for sterling and the continuation of Britain's role east of Suez.[21] As it turned out, efforts to support sterling were conducted by the Federal Reserve with no intervention from White House officials.[22] There is no doubt that the White House could have intervened to block the credit package or set political conditions for sterling support had it wished. But the Johnson administration did not choose to take such action.[23]

The British government's first attempt at defence cuts came in the shape of a 1965 defence White Paper. Given the Cabinet's views on Britain's international role, the government delayed any decision on international commitments. Instead, economies were made by cutting certain weapons projects which produced a modest saving of 56 million pounds.[24] The importance of the 1965 White Paper derives from the fact that it sparked a public expression of discontent by left-wing members of the Labour Party. Although Labour MPs voted with the government on the defence budget, twenty back-benchers introduced an amendment calling for 'greatly accelerated progress in the reduction of Great Britain's overseas commitments.'[25] In August 1966 seventy-seven Labour MPs called for a 25 per cent reduction in defence spending. In September a Labour Party conference resolution drew attention to 'the heavy burden on the national income involved by maintenance of outmoded military bases abroad.'[26] From that point domestic politics gradually began to impinge on and constrain international considerations concerning Britain's world role.

Aden: the First Abandoned

While political pressures for a reduction in overseas military spending were mounting in Britain, in Aden, Britain's principal military base in the Middle East, events took a turn for the worse. Since 1962 the British-protected South Arabian Federation of hinterland states and Aden had witnessed an increase in the activities of revolutionary nationalist movements. In 1963 British troops were used against 'dissident tribesmen' in Ad-Dali region, which provoked a series of assassination attempts against British officials. In September 1965, not for the first time, the Aden constitution was suspended and direct rule by the British governor was imposed. By that time, dissident political groups had built up forces with which they engaged British forces in guerrilla operations aimed at ending British occupation over the whole of South Arabia. Several attempts were made by the British government to achieve a peaceful solution to the conflict but all failed.[27] In the end, the Aden base, as historian Michael Howard put it, '... consumed more security than it could ever produce.'[28]

By early 1966 the British government had reconsidered Britain's role east of Suez.[29] As part of the February 1966 Defence Review it announced that it intended to withdraw British forces from Aden by 1968.[30] In the meantime, Wilson and the majority of the Cabinet maintained their support for a British world role.[31] Faced with growing left-wing pressure for a rapid withdrawal of overseas forces, the government sought to achieve a delicate balance between maintaining Britain's east of Suez commitments while still making large cuts in defence spending.[32]

The February 1966 Defence White Paper tried to achieve that balance.[33] In the White Paper the 1966 provisional defence budget of 2 billion pounds became a formal ceiling for the 1969–1970 budget. In addition to abandoning Aden, an order for the CVA 01 carrier, which the Navy believed to be essential for the east of Suez role, was cancelled. However, F-111 aircraft were ordered from the United States as a replacement for the carrier as a means of strengthening shore-based air capacity.[34] Furthermore, the White Paper set three criteria for a continuing British presence outside Europe: firstly, Britain would not undertake major operations of war except in co-ordination with its allies; secondly, Britain would not accept a defence obligation to another country unless that country were prepared to provide appropriate facilities for British troops; and thirdly, there would be no attempt to maintain defence facilities in an independent country against its wishes.[35]

With the British military presence in Aden drawing to a close, the Gulf was the only remaining area under British influence in the Middle East. On the surface the 1966 White Paper and subsequent government statements appeared to reaffirm Britain's presence there; the number of ground troops stationed in the Gulf was to be increased,[36] the British military bases in Sharjah and Bahrain were to be expanded,[37] and on 3 February Denis Healey declared that:

> We have no intention of retreating on any of our commitments. We intend to remain and shall remain fully capable of carrying out all the commitments we have at the present time, including those in the Far East, the Middle East and in Africa and other parts of the world. We do intend to remain in a military sense a world power.[38]

A few months later the foreign secretary, Michael Stewart, reiterated, 'We have neither the wish nor the intention to abandon the world east of Suez.'[39]

The criteria set out in the 1966 White Paper appeared to support the case for maintaining troops in the Gulf. The first, that Britain not engage in war activities without co-ordination with its allies, was vague, as it did not specify which allies: could they be the US, Australia or Kuwait?[40] The second, which stressed the need for countries to provide facilities for British forces, did not call Britain's presence in the Gulf into question as Britain already had military facilities in that area. The third, on the need for domestic consent if Britain were to maintain defence facilities, further underpinned Britain's role in the Gulf, as there was hardly any sign of local resistance to the British presence in the Trucial States, Qatar and Bahrain.[41]

However, a broader view of the situation may lead one to argue that 1966 marked the beginning of the end of the British presence in the Gulf. Since the end of British rule in India, the main purpose of the Aden base had been to support and enhance the British role in the Gulf.[42] Britain's military presence itself was relatively small – about 6,000 men. In the event of these troops engaging in combat activities, reinforcements and logistic supplies had to come from the southern Arabia base.[43] Although there was an increase in the number of troops in the Gulf following the decision to pull out of Aden it was only slight, from 6,000 to 7,000–8,000.[44] Without the Aden base British forces were vulnerable to attacks by regional powers.

With Britain's ability to defend Gulf commitments significantly reduced, some decision-makers began to question their merits. Although public statements attempted to dispel fears or hopes of British retreat, according to one source Michael Stewart warned the prime minister in private that Britain was 'in a posture of withdrawal,'[45] and Denis Healey began to reverse his position with regard to maintaining its commitments.[46] According to Healey there was no alternative to the Aden base. Construction of a new base at Masirah, an island off the coast of Oman, was considered for a short while, but the cost ruled out that option. Britain's air base in Cyprus was considered as a possible alternative for enforcing the Gulf presence, but difficulties in acquiring overflying rights from Arab countries rendered the option too impractical. From that point the question for Healey was not whether commitments east of Suez should be maintained, but rather the timing of the inevitable withdrawal. The chiefs of staff came to the same conclusion.[47] Healey still publicly opposed rapid pull out for fear of a sudden radical change in Britain's foreign policy.[48]

The domestic consequence of the Aden decision was a stepping-up of internal Labour pressure for ending all overseas commitments. Indications of further opposition from within the ruling party were notable. In May 1966 a cross-section of Labour MPs submitted a resolution to a Parliamentary Labour Party (PLP) meeting calling for a decisive reduction in commitments east of Suez, including the Gulf, by 1969–1970. The government succeeded tactically when the PLP chairman, Emmanuel Shinwell, blocked the motion on procedural grounds. Government critics then put the withdrawal motion to a vote in the next PLP meeting in June. In an attempt to demonstrate the government's strength, the meeting was attended by a large number of ministers and Labour peers, and the motion was decisively defeated (225 votes to 54 with 50 abstentions); the vote had been viewed in terms of party loyalty rather than of practical defence policy.[49]

Leaving aside party politics, macro-economic factors, in particular the persisting balance of payments deficit, were moving in a direction that would eventually influence a foreign policy change. The government was forced to reduce public spending. The prime minister announced in the House of Commons that public investment in the 1967–1968 budget would be substantially reduced, and the cuts of at least £100 million were to include both military and civil sectors.[50] In February 1967 a Defence White Paper announced a further decrease of £45 million in defence spending, with more cuts to be achieved by the end of June.[51]

The White Paper was to be put to a vote in the Commons in February 1967. Harold Wilson hoped that it would be more acceptable to the left than the previous ones; he saw it as the first defence White Paper '... to show economies in defence spending which were actually realised, with substantial further reductions in prospect.'[52] Nonetheless, to his surprise he faced the opposition of a substantial section of the PLP, '... going much wider than the traditional left,' who wanted more defence cuts and wanted them quickly.[53] The government then produced its own amendment to the White Paper which welcomed the existing Paper as a contribution to the continuing reduction of Britain's commitments, forces and overseas expenditure. When put to a vote the motion was approved by a majority of only thirty-nine, while sixty-two back-benchers abstained.[54]

With economic and political pressures at home, the Wilson government was pressed to clarify its position on the remaining commitments east of Suez. Where the Gulf was concerned, it still showed an unwavering resolve to maintain its position. When questioned on the matter in parliament in April 1967 Denis Healey used the old familiar argument of Britain's world role by arguing that, 'The Gulf is an area of such vital importance not only to the economy of Western Europe as a whole but also to world peace that it would be totally irresponsible for us to withdraw our forces from the area.'[55]

In June the foreign secretary also reassured the House of Commons that Britain would fulfil her Gulf commitments.[56] When the 1967 Arab-Israeli war erupted the prospect of further regional instability was used by advocates of the Gulf commitments as evidence of the importance of Britain's role in the world as a whole and in the Middle East in particular. George Brown expressed his 'particular concern' over Gulf stability arguing that, '... our forces are not in the Persian Gulf simply to protect our oil interests as such, but to maintain stability in the area.'[57]

During 1967 Britain's balance of payments deficit caused pressure on the value of the pound; as early as February the British government sought a multi-billion dollar long-term loan to support sterling. According to James Callaghan the idea originated from US bankers. But this time the matter was not left to bankers. Johnson administration officials had a different assessment of British policy.[58] After learning in the summer of 1965 about Britain's intention to limit the defence budget to £2,000 million by 1970 and to withdraw from Aden, US officials had become increasingly concerned about the future of Britain's international political and security role, which US Secretary of State Dean Rusk believed no other country could assume.[59] By September 1965 the implicit link between Britain's world role and American financial support was made clear to the British government. During a meeting with Wilson, George Ball, the US under secretary of state, told the prime minister that, '... the US regards the maintenance of Britain's commitments around the world as an essential element in the total Anglo-American relationship' including US support for the pound. Although Wilson insisted that such a link could not be made,[60] he assured President Johnson of Britain's continuation of its east of Suez role, albeit at a reduced level.[61] The US accepted Britain's withdrawal from Aden, but at the same time American officials pressed for a continuation of Britain's commitments in the oil rich Gulf and the Far East.[62]

In 1967 US officials were receiving messages that the Wilson government was considering a reduction of forces stationed in Singapore and Malaysia and total withdrawal by the mid-1970s. One US London Embassy telegram noted increasing sub-Cabinet ministerial agreement on more reductions east of Suez.[63] This notion was underpinned when Britain reapplied to join the European Economic Community. Prior to Wilson's arrival in Washington in June 1967 Dean Rusk wrote to the president, 'He comes to Washington at a time when the British ... appear to have arrived at a conscious decision as to Britain's future role in the World. The decision is to liquidate most of the overseas commitments remaining from the Empire and become an integral part of the European movement.'[64] In this context, US officials demanded that any further loans should be conditional on continuation of Britain's role east of Suez – a requirement that was unacceptable to the British government.[65]

During the first half of 1967, US officials persisted in their efforts to discourage Britain from changing its position in the Far East. In a message to George Brown, Dean Rusk warned the British foreign secretary of the 'devastating repercussions' which would 'strike at the very basis of [US] post-war foreign policy' should Britain decide to end its east of Suez role. US concern over a possible change in British foreign policy stemmed from the Johnson administration's preoccupation with Vietnam and its consequent effect on the domestic consensus over foreign policy. As American war efforts in Vietnam seemed to be heading into dire straits, Rusk told Brown, 'American opinion would not stand for picking up the abandoned British position,'[66] and in what appeared as a threat, President Johnson stated,

If the American Congress and people should ever conclude that we are alone among the great powers in dealing with problems in this area, there could be a revulsion here against our assuring or maintaining our commitments [e.g. NATO] that could shake the foundation of our policies.[67]

By that time the Wilson government too was preoccupied by domestic politics and Healey told US Defence Secretary Robert McNamara that he could not justify policies that were not in the best interests of Britain.[68]

In accordance with its promise to parliament in the February White Paper, the Wilson government announced new defence cuts in the July 1967 Defence White Paper. These included plans to reduce British forces stationed outside Europe in general including the Mediterranean, the South Atlantic and the Caribbean.[69] However, the biggest reductions were to be achieved east of Suez. After Aden, the British government's attention turned to the Far East. Some British politicians believed that the end of confrontation with Indonesia in 1967 would make reduction of Britain's military presence in the Far East more acceptable to the US, where the number of troops was cut by half (to 40,000 from 80,000) in preparation for a withdrawal from Malaysia and Singapore by the mid-1970s.[70] The aim, according to the July White Paper, was to bring the defence budget down to the 1966 target of £2,000 million.

While commitments in the Gulf were left intact in this document, the government's tone regarding the future of east of Suez had begun to change. Unlike previous White Papers which emphasised Britain's intention to maintain its east of Suez commitments, the 1967 White Paper declared the aim of British policy was, '... to foster developments which will enable local peoples to live in peace without the presence of external forces.'[71] However, a set date for total British withdrawal from east of Suez was difficult to predict. Healey told the House of Commons, 'Before we fix a date in this way, we must give our diplomacy a chance to construct a different basis for the security of the countries which we are leaving.'[72]

As late as November of 1967 the British government sent Goronwy Roberts, the minister of state at the Foreign Office, to the local rulers in the Gulf and the Shah of Iran to reassure them that Britain intended to remain in the Gulf for the foreseeable future.[73] Given the Labour Party's attitude to overseas defence spending this was a puzzling move. One explanation could be that the Wilson government hoped to win favour with the Americans because the Gulf was the only remaining strategically vital region to the US under British influence. Another might be that the British government genuinely felt that the Gulf was potentially unstable as many regional issues were not resolved.[74] A third possible explanation is that some members of the British government thought that by announcing withdrawal from Malaysia and Singapore by the mid-1970s the domestic political pressure on ending the Gulf commitments would ease. However, November 1967 witnessed the eruption of an economic crisis at home which was to modify earlier expectations.

At the end of November the sterling exchange rate fell sharply, which in turn led to a crisis in the world money markets. The immediate cause of the crisis, according to Wilson and Callaghan, was the foreign trade consequences of the closing of the Suez Canal following the 1967 Arab-Israeli war and the subsequent dock strikes in London and Liverpool.[75] In the absence of American help, the British government attempted to meet its economic obligations by accepting a loan from the International Monetary Fund. In taking the loan it subscribed to two fundamental IMF conditions: a devaluation of the pound to reflect market forces, and cuts in public spending to restrain domestic inflation.[76]

The Countdown to Withdrawal

Under these conditions the Wilson government went to work on the 1968–1969 budget. The Cabinet met on 4 January 1968. Not only was a major reduction in defence and overseas expenditure, which had been shrinking since 1965, deemed to be necessary, but also in social expenditure which had been on the rise since Labour took office.[77] At risk was both Britain's assumed world role and the ruling party's support for the government. As Wilson recalled, '... there was no guarantee that we would get a package of the required scale, with the necessary political balance, even through the Cabinet, let alone through the Parliamentary Party.' Wilson concluded that the task of passing an austerity budget without Cabinet resignations, '... was the most formidable test I had attempted in over three years of government.'[78]

During the Cabinet meeting the new chancellor, Roy Jenkins, proposed sweeping cuts in a number of areas. To the prime minister among those which presented the greatest difficulty were the cancellation of orders for the American F-111 aircraft, a speedier withdrawal from South-East Asia and immediate withdrawal from the Gulf. Predictably the foreign and defence secretaries, joined by a small number of Cabinet members, were opposed to further defence cuts, but they did not take a hard position on withdrawal from east of Suez. According to Cabinet member Richard Crossman, they merely asked to delay withdrawal until at least 1972, while their opponents wanted withdrawal completed by March 1971.[79]

When the issue was put to a vote in Cabinet the side opposed to maintaining the east of Suez commitments won by a large majority. The Cabinet met again eight days later. In the interim George Brown travelled to the US on 10 January to inform the Americans of his government's decision, and Goronwy Roberts returned to the Gulf to convey the same news to the Rulers and the Shah of Iran.[80] When the Cabinet met again Brown reported American dismay at the British decisions[81] and Johnson sent a letter to Wilson urging him to review the alternatives before taking a final decision. President Johnson suggested, '... a prolongation of your presence in the Far East and the Gulf until other stable arrangements can be put in place would be of help at this very difficult time for all of us.'[82] Nonetheless, the Cabinet was unshaken.[83]

On 15 January the Cabinet met for the last time to decide a final date for the completion of withdrawal before the announcement of the budget. Healey, Brown and their supporters, now in a minority, wanted to stay until 1972 while their Cabinet opponents maintained that withdrawal ought to be completed by March 1971. Wilson then offered a compromise by proposing a December 1971 deadline. The majority accepted that compromise.[84]

The following day the prime minister announced the budget in parliament and formally declared Britain's intention to withdraw from east of Suez by the end of 1971.[85] Wilson admitted to parliament that the decision involved risks, but economic realities, he argued, made these risks acceptable. East of Suez was not the only area for defence cuts; the order for F-111 aircraft from the US was cancelled, there were cuts in the Navy's aircraft carrier forces, and the Army was to be reduced with corresponding reductions of support facilities. In the 1968–1969 budget, the government hoped to make a saving of 110 million pounds,[86] with further reductions of another 110 million pounds planned in 1969–1970, and a another cut of 210 to 260 million planned for the 1972–1973 budget.[87]

The overall figures for the 1968–1969 budget indicate that the British government tried to make cuts across the board in all sectors of the economy. Economies were made in areas such as social security, education, health and welfare, housing and industry, giving total savings of £300 million.[88] For a socialist government they were especially hard decisions to take. To maintain overseas military expenditure in the face of internal Labour Party opposition and a reduction of welfare spending would have spelt political suicide. Although the financial cost of maintaining the Gulf garrison itself was relatively small,[89] the decision to withdraw troops was largely symbolic of money saving for domestic spending and efforts to improve Britain's balance of payments situation.

In parliament Conservatives reacted with sharp criticism,[90] on the grounds of dishonouring obligations to friends and allies in the Gulf who had been reassured less than two months earlier that Britain had no intention of withdrawing in the near future;[91] that the risks of instability in the Gulf, especially from Russian infiltration, were too high to be accepted; that British forces would be demoralised for a long period to come; and that Britain's world role, which Wilson continuously proclaimed, would disappear.[92] One member of the Opposition raised a noteworthy point of criticism by arguing that although the government had presented an economic case for withdrawing forces from the Gulf, a better case could be made economically for staying. According to Viscount Lambton, Britain's possessions in the Gulf as a whole added up to between £2,000 and £3,000 million, and Britain's annual income from the area was more than £200 million.[93] In that context the £12 million cost of maintaining Gulf stability seemed good value for money.

Some of the points which the Conservatives raised in criticism of Labour's decision were similar to those which the prime minister and some prominent members of his government had, since 1964, used to justify maintaining British commitments. However, in January 1968 the government's principal aim was to regain support from the PLP and to restore order among the ranks of the ruling party. Apart from a few individual negative reactions from members of the government,[94] only three Labour MPs voted against the budget,[95] and there were no Cabinet resignations. In other words the budget was a domestic political success for Harold Wilson. However, the international consequences of the British decision were far more complex.

After President Johnson's and Dean Rusk's response to George Brown's visit to Washington mentioned above, the first US public reaction came in the shape of a State Department statement which said, '... we regret the British government's announcement regarding its forces in South Asia and the Persian Gulf and the F-111 contract' but indicated, '... we have no plans to move in where the British pulled out.'[96] Although some US policy makers were anticipating an end to British military presence east of Suez, domestic constraints, notably the Vietnam entanglement, meant that there was no support for new commitments in the US. Furthermore, where Middle East questions were considered, it was the consequences of the 1967 Arab-Israeli war that received most of the attention of US policy-makers.[97] The ramifications of the British decision on the Gulf were not discussed in Congress and leading US journals had little coverage of the issue. Although some US officials anticipated a British withdrawal, one thing the Johnson administration lacked was a Gulf policy following the end of Pax Britannica.

In the Gulf itself, the small emirates whose external security had been guaranteed by Britain for over 150 years were most affected. To these emirates there was no regional alternative to the British security umbrella. The large Gulf Arab states, Iraq and Saudi Arabia, were no substitute. Iraq's pan-Arab ruling regime was perceived as a source of threat rather than regional stability, particularly following the former Qasim regime's threat to invade Kuwait in 1961. Saudi Arabia had unresolved territorial disputes with some of the emirates (Qatar and Abu Dhabi), and lacked the military might to play the role of protector of the Gulf. Iran had the military might but given its historical claims to Bahrain and the Hormuz islands was perceived by some as a greater threat than Iraq. The emirates were quick to express their regret over the British decision, and uncertainty about the future was natural. Mohammed bin Mubarak al-Khalifah, the director of the Bahraini Bureau of Information said, 'It was shocking.'[98] The Ruler of Abu Dhabi, Shaikh Zayid Bin Sultan al-Nahyan, and the Ruler of Dubai, Shaikh Rashid al-Maktoum, promptly offered to cover the financial cost of Britain's presence in the Gulf in an attempt to reverse Britain's decision.[99] The offer was quickly rejected by the British government.[100]

One could question why Britain did not accept the offer of cost-sharing of military protection, as it is not uncommon in inter-state security relations (the British presence in Germany and the US presence in Japan provide cases). When this question was raised in parliament, George Brown replied, '... much more than local cost would be involved. It would place a severe burden on the logistic backing required for our forces.'[101] Healey argued the same point: '... even with Gulf money it would not be possible to maintain British forces because the cost of presence must include military capability that might be needed to support it.'[102] The offer was not only rejected, it was not even considered seriously. A more convincing reason was given by Healey who, in an interview, remarked that such an offer was unlikely to receive wide support from members of the Labour Party as many of them were not attracted by Arab Gulf forms of government. He said, 'Germany was a democracy and a European ally, but the Gulf rulers were perceived as local dictators.'[103]

The Iranian Position

While Britain and the United States were debating the future of Britain's role east of Suez, Iran was witnessing the rapid growth of its national power. In the early 1960s the Shah had declared his country's intention to pursue a national foreign policy independent of East-West interests,[104] but it was not until the second half of the 1960s that Iran was able to put that policy into practice.

Prior to the announcement of the 1966 British Defence Review, the British ambassador in Tehran told the Foreign Office that the Shah was beginning to worry about the prospect of a British pull out from east of Suez. The Iranian prime minister, Amir Abbas Hoveida, told Sir Denis Wright that Iran would not tolerate a power vacuum left by Britain in the Gulf, '... so as to ensure that hostile forces did not take over in the area.'[105] From 1965 onwards Iran witnessed an annual economic growth rate of about 8–10 per cent and low inflation. Oil revenues were on the rise, matched by a rapid increase in military spending and expansion of the armed forces.[106] We shall examine the question of the influence of Iranian military power on foreign policy in later chapters; suffice it to say here that these changes were noticed by Iran's international allies, most notably the United States.

From 1964 Iran no longer received American grant aid; rather the US began to help finance Iranian military purchases through export-import bank credits, a development which, in the opinion of some analysts, reduced US ability to influence Iran's foreign policy.[107] The first credit package was for 200 million dollars for eight years at an interest rate of 5.5 per cent. However, US officials were concerned about the impact of military sales on the Iranian economy. According to one US official, 'The Shah had a big appetite for buying arms which had to be controlled.' For this reason the credit was subject to an annual review of the status of the Iranian national economy.[108] Soon afterwards Iran asked for another credit at lower rates. While supporting a new credit, US officials showed reluctance to change the interest rate. Iran's response was to warn the US that it would seek credits elsewhere. Defence Secretary McNamara recommended to the president that the US should not yield to 'the Shah's blackmail.'[109] But in 1966 a second 200 million dollar military credit was given to Iran for five years at a similar rate.

In 1965 Iran had delivered a warning to the US by signing a trade credit agreement with the Soviet Union at lower interest rates which sparked a series of credit agreements with the USSR and the East European countries. By early 1966 economic credits extended from the Soviet Union to Iran totalled 346 million dollars, including 289 million dollars to build a steel mill and to construct a gas pipeline to the Soviet Union through which Iranian natural gas would pass, which the Soviets accepted as payment of the credit. In January 1967 – probably the most significant development for the US – a 110 million dollar Soviet-Iranian arms deal was announced, followed by a 540 million dollar trade agreement. At the same time Iran had also taken 158 million dollars worth of credits from East European countries, mainly Romania.[110]

It can be debated whether what lay behind these agreements was an attempt to put pressure on the US, commercial logic – Iran was offered better terms by the Eastern bloc – or Iran's wish to improve its national security posture by enhancing relations with its neighbour, the USSR. The significance of the development for US-Iranian relations, however, was that by 1966 the US was convinced of the Iranian intention to adopt a new foreign policy.[111] At the same time the US had become concerned about the future of Britain's continuation of its overseas commitments. From that point a marked change in the US attitude toward Iran was noticeable. Its hallmark was a recognition of Iran's growing power.[112]

In 1967, on the recommendation of Dean Rusk and Robert McNamara, Iran was given a second 50 million dollar slice of its 1966 credit at a reduced interest rate of 5 per cent.[113] It was now believed that Iran could maintain a high level of defence spending without causing damage to its economy.[114] Many US officials saw the Shah's regime as stable and secure,[115] and were full of praise for Iran's impressive socio-economic development.[116] Moreover, Iran's improved relations with the Eastern bloc did little to bedevil US-Iranian ties. Although it discouraged Iran from extending links with the East, the US took a 'generally relaxed' attitude to Soviet-Iranian rapprochement,[117] and some decision-making circles even saw some benefits in closer Iranian-USSR relations. A CIA memorandum argued that these exchanges would end Soviet supported anti-Iranian propaganda, and would end Soviet efforts to topple the Shah's regime through whatever influence the Soviets had over left-wing groups in Iran.[118] Some members of the State Department also believed that the rapprochement would give the Shah an opportunity to crush leftist opposition groups,[119] thus making his regime more secure and a better ally of the West.

Furthermore, the US was convinced that although Iran had extended its relations with the East, the Shah would remain pro-Western as Iranian arms purchases from the USSR did not include sophisticated weapons,[120] and Iran would still remain dependent on Western trade and investment.[121] This idea was further strengthened when the US vice-president reported to Johnson that, 'He [the Shah] is fully aware of the danger of Soviet infiltration as a result of this influx of military equipment, and he has therefore very greatly strengthened his intelligence and security system.'[122] The fact that Iran was one of the few developing countries that publicly supported US operations in Vietnam helped preserve its image as a reliable US ally.[123]

To this point the Shah's brief attempt to play the Soviet card against the US seemed effective. He had gathered American support for Iran, while maintaining Iran's own national interest as his principle aim. The Shah visited Washington in August 1967, at a time when the US had learnt about Britain's intention to withdraw from the Far East and expected an end to its Gulf commitments to follow, and America, for its part, was handicapped by the ongoing Vietnam war. US officials sensed an increase of Iran's importance to US policy in the Middle East.[124] From that point the idea that American interest in the Gulf could be safeguarded by regional powers, mainly Iran and Saudi Arabia, gathered momentum all the way to the articulation of the Nixon doctrine.[125]

Having established close relations with the US and improved relations with the USSR, Iran began to express its independent interest in the Gulf and felt less concerned about the continuity of Britain's security role there. Iranian officials argued that Iran's main national security challenge came from the south.[126] Following the decision to withdraw from Aden in 1966, the Shah believed that Britain's days in the Gulf were numbered and from time to time would remind the British ambassador in Tehran of Iranian interests and territorial claims,[127] most notably to Bahrain which in 1957 Iran had made its fourteenth province with the right to a seat in the Majlis. According to one source, when Goronwy Roberts informed the Shah in November 1967 of Britain's intention to remain in the Gulf for the foreseeable future, the Shah did not voice any objections.[128] Simultaneously, however, the Iranian press launched a campaign critical of the British role in the region. On

16 November 1967 the semi-official newspaper, *Kayhan*, reminded Britain of its policy failure in Aden, and stressed that security in the Gulf could only be achieved by a full recognition of Iran's role as the main regional power.[129]

Unlike many regional players, by 1968 Iran had no reason to fear the consequences of Britain's retreat. As Prime Minister Amir Abbas Hoveida said, 'Iran does not feel concern or anxiety [over Britain's decision], we don't feel there will be a dangerous political vacuum in the Persian Gulf ... we face this historic new phase with great confidence.'[130] But the strongest expression of the Iranian attitude came in the Shah's first public statement on the issue on 12 March 1968 when he said,

> All countries can expect reciprocity from us for their attitude toward our country. The time has come for us to take reciprocal action to foreign attitudes. We will not be satisfied with showing friendship and receiving perhaps only a benevolent glance in return. I warn even our present friends that if they ignore Iran's interests in any respect, especially in the Persian Gulf, they should expect from Iran treatment befitting their attitude.[131]

Conclusion

Three trends set the stage for Iran to play a leading role in the Gulf from January 1968 onwards: Britain's diminishing overseas power, particularly in the area east of Suez; America's preoccupation with Vietnam and its reluctance to assume new commitments; and Iran's growing national power.

The British Labour government set out to play a world security role in order to maintain Britain's international status and guarantee other countries' co-operation in different fields. The most persistent issue at the time was American financial support. Soon after the new government announced its policy, however, opposition broke out within the Labour Party: with continuing economic difficulties this opposition grew rapidly. The government was forced to make one defence cut after another which weakened its position in the Gulf both politically and militarily, and in the end Gulf commitments could not withstand the rising tide of austerity.

The US pressed Britain to continue its east of Suez role but without much success as the British government gradually shifted its priority to domestic politics. US pressure on Britain reflected the difficulties America faced in extending its international security role, while the ongoing Vietnam war set domestic constraints on the Johnson administration's policy toward developing regions. By the end of 1967, US officials anticipated a British withdrawal from the Gulf, but difficulties in achieving consensus on foreign policy issues, together with the administration's preoccupation with the Arab-Israeli conflict, prevented the formulation of a policy to deal with the emerging situation in the Gulf. Instead they began to look to regional powers for a solution.

Out of the British decision and American indecision, a leading role for Iran in the Gulf was born. Iran at the time was witnessing rapid growth of its military and economic power matched by a new direction in foreign policy which provided for rapprochement with the East without damaging its relations with the West. By 1968 Iran was in a position to assert its own interests in the Gulf. The issues which most concerned Iran, and how they were dealt with in the early stages of Britain's withdrawal, are addressed in the next chapter.

3

From Gunboat Diplomacy to Compromise

'The departure of foreign forces from the Arabian Gulf,' declared President Arif of Iraq in March 1968 '... means that the area is returning to normal and is regaining legitimate rights which were usurped many years ago.'[1] Some two months later, the Shah told a Pakistani journalist that '... the withdrawal of Britain from the Gulf must be a real one,' and added that Britain must not use local agents 'to leave through the front door in order to return through the back door.'[2] Meanwhile, the Iranian press called for efforts to 'cut foreign hands from the Persian Gulf.'[3] The similarity in the rhetoric employed by these neighbouring, and generally hostile, states is striking. Most notable, however, is the shift in Iran's political language. The pro-Western tenor of Iranian discourse on foreign policy for the best part of the 1950s and 1960s had, by this time, given way to a more assertive and explicit resentment of external intervention in regional affairs very much in tune with the worldview of Cairo and Baghdad.

Iran and the radical Arab states could find common ground on a Gulf free from great power interference; but Iran never reached a rapprochement with the radical Arab camp, and nationalistic tendencies forced the two sides apart. The division between them, moreover, nurtured a disagreement over whether 'the Gulf' is 'Arab,' a view favoured by Iraq along with all Arab states, or 'Persian' as Iran maintained[4] while continuing to criticise Arabism in general, although the Arab threat was hardly real.[5]

The disagreement over the name of the waterway was, however, largely symbolic and made little difference to Iran's political interaction with the Gulf Arabs. The backdrop to the Gulf arena in the late 1960s was the ebbing tide of Nasserite pan-Arabism following the 1967 War. Iraq's own radical Arabism gained it antipathy from Iran and isolation from the Gulf Arabs. All serious attempts to resolve the Shatt al-Arab dispute were delayed. Hence, Iran focused on the issues and disputes which Britain would leave behind in the lower Gulf. How did Iran tackle these issues given the emerging regional context? And what was the role of external influence in the Gulf in an era of increasing regional autonomy?

Forming an Agenda

The new Gulf agenda was largely shaped by two players: Britain and Iran. Britain's main concern was to leave behind a 'viable state' and a 'stable regional structure.'[6] On 9 January 1968, during his trip to the Gulf to announce the pending British withdrawal, Foreign Secretary Goronwy Roberts is reported to have said that his government's policy was to encourage mutual co-operation among the Gulf states in matters of defence. No official statements were issued on a proposed defence pact.[7] However, Iran at the time was considering a regional pact to replace CENTO that would include Saudi Arabia, Kuwait and Pakistan,[8] while Saudi sources reveal that Britain had proposed a Saudi-Iranian defence agreement. The Saudi response was that such an alignment conflicted with Saudi Arabia's traditional policy which was opposed to formal bilateral alliances.[9] The Saudi document sheds light on the Saudi attitude to such an idea and on the limits to Saudi-Iranian co-operation and helps explain why the idea of a defence pact was not pursued vigorously.[10]

The viable state which Britain had in mind was a federation of the seven Trucial states – Abu Dhabi, Dubai, Ras al-Khaimah, Sharjah, Ajman, Umm al-Qaiwain and Fujairah – plus Bahrain and Qatar. The idea originated in Britain. As early as 1952 the British political resident in Bahrain, Sir Rupert Hay, had observed that the full independence of the Trucial emirates was inevitable in no more than two decades. The Foreign Office seemed to concur with this view and as a first step to independence a Trucial Council was created to discuss topics of mutual interest and adopt a common policy.[11] The Council met once or twice a year, but never developed into a form of federation. Nevertheless, in July 1965, the rulers of the Trucial states and of Bahrain and Qatar assembled for the first time in Dubai, and agreed to establish a Trucial Development Office. From that time onwards the idea of an Arab federation did begin to evolve although initiatives to actually establish one had to wait until 1968.

Once it had taken the decision to withdraw, Britain encouraged attempts to form the federation. It did not, however, try to impose it on the Rulers, and no long-term military protection was promised.[12] At this time Britain had no plans which could lead to its further involvement in the region – a policy one British official later described as 'defeatist,' although to others it was no more than a reflection of economic weakness at home.[13] The only British contribution to the Trucial States' security was a decision to develop the Trucial Oman Scouts, an internal military force composed of Arabs under British command, to become the nucleus of a federal army.[14]

Like their British counterparts, Iranian officials often dwelt on the idea of regional co-operation. At the time of Goronwy Roberts' January 1968 trip to the Gulf, an Iranian government spokesman announced that his country welcomed, '... any form of regional co-operation for the collective defence of the Gulf.'[15] Some two weeks later the Iranian prime minister said, 'Iran is naturally concerned with the security and stability of this region and is prepared to work with any other coastal country willing to cooperate toward this end.'[16] But to Iran the prospect of an Arab federation which included Bahrain hindered any practical development of 'regional co-operation.' Official Iranian statements often carried signals of Iran's determination to protect its own regional interests, and its desire to play a dominant Gulf role. Hoveida soon followed up his vaguely encouraging January statement with a qualification: 'In any case, the Imperial Iranian Government can undoubtedly protect its interests and rights in the Persian Gulf without allowing outside powers to interfere.' For the Shah there were, '... no problems with the Arabs unless they create some.' The only problem '... is to think that they should be heirs to British colonialism.'[17]

In the British Foreign Office, the response to these attitudes was mixed. Many in London were impressed by Iran's military might, and Iran's influence was perceived as a benign one which would not sabotage Western interests. Hence collaboration with Iran was viewed as a desirable way of guaranteeing peace and stability in the Gulf after British withdrawal.[18] Even so, Julian Bullard, who in 1968 was the British political agent in Dubai, noted the existence among his colleagues in the late 1960s of 'sentimental feelings' towards the abandoned Arabs at the end of empire – feelings mixed with concern over Iran's long-term intentions in the Gulf.[19]

Throughout these early attempts to establish a working agenda for the Gulf in the years leading to the British departure, Iran believed that any talk of long-term regional arrangements was premature before territorial disputes were settled.[20] To Iran, such issues were a priority and the Gulf Arab states and Britain, by suggesting new 'regional' structures, were getting ahead of existing attitudes in the region. The most apparent areas of dispute were the emerging conflict of Iranian-Arab territorial claims over Bahrain and the Hormuz islands. Linked to them was the formation of the federation of Arab emirates. Less apparent, but equally crucial, was a maritime dispute between Iran and Saudi Arabia. As events unfolded these disputes came to dominate the Gulf agenda.

The First Encounter

During the first two months of 1968 all the territorial disputes between Iran and the lower Gulf Arabs were brought to the fore. On 15 January, shortly before the Shah was due to pay an official visit to Saudi Arabia, the Emir of Bahrain visited the kingdom. The Iranian press was at the time full of the country's long-standing claim to the Bahrain. However, the Saudi ambassador to Tehran, Yussif al-Fawzan, believed that the Iranians were not serious, and told Riyadh that what was being said in the media was for domestic public opinion.[21] He thought that the Emir's visit would have no consequences for Saudi-Iranian relations – an analysis that was apparently confirmed when the *Observer* reported the next day that the Shah had given the Emir of Kuwait assurances that Iran would not claim Bahrain.[22]

The Emir of Bahrain was formally received as head of state by King Faisal, and it was decided during the visit that a causeway linking the two countries would be built.[23] A joint communiqué was issued stressing the strong historical bonds between the peoples of Bahrain and Saudi Arabia, Saudi Arabia's full support for the government of Bahrain, and the prospect of further economic co-operation.[24] The fact that Bahrain was only 15 miles away from the eastern coast of Saudi Arabia meant that good relations, and the island's independence, were Saudi security objectives. Indeed official British papers reveal that during this visit King Faisal assured Shaikh Eisa that, '… any attack on Bahrain would be treated as one on Saudi Arabia and met with all his country's resources.'[25]

To Shaikh Eisa, Saudi support was one way of ensuring his country's independence and in addition of gathering regional support to counter Iranian claims. Another option, proposed at the time by Anthony Parsons, the British political agent in Bahrain, was that Bahrain should apply for membership of the UN. Parsons could not see who would veto the application at the Security Council and assumed that such a move would have Arab support. According to Parsons, however, the emir did not want to move ahead of the Trucial states and Qatar as talks on a federation of nine members were about to get underway.[26]

Soon after Shaikh Eisa left Saudi Arabia the Saudi protocol department started to prepare for the Shah's arrival and in the streets of Riyadh processional arches bearing welcoming slogans were erected. But at the height of the preparations a message arrived from the Saudi Embassy in Bangkok saying that during the Shah's visit to Thailand Foreign Minister Ardeshir Zahedi had told a Saudi official that the visit might be cancelled.[27] Shaikh Eisa's visit and the language of the resulting communiqué were, said senior Iranian diplomat Amir Khosrow Afshar in an interview with the author, unacceptable to Iran, and the fact that Shaikh Eisa was given a head of state reception was a source of great anger at the highest levels.[28] The Shah, according to American sources, took the view that, had he gone to Saudi Arabia it would have been a public recognition that Iran had given up Bahrain, a position he was unwilling to take at the time. Although the American ambassador to Tehran tried to persuade the Shah not to cancel his trip, on 1 February it was announced that it would be postponed.[29]

The Saudi ambassador to Iran listed three reasons behind the cancellation: The *Observer*'s report from Kuwait that Iran had dropped her claim to Bahrain; the use of the phrase 'Arab Gulf' in a joint Saudi-Turkish communiqué following a visit by the Turkish prime minister to Saudi Arabia; and the Saudi-Bahraini communiqué.[30] When the Shah's personal envoy, Manuchehr Fartash, travelled to Saudi Arabia to convey the news formally,[31] the points he raised in conversation with Rashad Pharon, a senior adviser to King Faisal, confirmed that it had been the visit of the Emir of Bahrain, and the language of the joint Saudi-Bahraini communiqué that had provoked Iran. The Saudi-Turkish communiqué was ignored. Fartash had gone on to say that a public message from King Faisal to Iran would help dampen Iranian public anger. The Saudi government's response was that the reception of Shaikh Eisa was normal, given the historical ties between Saudi Arabia and Bahrain, and that there was not one word in the communiqué directed against Iran,³² hence there was not much to be explained and a message from King Faisal was ruled out.

Meanwhile, another disagreement flared up. Iran and Saudi Arabia had differences over offshore oil in the mid-Gulf dating back to the early 1960s and at the end of January the two countries were exchanging accusations that their respective oil companies were drilling in the disputed waters.³³ The Iranian minister of court, Asadollah Alam, requested a halt to drilling by both sides until a meeting could be held to negotiate the dispute. King Faisal soon agreed and on 31 January ordered the Saudi ambassador in Tehran to,

> Meet with Iranian officials immediately, and inform them that IPAC (Iranian Pan American Oil Company) is continuing drilling till this afternoon. We wish an immediate halt of drilling. The Saudi government on its side will order the Arabian American Oil Company (ARAMCO) to stop drilling temporarily till a meeting takes place.³⁴

The Saudi ambassador conveyed the message to the Iranian foreign minister and King Faisal agreed that an Iranian delegation should travel to Saudi Arabia.³⁵ In a telegram that arrived the next day the Iranian government concurred. However, the arrangement collapsed as soon as it was made when, on 1 February, an Iranian gunboat drove an ARAMCO drilling rig out of Gulf waters claimed by Iran. According to Saudi Arabia the rig, carrying sixty Saudis and Americans, had been sent to drill in an offshore concession leased by Saudi Arabia to the oil company.³⁶ At around the same time the USS *Pueblo* had been seized by North Korea. The North Korean government claimed that the American ship was in Korean territorial waters, while the United States maintained that it was sailing in international water (later it was revealed that the North Korean version of the story was true). Following the incident US ambassadors to friendly countries were ordered to describe the Pueblo affair as 'an act of piracy.' But when Herman Eilts, the US ambassador to Riyadh, approached King Faisal and asked for Saudi help to condemn the Korean action at the UN the King replied, 'Let me tell you about another act of piracy.' He went on to describe the Iranian seizure of the ARAMCO rig and the transfer of ARAMCO personnel to an Iranian vessel. According to Eilts this was how he first learnt of the affair, and he promptly contacted the US ambassador in Tehran to ease tension between the two countries.³⁷ As it turned out no great effort was needed because Alam had already informed the ambassador that as soon as the Shah heard of the seizure he had ordered the personnel to be released, and ARAMCO had been permitted to tow the rig away.[38] But the incident was enough to revive the old dispute.

During the first two months of 1968 a third development focused Iran's attention on local territorial issues. On 22 January the Ruler of Dubai, Shaikh Rashid Al-Maktoum, met with the Ruler of Abu Dhabi to discuss the proposed federation of Arab emirates, and then went on to Bahrain and Qatar.[39] The Emir of Bahrain, who was the first to announce publicly the plan to establish a federation, saw it as a Bahrain-Arab issue, '... which will not be decided by anyone for us.'[40] On 18 February Abu Dhabi and Dubai signed a union agreement,[41] and a Gulf emirates conference was held in Dubai attended by the rulers of Bahrain and Qatar as well as those of the Trucial States. Nine days later, on 27 February, an agreement was signed by the rulers of the Trucial States, Bahrain and Qatar on a united foreign and defence policy and the creation of a Supreme Council which was to be the highest policy making and legislative power of the federation. The agreement also created a Federal Council with executive authority to assist the Supreme Council, and a Supreme Federal Court. It stated that, 'Each emirate is sovereign over internal affairs which do not come under federal jurisdiction.'[42]

The document was more a declaration of intent than a plan for a fully formed federal state. Much was left unresolved, most notably a federal constitution and a detailed mechanism for the working of the federation. The agreement itself stated that the final agreement, '... shall come into force on 30 March 1968' allowing time for further rounds of talks among the Rulers.[43] Regional states, notably Saudi Arabia and Kuwait, were quick to welcome the Dubai agreement; however, the inclusion of Bahrain, Sharjah and Ras al-Khaimah, who were in dispute with Iran over the Hormuz islands, was enough to provoke Iranian anger. 'From the Imperial Iranian Government's point of view,' said the Iranian minister of foreign affairs on 1 April, 'the British Government cannot bequeath to others territories that it has – as history bears witness – severed from Iran by force and trickery. The Imperial Government reserves all rights in the Persian Gulf and will in no circumstances tolerate this historical injustice and imposition.'[44]

Diplomacy in Deadlock

Throughout 1968 the issue of Bahrain overshadowed other areas of dispute in the Gulf. Bahrain can on many levels be looked upon as different from the rest of the Gulf Arab emirates. According to the 1965 census it had a total population of nearly 182,203, mainly Arabs with just over 7,000 Iranians and a maximum of 15,000 Arabs of Iranian extraction.[45] This was a relatively large population when compared with the 80,000 population of Qatar and the 177,640 population of the seven Trucial States combined.[46] The level of education was also high as formal schooling had begun in Bahrain as early as 1929, and the rapidly diminishing oil reserves meant that economic problems were looming. Furthermore Bahrain had already displayed a preference for independence. With help from Britain, it had begun to achieve some international recognition as an associate member of UNESCO in October 1966, of the FAO in November 1967, and of the World Health Organisation in May 1968.[47] For all these reasons the British Political Resident in Bahrain did not believe that Bahrain would ever become a member of the Arab federation.[48]

The dramatic cancellation of the Shah's visit to Saudi Arabia assured Bahrain of international media attention, but also caused concern among many British and American decision-makers about how the issue might ultimately be resolved. Immediately after the cancellation, Asadollah Alam had told the US ambassador that the prospect of a rescheduled visit by the Shah, '... [did] not look good' and that the final decision would depend on Saudi reaction to Iran's objections on the Bahrain issue.[49] With that the prospect of an early resolution of Gulf disputes seemed gloomy; Iran and Saudi Arabia had taken extreme positions over the issue, and Iran was clearly vehemently opposed to the Federation of Arab Emirates. However, the offshore dispute between Saudi Arabia and Iran on the division of disputed waters in the Gulf prompted active contacts between the Gulf's two largest countries.

Early Attempts to Settle the Offshore Dispute

The offshore dispute dated back to April 1963 when the National Iranian Oil Company (NIOC) announced that certain offshore areas would be opened for international bidding. On 15 June that year Saudi Arabia protested the declaration on the ground that it constituted '... an infringement of the legitimate rights of Saudi Arabia in respect of the natural resources in the area opposite Saudi Arabia's territorial waters.'[50] The Saudi protest was ineffective as Iran granted an oil concession to the Pan-American Petroleum Corporation which overlapped with a concession already given by the Saudi government to ARAMCO. Thus, negotiations began in 1964 to resolve the dispute. The outcome was the Saudi-Iranian continental shelf agreement signed in Tehran in December 1965.

The text of this agreement was never made public. However, in an article published in 1970, Richard Young, a legal adviser to the Saudi Oil Ministry, revealed that it covered three geographical segments of the Saudi-Iranian maritime boundary.[51] The first ran from the southerly terminus up the Gulf to the vicinity of al-Arabiyah island. This area caused no technical difficulty, as it has no significant off-lying islands, and an agreement was eventually reached that the boundary should be essentially the median line between the opposite mainland coasts. The second segment comprised the area surrounding al-Arabiyah and Farisi islands. Here there was a need to resolve the status of the islands themselves. This was accomplished by recognising Saudi Arabia's sovereignty over al-Arabiyah and Iran's sovereignty over Farisi. Between the two islands a local median line was adopted separating their respective territorial seas. The third segment, the northernmost sector, faced the negotiators with the greatest obstacles, mainly stemming from the location of Kharg island and oil concessions in the area. Iran had granted concessions according to a median line using Kharg as a base line. On the other hand, Saudi Arabia's concession boundary followed the median line between the opposite mainlands, giving no effect to Kharg. In the end a compromise was achieved giving Kharg 'half effect' status for determining the relevant part of the offshore boundary.

A few months after the December 1965 agreement was signed, however, an Iranian concessionaire discovered oil in the Feyerdoon field in the northern segment of the disputed area.[52] Conservative estimates of oil reserves were about 10 billion barrels, lying mostly on the Saudi side of the 1965 boundary.[53] At that point Iran voiced its wish to alter the terms, and consequently it was never ratified.

On 7 February, just a week after the seizure of the ARAMCO oil rig, an Iranian delegation was dispatched to Dahran to meet the Saudi oil minister, Ahmed Zaki Yamani. It was lead by the government parliamentary secretary, Amir Teymour, who had reportedly played a role in the negotiations of December 1965, and included a number of NIOC officials. After a day of talks the Iranians accompanied Yamani to Riyadh for further discussions where the Iranian side are reported to have put forward the idea of a Saudi-Iranian joint venture in the disputed area – a proposal rejected by the Saudis.⁵⁴ According to a Saudi minute, the Iranian negotiator, Amir Teymour, adopted a tactical position in the talks, invoking domestic constraints by suggesting that Iranian public opinion would not accept the 1965 agreement and parliament would not ratify it (we should bear in mind that this dispute was not a major domestic issue in Iran nor did the Iranian parliament possess enough power to oppose the government). The Saudis suggested arbitration – a proposal the Iranian delegation referred to their government in Tehran and refused the next day, arguing that arbitration would complicate matters and it was better to arrive at a solution through bilateral negotiations. The Iranians stressed yet again that the problem was not economic but 'political,' a coded reference to public opinion.⁵⁵

An undated Saudi document suggests that the negotiations were subsequently taken to a higher level. In a conversation with Yamani in Tehran the Shah again suggested a joint venture. Yamani, however, repeated his objections to the idea, this time arguing that it would lead to managerial complications and that a joint venture had been rejected by Saudi Arabia as early as 1964. Furthermore, a joint venture would be unfair to Saudi Arabia as most oil lay on the Saudi side of the 1965 median line. Yamani ended his trip to Iran with no clear result.⁵⁶

Breaking the Ice

At the end of February 1968 an agreement on the maritime boundary dispute seemed unlikely in the light of strained Saudi-Iranian relations. It is nevertheless clear that at this time Iran was trying to initiate some movement to break the ice with Saudi Arabia and to improve its relations with Britain and the United States. Although the Shah told US officials that he believed their government was taking sides with Saudi Arabia on the Gulf water dispute, he began to refer to the long-term importance of good relations with Saudi Arabia which '... could become the nucleus for stability and progress in the Persian Gulf.'⁵⁷ A similar attitude prevailed on the Saudi side as the US ambassador in Riyadh, Hermann Eilts, had reported at the beginning of February. Although disappointed with the cancellation of the Shah's visit, King Faisal, he told Washington, still hoped that the problems that had arisen between the two countries could be managed through direct discussions. Secretary of State Dean Rusk in response asked Meyer to convey the King's mood to the Shah. For some three months, however, both the Shah and King Faisal refrained from making public statements which might improve the atmosphere.[58]

The Shah had, from time to time, hinted to certain British officials that a resolution of the Bahrain issue was not impossible. Indeed, during his January tour of the Gulf, Goronwy Roberts had, according to Saudi sources, indicated that the Shah, as he understood it, would not pursue his claim to the island.[59] At around the same time, Abbas Aram, the Iranian ambassador to London, had conveyed a message from the Shah to Saudi and British officials that there was no need to raise the Bahrain issue as the Shah could not antagonise public opinion by dropping the claim but wanted to resolve the problem with King Faisal during his planned visit to Saudi Arabia. The Shah's position, however, was not widely known and was thoroughly at odds with Iran's public pronouncements. At that point, even the British Political Agent in Bahrain was not aware of it,[60] and within the Shah's inner policy circle Amir Khosrow Afshar, who knew where his monarch stood, did not believe that he would have made it clear to Western diplomats since that would weaken Iran's position.[61]

Sir Denis Wright has recently revealed that, as early as 1955, when he was serving as chargé d'affaires in Tehran, the Shah had made no secret of his lack of interest in Bahrain.[62] But he faced a problem, neatly summed up by Sir Denis in an undated entry in his memoirs,

> Occasionally the Shah would raise the question of Bahrain with me. He would say that because the pearls had run out and the oil was running out he had no interest in acquiring the island but, because of Iran's historic claim to the place, he could not go down in history as the King who had abandoned his heritage without good cause; in other words, some face-saving formula.[63]

The question that faced the Shah in this period was not whether, but how and when, Iran could drop its claim to the island.

An American document pinpoints early February 1968 as the date when the Shah explicitly began to convey his lack of interest in the Iranian claim. In the course of a meeting with the American national security advisor, Walt Rostow, held on 9 February, the Shah said that he '... would not use force to gain Bahrain,' adding that, '... pearl and oil industries are no longer [a] great prize ... [and that the] island is infested with Arab nationalist trouble-makers.' However, he stressed that Iran's claim was 150 years old and could not be dismissed without some justification.[64] A plebiscite was discussed but no clear solution was indicated. Significantly perhaps, Armin Meyer, who was present at the audience, recalls that the Shah did not actually insist on a plebiscite and was open to suggestions for an adequate face-saving device.[65] On the mid-Gulf oil reserves the Shah proposed the solution that would be put to Saudi Arabia two weeks later, namely that the way out was a joint venture with Saudi Arabia. Given that it was known that 'enormous reserves' had been discovered in the disputed area, it would, he said, be politically impossible to ratify the 1965 median line.[66]

In mid-March, the US ambassador began to elaborate a solution to the Bahrain question. Meyer believed that the Shah could save face over the claim only if the contested islands near the Strait of Hormuz were given in exchange. In a telegram to Dean Rusk dated 15 March 1968 he argued that '... unless these concessions [are] made to [the] Shah, he will in our view take unilateral action with regards to mid-Gulf oil, which no one can prevent and which can only lead to permanent feuding across the Gulf.' Meyer also recommended that Bahrain stay out of the proposed Arab federation.[67]

At an audience with the Shah, Meyer put forward what he saw as a possible deal on Bahrain: a clear secession (through British auspices) of the Tunbs and Abu Musa islands to Iran and a joint Saudi-Iranian venture in the mid Gulf for oil exploration on both sides of the 1965 median line; as a reciprocal gesture Iran would relinquish its claim to Bahrain.[68] There is no evidence to suggest that the Shah agreed to such deal, or that the US ambassador informed Britain of his proposal. In April, however, the Shah made a similar offer to the British ambassador who, in a telegram to the Foreign Office, reported that the Shah had said he did not wish to occupy Bahrain, '... but since every Iranian had been brought up to regard Bahrain as Iranian territory he must have some quid pro quo.' The Shah suggested a plebiscite to '... get him off the Bahrain hook plus acquisition of the Tunbs and Abu Musa.' Sir Denis Wright made it clear, there and then, that Britain was opposed to such package deal.[69]

Soon afterwards an American source speculated that another party, namely Morocco, had become involved in the attempt to mediate betweem Saudi Arabia and Iran. In late April, during a visit to Iran by King Hassan, it was reported that a

Moroccan delegation had left Tehran for a day mission to Riyadh.[70] Although Morocco was not usually involved in Gulf affairs, King Hassan had close friendships with both the Shah and the Saudi royal family. Furthermore, before King Hassan's visit, the Moroccan ambassador in Tehran had told his Saudi counterpart that he sensed the Iranians regretted the deterioration of their relations with Saudi Arabia, and that the Iranian foreign minister had met with him twice in an attempt to find a 'way out.'[71] In recent interviews with the author both Zahedi and Afshar have played down the part taken by Morocco and said that King Hassan's visit was planned long before the Saudi-Iranian rift.

It may, then, have been coincidental that, at the beginning of May, soon after the Moroccan delegation's visit, King Faisal sent a public message to the Shah through an interview with the Kuwaiti newspaper *Al-Siyasah* in which he said that the Shah would be welcome to visit Saudi Arabia whenever he chose, and stressed the existence of '... mutual rights on the Gulf for all countries concerned.' The Arabs of the Gulf, the King went on, would not take any action against Iran's interests in the region.[72] The statement was received positively by the Iranian press and four days later the Shah responded by announcing that he would go to Saudi Arabia at the first opportunity.[73] The Iranian foreign minister reported to the US ambassador the 'good news' of a rescheduled visit by the Shah,[74] which came, he said, as a result of 'on-going contact' between the two countries.[75] Most of these contacts are undocumented in the Saudi archives, or indeed elsewhere, and therefore difficult to track.

Another possible explanation of this development is more straightforward, but again undocumented, namely Saudi-Iranian diplomacy. In mid-April the US ambassador to Riyadh had told Omar Saqqaf, the Saudi minister of state for foreign affairs, that the climate was right to patch up differences with Iran, and suggested an audience between the Saudi ambassador and the Shah to explain Saudi Arabia's position over Bahrain.[76] According to Eilts, 'My idea was to have the Saudi Arabian ambassador see the Shah so the matter would not be seen [by the Shah] as imposed by the US.'[77] Just a few days later Afshar informed Armin Meyer that Maroof al-Dawalibi, an adviser to King Faisal and former prime minister of Syria, was to visit Tehran in the near future.[78]

When he met the Shah in early May, Dawalibi began to explain that pushing Iran's claim to Bahrain would endanger Iranian relations with the entire Arab world. But to Dawalibi's surprise the meeting was not a long one. The Shah had made up his mind to make a commitment to Saudi Arabia on his intentions over Bahrain; he told the Saudi envoy to inform King Faisal that he had dropped his claim and to convey his wish to visit Saudi Arabia in the near future. On his way back, Dawalibi made a stop in Manama to placate Bahrain's fears of Iranian intentions.[79] Denis Wright had no knowledge of this Saudi-Iranian communication,[80] and Anthony Parsons only heard about it from the Emir of Bahrain.[81]

It is difficult to explain why the Shah chose to inform the Saudi government of his position on Bahrain in May 1968, as no evidence can be found of exchanges between the two governments before Dawalibi's trip. However, days after Dawalibi's return an informed Iranian source told the Saudi ambassador that the Shah had indeed sent a telegram formally conveying his wish to visit Saudi Arabia.[82] A few days later Abbas Aram informed the Saudi ambassador in Tehran that the Shah would touch down in Saudi Arabia on his way to Africa.[83] The visit took place on 3 June 1968 when the Shah made a stop-over in Jeddah on his way to Ethiopia. This short visit, however, was largely symbolic of a resumption of meetings at the highest level rather than an occasion designed to achieve specific agreement on particular issues.[84]

Conflict Resolution

As prospects for the resolution of the Bahrain issue began to seem promising in the Spring of 1968, the terms of a possible compromise over the Gulf offshore oil began to emerge. In March the president of ARAMCO, Thomas Barger, presented a proposal for the resolution of the Saudi-Iranian oil dispute to the US government. Barger echoed the Saudi idea that a joint venture would involve 'management complications for ARAMCO and IPAC.' Instead, he suggested a geographical or economic division of the disputed area. Barger divided the area into zone A for Saudi Arabia and zone B for Iran, and suggested that proven reserves would be equally divided. Armin Meyer believed that such a proposal could be 'sold' to the Shah if 'the Saudis buy it.'[85]

At this stage a response came from Washington that encapsulated the Johnson administration's attitude toward the Gulf. The State Department believed it would not be desirable for Meyer to mention the Barger proposal to the Shah, or elsewhere in the Iranian government, for the time being. In explaining this policy the secretary of state saw the aim as getting the Saudis and Iranians to negotiate

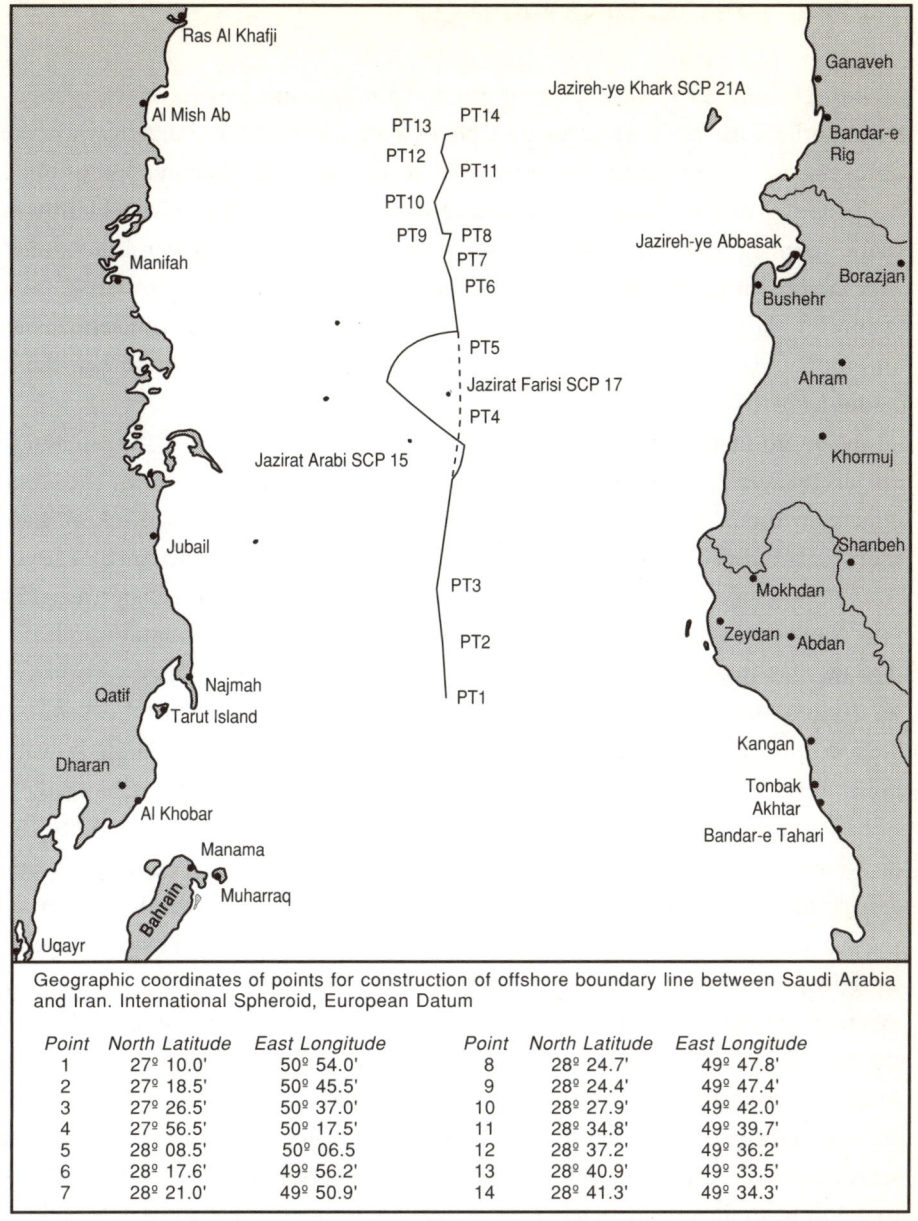

Map 1: The 1968 Final Offshore Boundary Line between Saudi Arabia and Iran

Source: Adapted from a map held in the Saudi Arabian Oil Ministry Archive which forms part of the Offshore Boundary Agreement between Saudi Arabia and Iran

bilaterally; only then would a number of solutions be mentioned. 'If it was mentioned now,' Rusk believed, '... it would be interpreted [by the Iranian government] as taking sides with ARAMCO.' Rusk added that Barger had already mentioned his proposal to the Saudi oil minister Yamani.[86] An even clearer statement was made about America's position when a State Department memorandum argued that the US should stay out of internal Gulf affairs and do no more than '... keep reminding both of them [Faisal and the Shah] that the best way to keep Nasser and the Russians out is to work together.' The US should make its views heard but '... not think in terms of a major US program.'[87]

In fact no major US programme was needed to resolve some of the outstanding disputes in the Gulf since regional powers had begun to carry out the work effectively themselves. On 29 July negotiations between Iran and Saudi Arabia on the Gulf oil dispute were resumed in Taif, a city in the western province of Saudi Arabia. An agreement was reached to divide the 'oil in place' equally between the two countries, a solution along the lines of Barger's recommendations. Thus a new median line was ultimately worked out. (see map 1) The revised section, referred to in the 1965 agreement as the third section northernmost of the disputed area, ran in zigzag fashion until it intersected the boundary of the Saudi-Kuwaiti neutral zone. The other segments of the 1965 agreement were left unchanged.[88]

Saudi sources confirm that the Iranian delegation agreed in principle to the division reached at Taif. During a meeting with Dr Manouchehr Eqbal, the managing director of NIOC, King Faisal stressed the legality of the Saudi position in the oil dispute. The King also sent Yamani to Tehran in August in the hope of bringing an end to the dispute in order to '... focus on other essential matters.'[89] When Yamani arrived for the talks, however, an unexpected last minute obstacle developed: the Iranian negotiators had changed their position, arguing for a division of 'recoverable oil' or proven oil reserves and not the 'oil in place.'[90] The Saudi side argued that such a division was technically difficult as there was no way in which accurate estimates could be given on the amount of oil reserves unless actual drilling took place in certain areas. Yamani reported home that the negotiations were difficult, and the issue seemed to have reached a deadlock, but that he was due to meet the Shah the following day.

During this meeting Yamani explained the Saudi position to the Shah who, according to Ardeshir Zahedi, had been briefed by the Foreign Ministry that Saudi Arabia had stronger legal claims.[91] Once more, the Shah gave priority to long-term stability in Saudi-Iranian relations instead of immediate gains. He accepted Yamani's case and a map was promptly initialled on the basis of the understanding reached in Taif.[92] On 21 August, when a map showing the newly agreed boundary line was initialled in Tehran by Yamani and the Iranian finance minister, Jamshid Amouzegar,[93] an Iranian official told the Saudi ambassador that the new Continental Shelf Agreement would be signed on 24 October and would be presented to the Iranian parliament on the 27th to coincide with Yamani's next visit to Iran.[94]

The successful resolution of the Saudi-Iranian dispute further reinforces the idea that regional players had the ability to resolve their disputes without outside intervention provided they had the political will to do so. But would this impression hold in the case of Bahrain?

Resolving the Bahrain Issue

On the eve of an audience with the Shah on 2 June 1968, Denis Wright wrote, 'Brooding about my coming audience on Sunday and the unsatisfactory hand I have to play. Bahrain, the Tunbs, Abu Musa and Sirri will be graven on my heart, also the Union of Arab Emirates ... .' After the meeting Wright noted that, 'I put to the Shah various of HMG's ideas for settling the islands problem in the Persian Gulf. Package deals; median line plus islands; non militarisation; arbitration; condominium etc. Not a bad meeting though there is a long way to go yet.'[95] To Wright it was 'not a bad meeting' because the Shah did not reject any of the ideas put to him; but he showed no enthusiasm for any of them either.[96]

On the federation, the Shah had already clarified his position, which in its essentials had not changed. In an interview in May with the Kuwaiti journal *Al-Ra'y al-Amm* he had said that Iran did not oppose the Arab federation, '... as long as historical and territorial rights are observed in its foundation. There is a possibility that the federation could inherit the old British colonial policy, which opposes the interests of Iran.'[97] Speculation was by then growing that attempts to establish the federation were facing difficulties. The 30 March date for the Dubai agreement to come into force had come and gone without a Supreme Council meeting and no explanation had been given for the inaction.[98]

Details of difficulties facing the federation will be discussed in a later chapter. Suffice it to say here that they were presented by the Iranian media as a response to Iranian unease and Tehran Radio continued to speak of the federation as a British plot to maintain its imperialist policy, which Iran could not tolerate.[99] But a meeting of Gulf rulers was eventually convened on 8 July and an agreement on the functions of federal institutions was issued.[100] According to the press a spirit of compromise was in the air. There was agreement on a revolving chairmanship for each Supreme Council session; a Provisional Union Council was set up, headed by the deputy ruler of Qatar, Shaikh Khalifa bin Hamad al-Thani; and Abdulrazaq al-Sanhuri Pasha, an Egyptian lawyer and author of the Kuwaiti constitution, was asked to draft a federal constitution. Divisions over the location of the capital, however, and decisions on foreign and defence policy, were left for a second round of negotiations to be held in Doha on 20 October.[101]

When the results of this meeting were announced, the Iranian foreign minister again described the federation as a 'manifestation of colonialism' and indicated that the inclusion of Bahrain was unacceptable.[102] The available evidence does not, however, suggest that such public criticism was matched by any active attempt to subvert the process of federation. Rather, direct contact between Iran and some of the rulers was resumed in the wake of this meeting. Iran, however, remained circumspect about how such contacts might be interpreted and an editorial in the Iranian newspaper *Ayandegan* argued that co-operation with the Gulf rulers did not mean that 'Iran will sacrifice its interests for any consideration.'[103] Indeed in August, when the Crown Prince of Ras al-Khaimah, Shaikh Khalid bin Saqar, visited Tehran, British sources reveal that he could find no room for negotiation on the Tunbs.[104] Such caution reinforces the idea that Iran's priority at the time was the resolution of the Bahrain issue.

Publicly, Iran continued to maintain a hard-line on the island. In June, the Iranian representative at the United Nations said that it was as rightfully Iranian as 'Gibraltar is Spanish,'[105] while his Saudi counterpart emphasised Bahraini independence. In August month-long demonstrations, organised by a pan-Iranist party, were held throughout Iran in support of the claim to Bahrain,[106] while the Iranian press protested a statement made by Goronwy Roberts in a Kuwaiti newspaper, *Al-Siyasah*, which referred to Bahrain as an independent state.[107]

Despite such declarations, in private a deal on Bahrain was being prepared.[108] An American Embassy telegram reveals that at the end of July the Shah had, for the first time, advanced concrete options for resolving the issue by proposing to Armin Meyer that it should be taken to the Security Council in the form of a complaint against Britain, or to the International Court of Justice (ICJ). The ambassador discouraged the Security Council option and agreed to have the US Embassy's legal experts examine the feasibility of the ICJ case and prepare an 'unofficial' study to be presented to the Shah.[109] Meanwhile, Asadollah Alam apprised the Shah of another possibility: namely that Iran could give up Bahrain in return for the three islands of Hormuz. Alam had added that this option had been suggested to Denis Wright, but Wright, '... had been avoiding the Shah due to the inadequacy of London's response to his endeavours.'[110]

Despite Meyer's insistence on more US involvement, the State Department re-emphasised its Gulf policy. Dean Rusk stressed that he preferred to have the British continue to take the lead in attempting to resolve the problem posed by the Iranian claim to Bahrain, '... as you know,' said Rusk, 'Ambassador Wright had instructions to probe [the] Shah's intentions and desires. We understand he [has] requested an audience with the Shah for the next few days. We see real risk in our becoming involved in terms of our relations with all parties to dispute.'[111] In response, Meyer argued that the British were not doing very well, and that a solution must be provided before the Gulf rulers' meeting scheduled for December. If not, Meyer warned, '... he [the Shah] is likely to go further down a road which is difficult to escape, [one] which he does not want to go, and which leads to trouble for all of us.' The US ambassador reiterated that the International Court of Justice option seemed worth exploring as it would provide face-saving for the Shah, although the British and the Bahrainis might not like it because it would involve tacit acknowledgement of Iran's claim.[112] There is no evidence to suggest whether the State Department responded to Meyer's message or whether it revised Washington's policy.

Meyer was right to inform the State Department that Britain's efforts were encountering difficulty, for on 5 August the Shah told Denis Wright that none of the ideas he had put forward at the 1 June audience were acceptable. Instead he insisted on a 'referendum' or 'plebiscite' in Bahrain.[113] Anthony Parsons later recalled commenting at length to the Foreign Office on the idea of a plebiscite, which he opposed fearing that it would be turned by pan-Arabists in Bahrain into a plebiscite on the choice between Bahraini ruling family or a republic. According to Parsons London accepted his view, and the idea was not put to Shaikh Eisa.[114]

Sir Denis Wright conveyed his government's position on a plebiscite to the Shah who could not understand Britain's reservation; to him it was a simple way to resolve the dispute. The Shah took the argument a step further: '... within the next few years,' he told Wright, 'it would be impossible to avoid introducing democratic process in Bahrain. Sooner or later therefore these revolutionary forces we feared so much would be able to have their say.' Sir Denis tried to put different alternatives for the expression of the people of Bahrain of their wish for independence, such as a petition to the Emir by heads of different religious and racial groups, or through a poll of a cross section of Bahrain's population; but none of this was enough to enable the Shah to tell his people that the majority of Bahrainis did not want to be part of Iran.[115]

As both British and US efforts toward resolving the dispute were not moving forward, Iran took a different route to conflict resolution: a return to the bilateral and regional levels. Towards the end of 1968, the first documented meeting between Bahraini and Iranian officials took place to resolve the issue.[116] The meeting was convened in Switzerland as a result of a Kuwaiti initiative.[117] Shaikh Khalifah bin Salman al-Khalifah, who was both the prime minister and Shaikh Eisa's brother, headed the Bahraini delegation, while Amir Khosrow Afshar represented Iran.[118] According to Eric Jensen, who was to become the political officer to the UN secretary-general's 'good offices' mission to Bahrain, the Iranians proposed 'referring the dispute to the Security Council as a colonial issue under Article 34 and 35 of the UN Charter, to a special committee of the General Assembly, or alternatively as a legal issue to the International Court of Justice.' The Bahrainis rejected these proposals on the ground that they could not be considered applicable to Bahrain, which was, they maintained, an independent state and not subject to treatment as a decolonisation question. Instead the Bahraini side proposed that a relevant regional body, or a head of state friendly to both sides, be invited to mediate.[119] Iran rejected such claims, and the two meetings ended with no tangible results.[120]

The Compromise

Iranian efforts at the regional level did not, however, stop at meetings with the Bahraini delegation. On 9 November 1968 the Shah made his rescheduled state visit to Saudi Arabia. The joint communiqué issued at the end of his five-day stay made no reference to Gulf disputes but instead dwelt on Islamic solidarity and the Arab-Israeli conflict. However, prior to the Shah's arrival, Iranian officials told the Saudis that the Shah would raise three issues with King Faisal: Bahrain, the islands, and the Federation of Arab Emirates.¹²¹ Moreover, the Iranian newspaper *Ettela'at* speculated that the purpose of the Shah's visit was to resolve the issues of Bahrain and the federation.¹²² Once the talks were over, the Western press reported that the Shah had decided to drop his claim to Bahrain,¹²³ while according to the Iranian press the Riyadh talks had reached an unofficial agreement on Gulf matters.¹²⁴ In an interview with the author, Ardeshir Zahedi confirmed that an agreement to end Iran's claim to Bahrain was re-emphasised during the talks, but there was no consensus on a method to achieve it as Iran still saw a plebiscite as the sole option.¹²⁵

It was not until the following month that the first evidence of a breakthrough appeared over a means to end the Iranian claim. The Shah still maintained his position on a plebiscite to determine whether the people of Bahrain wished to become part of Iran or to seek independence. But when the proposal was eventually put to the Emir, Shaikh Eisa felt that such a suggestion infringed on his sovereignty. On 14 December, Armin Meyer summarised these positions and sent the following suggestions to Washington:

1. Shaikh Eisa requests a third party to assist him to conduct a 'census.' Each inhabitant should be asked, among other things, what he considers his nationality to be;
2. With support from Saudi Arabia and Kuwait, Shaikh Eisa should ask the Shah to accept the result of the census as an indication of the population's political desire;
3. In return, Meyer believed, Iran should be allowed to announce 'exclusive rights to fortify the Tunbs and Abu Musa,' rather than Iranian sovereignty over the islands, and possibly a Bahrain-Iranian treaty of friendship and commerce might be made at the same time. The American ambassador went on to say, '... it would help also if Bahrain declares that military facilities vacated by Britain would not be made available to non-Gulf states.'¹²⁶

The response to Meyer's suggestions is unknown, and no evidence has been found that his recommendations went beyond the State Department and the White House. However, it is likely they would have met with opposition from Britain and the Bahraini authorities. Britain would have been opposed to linking Bahrain to the islands dispute, and the Bahraini government would have objected to a plebiscite. But during the same month, on 7 December, Iranian senator and publisher of the daily newspaper *Ettela'at*, Abbas Masoudi, paid a visit to the British ambassador. Denis Wright recalls telling Masoudi, '... why we could not fall in with the Shah's wishes for a referendum.' He suggested that 'one way out might be to ask the United Nations to sound out public opinion.' But 'I had no authority for making this suggestion, apart from a single sentence in one Foreign Office telegram saying in certain circumstances they might possibly consider resort to the United Nations.'[127]

Two days later Masoudi told Wright that the Shah liked the UN idea.. The Foreign Office then began consulting Britain's representatives at the UN and in Bahrain.[128] The new head of the Arabian Department at the Foreign Office, Sir Antony Acland, believed that, 'We had to think of a way with the Iranians, and with the Bahrainis, of achieving this legal expression of the will of the people of Bahrain in a manner which was effective, in a manner which would enable the Shah to accept the outcome.'[129]

After a two-week silence Wright received instructions to propose a way around the obstacle of a plebiscite or referendum to the Shah – namely to ask the UN secretary-general, U Thant, to 'ascertain' the wishes of the Bahrainis. On Christmas Eve Wright met the Shah and put the idea to him, explaining that he had not yet received the agreement either of Bahrain or of U Thant. The Shah thought the idea was 'constructive,' although he said that he needed time to prepare Iranian public opinion for such a decision.[130]

Private discussions between Afshar and the British ambassador about the means through which the good offices of UN secretary-general might be exercised got under way within days.[131] But in the New Year the Shah made a public statement that took all concerned, whether his close associates, or British and American officials, by surprise.[132] At a press conference held in the Indian capital, New Delhi, on 4 January 1969 he announced that Iran would not use force to regain what belonged to it by right, 'It prefers to see the Bahraini people make their own free choice.'[133] Implicit in this statement was the Shah's acceptance of the UN option as put to him by Britain.

Some of the Shah's aides thought that a public statement of this kind was premature and were concerned to such an extent that Zahedi attempted to block the news from reaching the international media; but the Indians had already made the text of the press conference public.[134] The Bahraini authorities, on the other hand, were pleased, as was the British Political Agent there. Once again a single unplanned move from the Shah had set the resolution of a long Arab-Iranian dispute on track. The remaining difficulties were purely procedural.

Sealing the Deal

Throughout 1969 and the early months of 1970 Iranian, British and UN officials looked for practical ways to implement the Shah's commitment to resolving the Bahrain question. A number of obstacles had to be surmounted before the procedure itself could be launched. The first was the terms of reference under which the UN secretary-general's mission was to operate. The Bahrainis opposed the terms of reference originally proposed which described the Bahrain issue as a 'dispute' between Britain and Iran under articles 34 and 35 of the UN Charter which deal with settlements of disputes between member states.[135] Bahrain already considered itself a state, but since Iran did not recognise it as independent, the Bahrainis were prepared to approach the UN secretary-general through Britain '... which was entrusted with the conduct of Bahrain's foreign relations.' Eventually the terms of reference were spelled out omitting the use of the word 'dispute' and made no reference to Iran or Britain:

> Having regard to the problem created by the views of the parties concerned about the status of Bahrain and the need to find a solution to this problem in order to create an atmosphere of tranquillity, stability and friendliness throughout the area, the Secretary-General of the United Nations is requested by the parties concerned to send a Personal Representative to ascertain the wishes of the people of Bahrain.

Bahrain, Britain and Iran accepted that the findings of the secretary-general's representative were subject to endorsement by the Security Council. Other problems facing the UN mission included the procedures to be followed in assessing public opinion in Bahrain since the Bahrainis maintained their opposition to a formal plebiscite.[136]

To the Shah a speedy settlement of the Bahrain issue 'was essential' if Saudi Arabia and Iran were 'to get together and stand up to the increasing penetration of the area.'[137] In August the Emir of Bahrain visited Britain before going to the US.[138] Upon his return he publicly accepted the idea of a UN commission to ascertain the wishes of the people of Bahrain.[139] However, many technicalities had to be worked out.

In December 1969 a meeting took place in Geneva between three Bahraini representatives, Sir Geoffrey Arthur of the UK (later political resident in Bahrain) and two UN officials – Vittorio Winspeare Guicciardi, an Italian diplomat and director-general of the UN office in Geneva, and Dr Ralph Bunche, the under-secretary-general for special political affairs. The general procedure of the mission was agreed at this meeting, which has been described as a success.[140]

A last minute hitch occurred over the Iranian draft letter to U Thant asking him to use his good offices in resolving the Bahrain issue. The Foreign Office had objected to the original Iranian draft believing that it stated the Iranian case in a manner which may be offensive to Bahrain. A Bahraini protest might, the British feared, jeopardise the whole UN exercise.[141] On 5 February Sir Denis Wright was sent to see the Shah and Afshar in St Moritz where he reached an agreement with them on the text of the letter.[142]

In March 1970 Iran formally presented a note to U Thant requesting the UN secretary-general to ascertain the political views of the Bahraini population.[143] Soon after, U Thant made an official announcement regarding the exercise of his good offices in Bahrain and appointed Winspeare Guicciardi as his personal representative. Winspeare was to submit '... his findings in the form of a report to the Secretary-General who would transmit them to the Security Council for reconsideration and endorsement.'[144]

To Eric Jensen, the political officer to the secretary-general's mission, the 'quiet approach' adopted in dealing with the Bahrain dispute, '... made it possible to avoid public confrontation of the parties in the [Security] Council or elsewhere, where they would be tempted to express intransigent and rigid positions.'[145] Jensen's fear that the process set in motion to resolve the Bahrain dispute was being subverted by public debate was by no means unfounded as the Soviet ambassador to the UN criticised the failure to consult with other members of the Security Council beforehand. But in the end the USSR took no steps to impede the implementation of the secretary-general's good offices mission.[146]

Ardeshir Zahedi made a statement to the Iranian Majlis on 29 March regarding the future of Bahrain in which he spoke at length about Iran's claim to the island since the 19th century and repeated the claim Iran had made to the League of Nations in the 1920s. Zahedi then went on to say:

> As the honourable Deputies are aware, Britain will leave the Persian Gulf in 1971. It might be presumed that the practical obstacles for the return of Bahrain to Iran would then have been removed and that Iran could, after Britain's withdrawal, send troops to occupy the island. It should be borne in mind, however, that during this long period there might have been changes in Bahrain's demographic composition which could have affected the real wishes of the majority of the inhabitants and of which the Imperial Government may not at present be aware. It was on the basis of these considerations that the Shah, in his New Delhi press conference on 14th Dey 1347 [January 1969], declared a logical policy acceptable to the world with regard to solution of the Bahrain problem.

Zahedi confirmed that if the report of the fact-finding mission was approved by the Security Council Iran would accept it. He also announced that U Thant had accepted Iran's request 'a few hours' before his speech.[147] Asadollah Alam thought Zahedi should have also taken the opportunity to stress 'that the Gulf is absolutely vital to Iran.'[148]

Shortly afterwards, the UN announced that U Thant was to send Winspeare to Bahrain;[149] he arrived on 30 March.[150] The Secretary-General's Mission was small consisting, apart from Winspeare himself, of a principal secretary, a political officer, a public relations officer/interpreter, an administrative assistant and a security officer.[151] Upon his arrival Winspeare was provided by the Bahrain authorities with a list of 'clubs' representing various aspects of social and community structure, where he was to meet their representatives. The intensive consultations and meetings took three weeks. The responses came both orally and in writing.[152] Having decided not to hold a referendum, in other words:

> ... not to put precise questions, precise alternatives, which would have been nearly impossible for the people to reply to, the negotiations were rather open conversations and discussions more than asking direct questions, do you want this or do you want that, do you want Iran or do you want Bahrain.

Winspeare admitted that the second question was not put to the Bahrainis as it would have led them to believe that they were an independent state. Therefore, as mentioned above, the Mission's terms of reference 'were rather general, and spoke of the problem created by the different views of the parties concerned without mentioning them' and stressed the need 'to find a solution to this problem in order to create an atmosphere of tranquillity, stability and friendliness throughout the area.'[153]

According to a member of the UN mission Bahrain lent itself to this unusual consultation of public opinion, in particular because of its small territory and population. In addition, its social structure, according to the secretary-general's note to the Security Council, was divided into the following categories: religious leaders, municipal councils and other administrative committees, welfare societies, clubs and other community centres as well as professional groups, sports and recreational associations.[154] In concluding his report, Winspeare stated, 'My consultations have convinced me that the overwhelming majority of the people of Bahrain wish to gain recognition of their identity in a full independent and sovereign state free to decide for itself its relations with the other states.'[155]

Just as the Winspeare report was about to be issued by the secretary-general, a last minute difficulty arose. Bahrain did not agree on using the term 'the Persian Gulf,' while Iran insisted it was '... sanctioned by over 2,000 years of usage and had until quite recently been applied even in Arabic atlases,' and objected to using neutral language such as 'the Gulf.'[156] In the end Bahrain did not maintain its objection which might have jeopardised the conclusion of the report. The Security Council meeting took place on 11 May 1970 and the draft resolution was adopted unanimously.[157]

In a step aimed at normalising relations with Iran's new small neighbour, a goodwill mission lead by the Foreign Ministry's political under-secretary, Manuchehr Zelli, left for Bahrain in May 1970. The delegation included a deputy information minister, a number of Foreign Ministry officials, representatives from the Majlis and the Senate, and a number of journalists.[158] This visit had an additional objective, namely to present Iran's handling of Bahrain as a testimony to its official policy in the Gulf which was, according to some members of the Iranian press, the most significant point in the manner in which the Bahrain issue had been resolved and a confirmation of Iran's clear and peaceful policy in the region,[159] a conviction echoed by Prime Minister Hoveida and Abbas Masoudi, the publisher of *Ettela'at*.[160]

Conclusion

The efforts to resolve disputes in the Gulf during 1968 demonstrated the unprecedented role of dominance played by regional powers. As the strongest regional military power, Iran was in the best position to influence the outcome of events. Contrary to what its public statements might have suggested, Iran did not choose to pursue its interests without reference to neighbouring states. In particular, efforts to reach an accommodation with Saudi Arabia were central to Iranian activities.

The Iranian claim to the Hormuz islands faded for a time into the background during this period while the Saudi-Iranian maritime dispute and the Iranian claim to Bahrain became the focal issues. The largely bilateral nature of the maritime dispute did not mean that the Bahrain issue was not strongly influenced by the status of Saudi-Iranian relations. No direct link can be established between the two issues, but any improvement achieved in one greatly enhanced the chances of progress in the other. The Bahrain dispute flared up as a result of a Saudi decision to welcome the Emir of Bahrain in Riyadh while the Shah's visit to the kingdom was impending, and informally ended with a message from the Shah to King Faisal in May 1968. It was not until then that negotiations over the division of mid-Gulf oil were resumed. Their successful conclusion improved the political climate in which the Shah had to consider practical steps to end Iran's long-standing claim to Bahrain, gracefully, and with a minimal domestic backlash.

One characteristic of the period covered by this chapter is that several Iranian decisions, which proved to be keys to the outcome of events, came as a surprise to many outside as well as inside Iran. Among these were the cancellation of the Shah's visit to Saudi Arabia in February, the despatch of a message to Saudi Arabia indicating Iran's willingness to drop her claim to Bahrain, the settlement of the maritime dispute and, finally, the decision to go public, in New Delhi in January 1969, with the promise that Iran would let go of Bahrain if the people of Bahrain so wished. The timing and exact reasons for these decisions are difficult to explain as they reflect the personal character of Iranian foreign policy at the time. Many are attributed to the Shah's 'mood' and 'personal calculation.' Hence we can only throw light on the context in which they were made.

Britain's weakening power in the Gulf and the American lack of interest in assuming the old British role are also evident in the narrative of events: both powers had a limited influence on the outcome of the events of 1968. Indeed progress in dispute resolution seemed to occur when Iran took diplomatic initiatives at a regional and/or a bilateral level. US oil interests in the maritime dispute, security concerns over the end result of the Bahrain dispute, and Britain's eagerness to see a peaceful resolution to Gulf disputes before the end of 1971 notwithstanding, these powers' roles were secondary. British and US initiatives came to assist Iran after the Shah had agreed on a particular course of action. A clear example of this was Britain's suggestion for settling the Bahrain dispute through the good offices of the UN secretary-general to ascertain the wishes of the people of Bahrain, to which the United States then gave its blessings. A number of procedural obstacles faced the UN mission in Bahrain, but it was political will on all sides that helped overcome such problems.

With Saudi-Iranian relations back on track, and Iran's claim to Bahrain en route for a final settlement, the remaining issue was the Hormuz islands. At the same time, however, the position of outside powers, in particular that of the US, began to change with the election of Richard Nixon.

4

The Nixon Doctrine: Iran and the Gulf

US policy carries a multiple significance for interactions among Gulf states. In a multifaceted period of Gulf history that witnessed an end to Pax-Britannica, America's choice of its course of action could have influenced the Gulf states' inter-regional relations and position in the world. As the US had strong ties with the Gulf's two largest countries, Iran and Saudi Arabia, it could have attempted to play a more assertive role in Gulf security. Such an approach might well have proven to be a divisive force in the region, as Gulf states would each have reacted differently. Some, one could argue, may have grown closer to the radical Arab camp or even the USSR in order to counter direct US control. In other words, the Gulf would have been sharply divided along cold war lines. However, the Johnson administration chose not to succeed the British and the Gulf began to acquire an autonomy of its own.

In January 1969 Richard Nixon was sworn in as President of the United States. Unlike his predecessor, Nixon had an international outlook dating back to his period as vice-president to Eisenhower. This meant more US attention to the Gulf and other third world regions. However, with the ongoing Vietnam war, the national mood of opposition to more involvement overseas was at its zenith. The change of president did not alter the US domestic scene, but the manner in which the new president dealt with impending challenges in a region believed to be of great interest to the US seemed not only to determine US relations with the region, but above all how a particular ally of the US viewed itself.

An Intimate Relationship

Nixon's recognition of Iran's 'vital' role in the Middle East long preceded his presidency. As vice-president he had visited Iran a number of times during the 1960s on his way to and from the Far East, and had developed close personal ties with the Shah and high ranking Iranian officials.[1] But before his encounters with Nixon, indeed as early as 1960, the Shah had attempted to articulate his own conception of Iran's security:

> Such countries as mine must strive for the security which is their first essential for advancement. Freedom-loving peoples sometimes forget – but the Communist powers never forget – that most of the world's economically undeveloped countries are also militarily undeveloped. Communism seeks to exploit not only the political, economic and social weakness of the emerging lands, but also their military vulnerability. If a country fails to secure its defences, the Communists play with it as a cat does with the mouse. During the Azerbaijan crisis, and again in Mossadegh's time, we Persians found ourselves in the unhappy role of the mouse. We resolved never again to be so unprotected.[2]

According to the US ambassador Armin Meyer this was a message repeatedly conveyed to the US during Nixon's informal visits. Meyer recalled one particular occasion in 1967 when Nixon held a one-to-one meeting with the Shah. Afterwards Nixon told Meyer that the Shah explained his wish to seek American support only in case of an outbreak of hostilities with the Soviet Union, 'But if Iran had a quarrel with Iraq, Iran would like to be able to take care of itself.' Nixon concurred with that view.[3]

The personal relationship between Nixon and the Shah is vividly reflected in their exchange of letters when Nixon became president-elect. Replying to the monarch's congratulatory message, Nixon stressed the continuation of close ties between Iran and the US and recalled, '... with pleasure your wonderful hospitality to me in Tehran in April 1967 and [I] have continued to follow with admiration your country's progress at home and constructive statesmanship internationally.'[4] Nearly a month later the Shah received a second message in which Nixon said, 'I thought it might be useful, before I take office next week, to tell you once again of my close feeling for Iran and my high regard for you. I hope that in the years ahead you and I will be able to exchange views directly, and in a spirit of frankness and candor. For my part, I shall always be ready to give your wise counsel and advice my immediate and most serious consideration.'[5]

The seeds of close co-operation between Iran and the US in the Gulf had been laid in the later part of the Johnson administration. The Shah had met members of the Johnson administration for the last time in June 1968. Before Secretary of State Dean Rusk was due to meet the Iranian monarch on 12 June, Stuart Rockwell, the assistant secretary of state for Near East and South Asian Affairs, wrote in a briefing memorandum, 'You might tell the Shah that we count on him, the British and other states of the region to resolve [Gulf issues] amicably, that we believe Saudi-Iranian co-operation is particularly important to any future arrangements, and that we are encouraged by reports we have received of his meeting with King Faisal in Jiddah on June 3.'[6] In a Congressional hearing the assistant secretary of defence for international security affairs, Paul Warnke, stressed that Iran was a stabilising factor in the region and had no designs against neighbouring states, but instead felt threatened by radical Arabs.[7] This degree of continuity between the Johnson administration and Nixon's initial view of the Gulf is confirmed by US ambassadors to Iran and Saudi Arabia at the time.[8]

If there was to be an addition to the incoming Nixon administration's Gulf policy, it had to be placed in the context of the challenges America was to encounter abroad. These came from two directions. The first was domestic in the shape of strains caused by the Vietnam war. The second was international and included the development of the USSR's nuclear arsenal and its achievement of strategic parity with the US, the rise of Europe and Japan as economic powers and China's emergence as the coming power in the Far East. All of this prompted Nixon to promise a 'fresh approach' to deal with a new and more pluralistic world order.[9] But to form and implement a fresh approach to the world, Nixon believed some modification in the US government's foreign policy decision-making process was in order.

The White House and the Bureaucracy

From the outset the new president gave foreign policy decisions high priority and attempted to assert direct authority on policy making. Nixon argued, 'A case might be made for government by consensus in domestic policy. It will not work in foreign policy. A President is elected to lead. Government by consensus is not leadership, it is followership, designed to produce outcomes not that are right but that most people will support.' He went on to say that, 'Major foreign policy decisions should never be decided by votes in Cabinet or even the National Security Council.'[10]

Nixon believed that one of the main impediments to the president playing a direct role in foreign affairs was the large US government bureaucracy. Both Nixon and his chosen National Security Advisor, Henry Kissinger, had shown a degree of suspicion of the bureaucracy. The president was opposed to the idea of the bureaucracy presenting him with a single option or a set of options.[11] Kissinger argued in his memoirs, '... a large bureaucracy, however organized, tends to stifle creativity. It confuses wise policy with smooth administration.'[12] In an earlier work Kissinger wrote, '... it is dangerous to separate [policy] planning from responsibility for execution.'[13] In a later article he questioned the bureaucracy's ability to guarantee secrecy in the foreign policy decision-making process as, '... an unpopular decision may be fought by brutal means, such as leaks to the press or to congressional committees. Thus, the only way secrecy can be kept is to exclude all those who are theoretically charged with carrying it out.'[14] The new national security advisor had also argued that the large size of the bureaucracy led to fragmentation of the policy process as a result of a series of conflicts among the agencies involved.[15]

Hence, Nixon attempted to avert much bureaucratic intervention by focusing on 'revitalising' the role of the National Security Council (NSC) in order to enable the White House, and ultimately the president, to have a hands-on role in foreign policy making. In the words of one analyst, Nixon aimed at, '... shifting the decision-making center of gravity from the bureaucracy to the White House.'[16] In Nixon's own words, 'I planned to direct foreign policy from the White House.'[17]

The NSC was set up in 1947 by the National Security Act which stated the Council's purpose:

'... to advise the President with respect to the integration of domestic, foreign, and military policies relating to the national security so as to enable the military services and other departments and agencies of the Government to cooperate more effectively in matters involving the national security.[18]

However, the practical role of the NSC changed with each president. According to a Kissinger aide, Harry Truman 'ignored it' as he believed that the system was set up by the Republican-controlled Congress '... partly as posthumous revenge against Franklin Roosevelt's free-wheeling solo diplomacy.' Consequently, after the first meeting of the NSC he never attended another. Eisenhower used the Council as formal presidential staff to help co-ordinate policies set by the bureaucracy; Kennedy deemed his predecessor's system too bureaucratic and wanted to assert presidential leadership, but made minimal use of the NSC in that respect.

When President Johnson took office he attempted to push policy options to a sub-committee group chaired by the deputy secretary of state below the National Security Advisor. The secretaries of state and defence would also meet informally or their ideas would be communicated through their deputies at the sub-committee group.[19] The end result would be a paper presented to the president by National Security Advisor Walt Rostow, laying out different points of view and recommending a course of action. The conclusion would be discussed at an informal meeting between the president and members of the NSC known as 'the Tuesday Lunch.'[20]

During the presidential campaign of 1968 Nixon promised to reform the decision-making process. The idea of restoring 'the National Security Council to its pre-eminent role in national security planning' was promised by Nixon in a radio speech on 24 October.[21] The promise was repeated during a post-election preliminary meeting at New York's Hotel Pierre,[22] but no specific plans were outlined.

The details of the new NSC system were the work of Harvard's Professor Morton Halperin who had served as under secretary to the defence secretary Clark Clifford,[23] and General Andrew Goodpaster, a former assistant to President Eisenhower.[24] The recommendations were presented to Nixon in the shape of a document entitled 'National Security Decision Memorandum' (NSDM2) at the end of December 1968.[25]

The plan recommended the establishment of a network of interagency committees below the NSC level. The interdepartmental groups chaired by the under secretary of state in the Johnson administration were to be replaced by interdepartmental groups and an Undersecretaries' Committee under the firm direction of the NSC Senior Review Group chaired by Kissinger. The interdepartmental groups were to supervise drafting of a National Security Study Memorandum (NSSM) which laid out policy options to the president via the Senior Review Group.[26]

Thus some argued that on most foreign policy issues Kissinger had the initiative and more influence over the president's decisions than any of his aides.[27] But to Kissinger the mechanism guaranteed that both he and the president could get involved in every stage of policy formation and get a clear idea of the range of options available for the administration,[28] or as a State Department publication put it, '... the purpose of these procedures is to bring the full range of choices to the President and his principal advisers – not to bury them.'[29]

In assessing these changes the *New York Times* stated, 'A *coup d'état*' could have hardly deprived the people's elected representatives more of their constitutional powers than this gradual process.[30] Congress found Kissinger a frustrating figure as the reorganisation plan shifted more influence to the NSC, while the national security advisor was not an appointment confirmed by Congress. Kissinger, therefore, could not be held accountable by Capitol Hill and managed to avoid testifying before Congressional Committees.[31]

This plan also provoked fury among some members of the State Department, in particular the new secretary of state William Rogers, who raised serious objections. However, on 20 January 1969 Nixon signed NSDM2 and the plan was effectively implemented.[32] Consequently, relations between the State Department and the NSC were strained and personal relations between Rogers and Kissinger were cold. According to one former member of the State Department, 'The two hardly spoke to each other.'[33] However, Kissinger and Joseph Sisco, the assistant secretary of state for the Near East and South Asia, on the one hand, and Harold Saunders, member of the NSC, and Alfred Atherton, an assistant to Sisco, on the other, developed channels of communications and a working relationship between the State Department and the NSC.[34] Publicly Rogers tried to emphasise the role the State Department was to play in the new NSC system through the participation in NSC meetings of the secretary of state and the under secretary, and the Under Secretaries Committee, and the Department of State's participation in the Interdepartmental Groups.[35]

Many emphasise that the powers of the new National Security Advisor increased tremendously as a result of these reforms.[36] Kissinger tends to underplay the relevance of these organisational changes to his influence on decision-making, arguing, 'My power did not depend on structures but rather on my relationship with the President.'[37] As he discovered when entering the White House, the president's daily schedule was, '... so hectic that he has little time for abstract reflection. Almost all of his callers are supplicants or advocates, and most of their cases are extremely plausible ... As a result, one of the President's most difficult tasks is to choose among endless arguments that sound equally convincing.' Therefore, Kissinger adds, '... a Presidential decision is always an amalgam of judgment, confidence in his associates, and also concern about their morale.'[38] In other words, Kissinger was to be the president's medium for filtering contending ideas, while Nixon himself retained great ability to make policy. Some reduce Kissinger's role to merely articulating statements on foreign policy to the press; as former CIA director Richard Helms emphasised, 'Nixon called the shots.'[39] To Nixon, however, almost all decisions had to fit in the larger context of a grand strategy.

The Guiding Doctrine

Prior to the president's trip to Asia in July 1969, Nixon and Kissinger had discussed the problem facing US policy when a US ally encounters a threat or aggression by a neighbouring country. This situation Kissinger called the 'gray area' between Soviet aggression against a US ally, in which case the US would intervene militarily, and internal instability or a civil war in which case the US would refrain from interfering.[40] To Kissinger there was no simple formula; the intention was to develop ideas dealing with this problem for a presidential speech sometime that summer. On 18 July 1969 Kissinger recalled sketching the administration's philosophy for post-Vietnam Asia:

> The issue of the nature of commitments in the United States often takes the form of a discussion of legal obligations. But on a deeper level and on the level that had to concern the President, the relationship of the United States to other countries depends, of course, on the legal relationship but more fundamentally on the conception the United States has for its role in the world and on the intrinsic significance of the countries in relationship to overall security and overall progress.

What was important, the National Security Advisor added, was to understand, '... how these countries visualize their own future' as that future, '... will have to depend not on prescription from Washington, but on the dynamism and creativity and co-operation of the region.'⁴¹

With the future security order of South-East Asia in mind Nixon arrived in Guam on 25 July 1969 and made the following statement:

> I believe that the time has come when the United States, in our relations with all of our Asian friends, [should] be quite emphatic on two points: One, that we will keep our treaty commitments, for example, with Thailand under SEATO; but, two, that as far as the problems of internal security are concerned, as far as the problems of military defense, except for the threat of a major power involving nuclear weapons, that the United States is going to encourage and has a right to expect that this problem will be increasingly handled by, and the responsibility for it taken by, the Asian nations themselves.⁴²

This statement was not prepared by the president's White House staff; rather it was made at an informal background press briefing at the top of the Mar Hotel in Guam.⁴³ Kissinger was caught by surprise,⁴⁴ and it was during the following two years that the administration began efforts to expand on these guidelines and articulate them as a doctrine bearing the president's name.⁴⁵

To Nixon, '[The] central thesis [of the Nixon Doctrine] is that the United States will participate in the defense and development of allies and friends, but that America cannot – and will not – conceive all the plans, design all the programs, execute the decisions and undertake all the defense of the free world. We will help where it makes a real difference and is considered in our interest.'⁴⁶ In an attempt to reassure US allies the assistant secretary of state for East Asian and Pacific Affairs, Marshall Green, re-emphasised three propositions contained in the Nixon Doctrine:

1. The US will keep its treaty commitments.
2. The US will continue to provide a shield if a nuclear power threatened an American ally or a state whose survival was deemed to be vital for US interests.
3. In case of other types of aggression, the US shall look to the state directly threatened to assume the primary responsibility for its defence.⁴⁷

To a former member of the NSC the doctrine was not merely a result of the

Vietnam experience, but was also addressed to the left of US politics. It was the administration's way of saying foreign affairs still mattered, but the US need not dabble in regional disputes which might lead to direct military intervention.[48] Nixon reaffirmed that the doctrine was not '... a retreat from responsibility; it is a sharing of responsibility,'[49] and later stressed that the cause of the doctrine was the 'perception of the growing imbalance between the scope of America's role and the potential of America's partners.'[50]

The Policy

The immediate international challenge facing the Nixon administration was disengagement from Vietnam.[51] However, according to a senior member of the NSC, the Gulf was given special attention for three reasons: the possibility of Soviet insurgence after British withdrawal; its linkage to the security of the Middle East as a whole in the context of the Arab-Israeli conflict; and the question of access to oil.[52]

Nevertheless, interaction among the Gulf states was still not an issue in which either the State Department or the NSC attempted to get America involved. Richard Murphy, the director of the Bureau for Arabian Peninsular Affairs at the State Department 1970–1971, told the author that his office was a quiet place and that the State Department's attention was geared to the Arab-Israeli conflict.[53]

NSC Gulf policy, many believe, was largely influenced by Kissinger.[54] This view seems to be inaccurate as when Kissinger himself was asked about his conception of the Gulf in 1969 he answered, 'I did not have one,' and expressed his personal lack of knowledge about the details of Gulf issues, stating, 'I did not know how Saudi-Iranian relations worked, my priority was to get the Soviets out of the Middle East.' His primary interests were China, the USSR and NATO.[55] In other words, everything in the Gulf was seen through a Cold War prism, and the Nixon administration's main concern was the general power structure in the region and identifying the main forces.

The administration's policy was spelled out in a National Security Study Memorandum titled NSSM 66. This was the work of the interdepartmental committee at the NSC, submitted to the president on 12 July 1969. Since the document remains classified, its contents are in the realm of speculation or have to be taken second hand.[56] Harold Saunders, who participated in the deliberations which resulted in NSSM 66, says that the memorandum started with discussion of what the US should do after British withdrawal. The options ranged from the US succeeding Britain in the Gulf to total non-involvement.[57] To Peter Rodman, also an NSC member, the basic conclusion of the memorandum was that the best option for the US was to rely on Iran and Saudi Arabia to work together as guardians of the Gulf.[58] The same idea was later made public by US Under Secretary of State Joseph Sisco.[59] This came to be known as the 'Twin Pillars' policy.[60]

Saudi Arabia and Iran had, it will be recalled, come to a *modus vivendi* following the resolution of the Bahrain dispute and the division of the mid-Gulf oil.[61] (see Chapter 2) Nevertheless, the two countries were wide apart in terms of military power; Iran had a 150,000 man army, with a growing navy and air force, while Saudi Arabia had an army of only 30,000, mostly for domestic security, no navy, and a weak air force. To some this military power gap meant that the burden was unequal.[62] Others argued that the policy was misrepresented and was '... more of a one pillar and a half.'[63]

Some US policy-makers envisaged different functions for the two allies. Saudi Arabia would, they believed, be most effective in ensuring stability in the lower Gulf, not through military means but rather by political mediation and conciliation, and guarding against Nasserite penetration in Arabia.[64] Iran, in this scenario, would play a larger military role as a naval power to succeed Britain, and a force against hostile regional powers, mainly Iraq.

To this extent the Gulf policy of the Nixon administration seemed to offer little more than the policy the Johnson administration had initiated. However, the US under Nixon began to think of keeping Iraq, the USSR's chief ally in the Gulf, in check by helping Iran build its military capability to 'Show other Middle Eastern states that it does not pay to be a Soviet ally.'[65] This was Nixon's main addition to the question.

Thinking Strategy

From the early months of the Nixon administration the Shah was making an impression on the president's main aides. Both Kissinger and Helms were impressed by his geo-political outlook.[66] In his book *Mission For My Country* the Shah argued,

It is more than coincidence that throughout recorded history most of the important Middle East military campaigns have either originated in my country or have directly affected her. Today, speaking geographically and strategically, it is no exaggeration to dub Iran 'the centre of CENTO.' And since CENTO is the centre of NATO-CENTO-SEATO, my country is in a way the keystone of the whole structure.[67]

Kissinger's own memoirs take that impression a step further. America's position on Iran, he wrote, '... was based on a cold-eyed assessment that a threat to Iran would most likely come from the Soviet Union, in combination with radical Arab states, which is only another way of saying that the Shah's view of the realities of world politics paralleled our own.'[68] Moreover, like many in the US at the time, Helms saw the Shah's domestic position as 'strong and stable.'[69]

The Shah flew to the US in April 1969 on the occasion of General Eisenhower's funeral, but during this trip he and the president found little time to exchange views.[70] It was not until October 1969 that an official visit was arranged. Evidence of what went on in the Shah's discussions with members of the Nixon administration is scarce. Officially, however, it seemed that Gulf security was not a major topic, as neither the suggested text nor the final draft of the Shah-Nixon communiqué referred to the area.[71]

The press reported, however, that the talks centred on the Gulf and defence issues, and that Iran was seeking a 200 million dollar loan to purchase US weapons, including Phantom jets, over five years.[72] The *New York Times* claimed the Shah was hoping to buy 100 million dollars worth of US jet aircraft annually with proceeds from increased sales of Iranian oil in the US, but no final agreement was reached. It was also reported that Iran was pushing the issue of the defence burden it would bear after the British pulled out so as to gain US government support for more credit facilities and increased oil sales to the US.[73] Official records confirm that the Shah wanted the US government to pressure US companies to increase their oil lifting from Iran in 1970, but members of the consortium declined the request.[74] The diary of his court minister, Asadollah Alam, confirms that the agenda of the Shah's US visit focused on oil, Iran's role in the Gulf and various other military matters.[75]

This was all taking place at a time when the mood of self-reliance was gaining momentum in Iran itself. After returning from Washington the Shah began preparing public opinion for new responsibilities and the 'enormous' defence expenditure which would follow the British withdrawal. This sense of responsibility stemmed from the Shah's view of the world, as he told the Iranian parliament in October 1969,

> I should say that the world's situation is, unfortunately, very disturbing. It is for this reason that we are forced to increase our defence capabilities – especially because others are doing this with increasing determination around us – while continuing to strive for general and complete disarmament until the day this idea is achieved.[76]

In response to claims made by some Arab countries about the 'Arab' nature of the Gulf, the Shah answered,

> This means that the islands we have in the Persian Gulf cannot belong to Iran since Iran is alien to the Gulf. It means that this country's oil wells in the region, around [Kharg island] and elsewhere, are all 'usurped property.' One could only remain silent in the face of such a system of logic. But this is verbal silence only ... The real answer lies in our material and military preparedness which also provide the final answer. This is not a matter for verification.[77]

The Shah's ultimate aim was expressed in September 1970 as he told an audience at the Command and Staff College that,

> Should something happen to this country [we] must be able to face any considerable regional event on [our] own. Despite the friendship and alliances we may have with other countries, we rely exclusively on our own power in such events. This is a rational attitude.[78]

Iran and Arms

Iran's military relationship with the US goes back to the Second World War with the establishment of the US Military Mission to the Imperial Iranian Gendarmarie (GENMISH) in 1943. Later, as the continuation of GENMISH, a US Army Mission Headquarters (ARMISH) was established in 1947 to assist and advise the Iranian army. In 1950 a Mutual Defence Assistance Agreement was reached. On the basis of that agreement the US provided 687 million dollars in grant aid to

Iran between 1950 and 1965, an average of 45 million per year.[79] An American Assistance Advisory Group (MAAG) was established to administer the military assistance grant programme. In 1958 a decision was taken to consolidate ARMISH and MAAG into a single organisation. This was completed by 1962 and came to be known as ARMISH-MAAG which was charged with '... advising the Iranian Armed forces on weapon procurement, processing foreign military sales and assisting Iran in assimilating the equipment purchased from the United States.'[80]

The Kennedy administration kept Iran's military purchases in check, with the president informing the Shah during visits to Washington in March 1962 that, '... future US aid would emphasise long-term economic development rather than military strength.' One Kennedy military adviser, Theodore Sorensen, argued that military assistance to Iran resembled '... the proverbial man who was too heavy to do any light work and too light to do any heavy work'; in other words an enlarged Iranian army would be too little for the Soviet Union and too big for internal security.[81]

From the mid-1960s the Shah negotiated arms deals with both the east and the west. In 1966, Iran and the USSR had signed an arms agreement just a few weeks before the US and Iran reached an agreement for the supply of 30 F-4 Phantom fighter jets. Sixteen more were sold in October 1967 at a net worth of approximately 180 million dollars.[82] These were the first advanced fighter planes sold to Iran.[83]

By the end of the Johnson administration improvement in Iran's economic performance meant the socio-economic consequences of arms purchases were less of a concern to US policy-makers. This trend continued throughout the Nixon administration.[84] By then Iran could afford such purchases, as oil prices began to rise from 1969 onwards and Iran began to purchase arms through the export-import bank system rather than grant aid, which was terminated in 1967.[85]

Early in the Nixon administration the White House showed more inclination to sell arms to Iran than its predecessor. While no initial large US commitment for an increase in such sales was made, with talk about the need for US allies to be able to defend themselves against regional Soviet proxies, the US commitment was implicit. According to Alfred Atherton many regional experts in the State Department were unhappy about the potential upward trend in arms sales,[86] as some believed it might be provocative to neighbouring counties.[87] But strong support from the White House for the policy overcame any opposition from the State

Department or even the Pentagon.[8] The prevailing view of Iran in Washington was articulated by Kissinger,

> Britain at the end of 1971 had just completed the historic withdrawal of its forces and military protection from the Persian Gulf at the precise moment when Iraq was being put into a position by Soviet arms to assert traditional hegemonic aims. Our friends – Saudi Arabia, Jordan, the Emirates – were being encircled.

Therefore, it was important for Western interests that,

> ... the regional balance of power be maintained so that moderate forces would not be engulfed nor Europe's and Japan's (and as it later turned out, our) economic lifeline fall into hostile hands. We could either provide the balancing force ourselves or enable a regional power to do so.[89]

This assessment fitted the Iranian line of thinking at the time.

Threat Perception

To General Toufanian, the Shah's main arms procurement aide during the 1960s and 1970s, the threat to Iran since the mid-1940s had come mainly from its northern borders, and Iran's defence strategy concentrated on the protection of the Zagros mountains. However, the 1958 coup in Iraq prompted Iran to give serious consideration to defending its southern boundaries, and especially to rebuilding the navy destroyed during the Second World War. It was believed warm Soviet relations with the new Iraqi government meant that, 'The USSR had jumped over the Zagros into the Persian Gulf.' In addition, by 1958 the Soviet naval presence in the area was perceived to be greater than that of the US: the USSR had twenty-four ships in the Indian Ocean while the US had only a small naval presence in Bahrain although American destroyers would visit the Gulf from time to time.[90]

In 1961 the Shah ordered the commander of the Iranian navy to work on a plan for the expansion of his force. The outcome was a ten-year plan to purchase destroyers, hovercraft, aircraft and troop carriers. In addition to expanding training facilities and the port of Kharg in the northern segment of the Gulf, the ports of Bushehr, with its road links to the great inland cities of Shiraz, Isfahan and Tehran, and Bandar Abbas situated at the mouth of the Gulf, were also to be expanded.[91]

With the dispute over the control of the Shatt al-Arab inflamed after the 1958 coup in Iraq,[92] and the influx of Soviet naval arms into that country, especially the Komar Class missile boats used by Egypt to hit Eilat,[93] the ten-year plan was condensed into five years. According to Admiral Farajullah Rasa'i, the commander of the Iranian Navy at the time, Iran tried to follow a policy of diversification in naval arms procurement to prevent total dependence on a single country for logistics. Hence destroyers were bought from the US, fast patrol boats from Britain, and patrol boats from France carrying US Harpoon missiles.[94]

By the mid-1960s Iran had begun to make more ambitious plans for its build up of the army and air force with the acquisition of more sophisticated weapons such as American M-60 tanks in 1965 by way of an up-grade from the M-47 supplied to Iran in the late 1950s.[95] Between 1968 and 1970 Iran bought airfield equipment and surface-to-air missiles from Britain, helicopters from Italy, France and the US, and anti-tank missiles from France.[96]

Toufanian relates that the Shah had a particular passion for the air force which he believed to be the most effective means of protecting Iran's nearly 5,000 mile-long border: 'The Shah was a pilot and I was a pilot so it was natural that the air force would be given priority.' General Toufanian also argued that with Iran's large territory, 'We could not support every gate with a division, protection from the air was far easier.'[97] In October 1967 Iran purchased sixteen more F-4 Phantoms, the most advanced US fighter plane in operation,[98] which were paid for, over four years, by a US 200 million dollar loan.[99]

According to one source the defence decision-making process in Iran was uncomplicated: the Shah would decide on all major purchases, and General Toufanian would implement his decisions.[100] The mechanism of arms purchases, according to another source, worked as follows: once briefed by US arms manufacturers Toufanian would inform the head of MAAG of Iran's military requirements. The request then went to the US ambassador who would send it to Washington for deliberation between the Pentagon, the State Department and the NSC.[101]

The sales of arms to Iran did not go without criticism in America. By the late 1960s the US Congress was showing some reluctance to support sales to third world regions.[102] The basic premise was that arms supplies could eventually lead to US military intervention.[103] Such reluctance illustrated what Peter Rodman saw as 'a revival of isolationism mixed with liberal humanitarianism,' as manifested in Senator Mike Mansfield's call for the reduction of US forces in Europe.[104]

However, Michael Van Dusen, who had served on various Congressional committees dealing with foreign affairs since the early 1970s, disagrees with Rodman's assessment. He argues that members of the Senate such as Mansfield were not advocates of 'isolationism' but believed that the number of US troops in Europe, nearly 300,000, exceeded their operational need on the ground. Furthermore, it is argued that Senator Mansfield saw America's future interest as best served by focusing on the emerging powers in Asia.[105]

Moreover, Seth Tillman, assistant to Senate Foreign Relations Committee Chairman William Fulbright, argued that the Senate was not looking seriously into Gulf issues until 1973, prior to the October war, when the possibility of US military involvement to protect oil supplies was debated.[106] Congressional materials confirm Tillman's impression as the security of the Gulf was seldom discussed in the Senate or the House of Representatives during this period. This could be partly attributed to lack of familiarity with Middle Eastern affairs in Congress in the early 1970s. Indeed Van Dusen was 'Shocked by the lack of knowledge about the region in the House of Representatives,' and points out that some members of the Foreign Relations Sub-Committee thought Iran and Iraq were 'The same country but spelled differently.'[107]

According to Tillman there were only a handful of politicians who did not agree with the administration's approach toward Iran such as Senators Fulbright, Paul Findley and George McGovern, and Congressman Lee Hamilton.[108] Consequently, although critical of the decision-making process regarding arms sales, Congress never seriously challenged the substance of US policy toward Iran.[109]

The fact that arms sales to Iran went through Congress almost unopposed could also be attributed to efforts by the Iranian Washington Embassy to build support. Top Iranian diplomats, highly skilled in public relations, such as Houshang Ansary, Amir Aslan Afshar and later Ardeshir Zahedi, were appointed to Washington during the late 1960s and early 1970s. They preferred building support from the top by concentrating their lobbying efforts on senior members of Congress through personal contacts and extravagant events at the Iranian Embassy, rather than work at Embassy-Congressional staff level. Van Dusen reveals that until the revolution of 1979 he had only met twice with Iranian Embassy staff.[11]

The Arms Sales Bonanza

The stage was now set for a take-off in Iranian arms purchases from the US. This rapid increase did not take place until after 1973, but Iran's request for more sophisticated weapons came before the accelerated programme got under way. According to the *Herald Tribune*, in 1968 Congressional sources revealed that Iran sought to step up its arms purchases from the US from 50 to 100 million dollars a year for the coming five years. Reportedly the Johnson administration did not, at first, want to make such a long-term commitment, but was willing to consider the deal if subject to annual review.[111]

In 1971 Iran bought 700–800 British Chieftain tanks.[112] Although Britain did not sell this weapon to Israel and Libya because of sensitivities over the Arab-Israeli conflict, the Foreign Office decided that Iran should not be regarded as part of that conflict and the sale was completed.[113] Iran expanded its transport force by buying 30 US-made C-130 planes in December 1970.[114] In early 1972 Iran purchased US-made TOW missiles and enhanced its air force with a purchase of 30 F-5s fighter bombers[115] to add to the thirty F-4s and 100 F-5s it already possessed.[116] During 1971 the navy was strengthened with four British-made naval patrol hovercrafts and Seacat missiles.[117] The navy, though lacking in experience, outclassed those of Iran's Arab neighbours.

The Iranian army also had a qualitative edge over its nearest Arab rival, Iraq. At the time when Chieftain tanks were being delivered to add to the M-60 tanks already in Iran's armoured force, they were believed to be superior to the Soviet-made tanks used by the Iraqi army.[118] In terms of manpower, in 1971 Iran had an army nearly twice the size of Iraq's and over four times the size of Saudi Arabia's (see Table 1). By the end of 1971, according to one US official, Iran had already achieved a 'credible deterrent' against any aggression in the Persian Gulf.[119]

Table 1
Iran, Iraq and Saudi Arabia: Military Manpower (in thousands)

Country	Army	Navy	Air Force
Iran	181,150	9	22
Iraq	9,585	2	8
Saudi Arabia	4,135	1	5

Source: IISS, *Strategic Survey*, (1971), p. 44.

The increasing rate of Iran's military build-up was reflected in an increase in defence spending both in absolute terms and as a percentage of gross national product between the years 1968 and 1972, as illustrated by Tables 2 and 3.

Table 2
The Iranian Defence Budget 1968–1972

Year	Defence Budget ($)
1968–1969	495,500,000
1969–1970	505,000,000
1970–1971	779,000,000
1971–1972	1,023,000,000

Source: IISS, *The Military Balance*, issues covering 1968–1973.

Table 3
Iranian Defence Expenditure as a Percentage of GNP

Year	% GNP
1965	4.4
1966	3.6
1967	5.5
1968	5.6
1969	5.0
1970	7.1
1971	8.5

Source: IISS, *The Military Balance*, 1969–1970 and 1972–1973.

The trend was clearly to more armaments. By 1975, when the military deliveries and treaties agreed upon in 1971 were complete, Iran was to have 135 F-5 Phantom fighter jets to serve alongside those squadrons already in its possession. US credit was given to help expand facilities in the form of an airfield built at Jask on the northern coast of the Gulf of Oman, and another at Bushehr, nearly opposite the island of Kharg. Naval facilities in the Gulf were also being expanded; at the port of Bandar Abbas, near the Strait of Hormuz, a new naval base and airfield were added. A base for hovercraft was built on the island of Kharg, the hovercraft and troops stationed there being supported by a fleet of more than 200 helicopters.

The naval base at Khorramshahr, at the northernmost point of the Gulf, was to be enlarged.

The Iranian government was hoping to complete an army base south of Tehran in which about 850 US-made M-47 tanks were to be stationed, and it was reported that Iran would receive 55 transport helicopters and 134 general use helicopters.[120] Within months of Nixon's visit to the country in May 1972 it is claimed that a large increase in US arms sales had been promised,[121] as the US agreed to sell Iran its most advanced fighter plane, the F-14, at an estimated cost of two billion dollars.[122] It was also reported that Iran ordered British-made Clyde ships worth 12 million pounds, and there was speculation that an order of hovercraft might follow.[123]

Table 4

Arms Transfer Agreements and Deliveries under the Foreign Military Sales Programme

Fiscal Year(s)	Agreements	Deliveries
1950–69	741.2	237.8
1970	134.9	127.7
1971	363.9	78.6
1972	472.6	214.8
1973	2,171.4	248.4
1974	4,325.0	648.4
1975	2,447.1	1,006.1
1976	1,794.5	1,927.9
1977	5,586.9	2,433.1
1978	2,586.7	1,792.9
1950–78	20,751.7	8,715.9

Source: US Department of Defense, *Foreign Military Sales: Foreign Military Construction Sales and Military Assistance Facts*, (1978).

To give an idea of the magnitude of the increase in Iran's arms purchases in the 1970s, according to one source over 1.5 billion dollars was spent on arms between 1950–1972, while in 1973 alone Iran signed arms agreements worth over two billion dollars. Between 1973–1978 the total value of arms agreements was over 19 billion dollars (see Table 4).

The conventional wisdom is that during the Nixon-Shah meeting in May 1972 the US secretly agreed to supply Iran with 'virtually any weapon system it wanted' and promised to sell Iran either F-14 or F-15 fighter planes,[124] which to one American lawmaker represented, '... the most rapid build up of military power under peacetime conditions of any nation in the history of the world.'[125]

The idea that a 'carte blanche' had been given to Iran is contested by certain former members of the Nixon administration. Peter Rodman has argued that when it came to the sale of sophisticated weapons the US government bureaucracy still retained the ability to keep arms sales in check.[126] However, others argue that once the flow of arms was set in motion it was irreversible because a termination of US military supplies would not only have resulted in a deterioration of relations with Iran, but could also have led others to become suspicious of the US as a reliable source of military equipment.[127] Whether or not Iran was in fact given a carte blanche in 1972 – the question is still disputed – it is clear that the Nixon administration's attitude toward Iran had not changed significantly between 1969 and 1972. The great difference was that, from 1973 onwards, Iran had a large cash surplus to finance arms purchases.[128]

Conclusion

From the outset Richard Nixon was in favour of closer collaboration with Iran and enjoyed warm personal relations with the Shah. Nixon needed very little convincing to lead US policy in that direction. Change within the American policy making process only increased White House and presidential input in the final outcome of policy, allowing the personal contact and understanding between the Shah, Nixon and members of the Nixon administration to have more impact on US policy toward Iran and the Gulf.

US-Iranian collaboration took the form of increased reliance on Iran as the regional guardian of US interests, a policy consistent with the Nixon Doctrine. Although the frame of reference of the Guam statement was Asia, the Gulf was an arena for the Nixon Doctrine in practice, even before it was formally articulated. The immediate implication of the Nixon Doctrine in the Gulf was an up-grading and enlargement of the Iranian armed forces. The initial increase in arms sales to Iran was marginal compared with the years between 1972 and 1979. However, the early years of the Nixon administration witnessed a shift in US policy accepting the need to help Iran expand its military force. By that time Iran's military spending was already on the increase.

Military sales agreements between Iran and the US under Nixon did not necessarily reflect an immediate increase in Iran's fighting capacity as it took a number of years to deliver most of these weapons. But the mere expectation of more weapons to come after 1971 carried a political significance by adding to Iran's feeling of confidence and security. Moreover, the strength of Iran's expanding military force was clearly superior to that of its Gulf neighbours, including Iraq and Saudi Arabia.

While the Nixon administration was steering US policy toward recognition of the importance of the Gulf in a manner acceptable to US public opinion, American reliance on Iran alone meant that the US was concerned with the general position of the Gulf at the international strategic level, but was not involved directly with interactions among Gulf states. Britain remained in the midst of such interactions with little interest from the US.

Furthermore, while the US chose to rely on Iran as a regional protégé, Iran and the Shah did not see things in that context. This was another case of divergence between a superpower's international strategic aims and a local power's regional concerns. To the Shah, US support came at a time when Iran was aiming to develop sufficient military capability to preserve its security without relying on external help. The Shah impressed US policy-makers with his strategic outlook on the East-West conflict and America helped strengthen Iran to enable the country to stand against Soviet allies in the region. When it came to relations between Iran and the Gulf countries friendly to the US, Iran was left to its own devices and the Iranian monarch had his own agenda.

5

The Insoluble Disputes

Following the Shah's New Delhi statement on Bahrain in January 1969 a degree of wishful thinking took over among British officials. To Antony Acland, the head of the Arabian Department at the Foreign Office, the Bahrain settlement 'improved the atmosphere' for resolving the dispute over the islands of the Strait of Hormuz.[1] However, Sir Denis Wright recorded in his memoirs that, 'The euphoria of the Bahrain settlement success vanished within weeks as [the Iranian] press turned to the islands,'[2] an issue which had received little public attention prior to 1969.

The view in Tehran was different. As we have seen, the Shah had expressed his lack of interest in Bahrain as early as the 1950s. His repudiation of Iran's claim to Bahrain was, against this background, no more than a form of gesture politics aimed at placating Arab fears of Iranian intentions in the Gulf, which at the same time signalled the limits of the territorial compromise Iran was prepared to make.

A year had made a striking difference in Iran's Gulf policy. In 1968 Iran was adjusting to a new situation: the Gulf without an external hegemony. Its priorities were mixed, reactions to its territorial claims were unknown, and the result was incoherent policy. From 1969 onwards Iran was set on a specific goal: its supremacy in the Gulf. The symbol of this supremacy would be to secure the islands of Abu Musa, Greater Tunb and Lesser Tunb as part of Iran.

Buoyant American support for Iran's strategic role could only help its quest.

The introduction of the Gulf into the international strategy embodied in the Nixon Doctrine and the 'strategic' arguments which were made gave an intellectual rationale to Iran's Gulf policy. For this reason, after the inauguration of Richard Nixon, one could speak of a renewed Iranian power in the region without implying that Iran suddenly adopted an aggressive approach. This and the next chapter will focus on subtle changes in this scene giving primary attention to the islands. Other issues, although seemingly unrelated, will be considered in order to complete the picture of Iran's relations with the Arabs of the Gulf.

The Relevance of History

As in many other territorial disputes, Iran and the Arabs use historical facts in different ways to support their respective claims. While a detailed examination and weighing of these historical claims is beyond the scope of this book, an outline of some of the main arguments from both sides may be in order.

The Iranian claim to the Tunbs and Abu Musa rests on the contention that Persia owned the islands prior to British intervention in the Gulf in 1820.[3] However, some argue that evidence of ownership of these islands before the 19th century is inconclusive. In the 18th century, the Qawasim of Ras al-Khaimah had been active on the Persian coast of the Gulf, seizing the Persian port of Basidu in 1727. Yet, as Richard Schofield points out, '... political control at this time was marked by fluidity.' In 1737, reacting to these earlier Qasimi activities, Persia captured Qasimi positions approximate to the contemporary geographical location of Ras al-Khaimah. Although the Persians apparently obtained the submission of the rulers for a short while, no claim to Ras al-Khaimah itself was made.[4] A decade later, in 1747, the Qasimis seized the port of Lengeh on the Persian shores.[5] According to British records it was not until 1877 that Persia formally claimed the Tunbs and not till 1888 that a similar claim was made for Abu Musa.[6] Britain first recognised Qawasim ownership of Abu Musa during the 1870s, and the Tunbs a decade later.

The dispute was inflamed in 1904 when a proposal by a merchant shipping line to call at Abu Musa rather than Lengeh was announced. This led Britain to '... advise the Qasimi chiefs to place their flags on the islands, which was promptly done.'[7] The flags were soon removed by the Persian Customs authorities under Belgian management, who simultaneously hoisted the Persian flag.[8] Britain then warned Persia that action would be taken unless it backed down, which resulted in a speedy evacuation of the islands in June 1904.[9]

Another argument used to support the Iranian case is that during the late 19th century Abu Musa and the Tunbs were administered by a section of the Qawasim that had migrated to the Persian coast near Lengeh during the mid-18th century. From about 1877 till 1887, according to Iran, taxes were collected from the islands of Sirri and Tunb on behalf of the Qawasim headman in Lengeh who himself gave allegiance to the Persian government. The Qasimis, on the other hand, claim to have had '... uninterrupted possession of the island by the ruling family of Sharjah over a long and continuous period.'[10] It is argued, moreover, that even the Qawasim of Lengeh were independent of Persia and maintained close social and economic ties with the Arab side.[11]

A further contention advanced on the Arab side is that Lengeh did not come under Iranian jurisdiction until 1887 when the Qasimi ruler, Shaikh Qadib, was imprisoned by the Persian government. Qadib's descendant, Mohammad bin Khalifah, made a successful attempt to recapture Lengeh in 1898. His hold, however, did not last long as he engaged in fighting with the Persian navy which forced the Qawasim to return once and for all to the southern Gulf littoral.[12] By that time Persia had annexed Sirri, another island located in the Strait of Hormuz, a move in which Britain acquiesced since no great objections were voiced at the time.[13]

As a sign of Qasimi sovereignty over the island in 1906 Sharjah granted a mining concession for red oxide to two men living at Lengeh who claimed to be British subjects, Hassan Sumaih and his son Abdullah.[14] Britain objected to this arrangement when on 1 June 1906 the concessionaires entered into a contract with the German firm Wonckhaus. To guard against possible German intervention in the Gulf, Britain claimed that the concession was a breach of the 1892 treaty which committed the Gulf rulers, their heirs and their successors not to '... cede, sell, mortgage or otherwise give for occupation any part of their territory' without the consent of the British government. Hence Britain removed concessionaire workmen from the island by force.[15]

These developments, however, are seen by sources sympathetic to Iran as reflecting not any conviction on Britain's part of Arab rights to the island but rather a pragmatic change of policy, mainly to check Iranian expansion in the Gulf after the annexation of Sirri.[16] Iran lays emphasis on a War Office map presented by Britain to Naser al-Din Shah in 1888 showing the islands within Persian territory, as well as a map prepared by the Royal Geographical Society under Lord Curzon's supervision which was published in Curzon's book *Persia and the Persian Question*.[17] The Arabs, meanwhile, use documents from the British Residency in Bushehr as evidence that Britain recognised the Qawasim's ownership of the islands.[18]

In 1923 Iran, as we have seen, made efforts to refer the dispute to the League of Nations. The inter-war years saw Iran attempt to interfere with the customs of Abu Musa in 1925 and seize an Arab dhow in 1928. But for over a century Britain had guaranteed Qasimi control of the islands,[19] and in an effort to reach a compromise in 1932 Reza Shah's minister of court, Abdolhossein Taimourtache, proposed to Britain that his government would be willing to relinquish its claims to Bahrain if it were given the islands in compensation. In language similar to that used by Mohammad Reza Shah in the 1950s and 1960s, Taimourtache in effect told the British that Bahrain was not of great material interest to Iran, but his government could not abandon its claim without considerable compensation.[20] In 1935 Iran offered to renounce its claims to Abu Musa if Ras al-Khaimah would drop the claim to and administration of the Tunbs, and considered granting leasehold rights over the Tunbs to Ras al-Khaimah.[21] But these potential trade-offs were all rejected by the British and nothing ever came of them.

Nearly two decades later Britain tried to sponsor an agreement whereby Sharjah would recognise Iranian sovereignty over Sirri, Iran would recognise Sharjah's ownership of Abu Musa, and Ras al-Khaimah would be willing to sell the Tunbs to Iran. The Iranian refusal to sacrifice the claim to Abu Musa ended this attempt.[22] Overall, the issue lay dormant throughout the Second World War, and the late 1940s and 1950s when Iranian attention was focused on the 'northern tier' and CENTO. When the dispute resurfaced in the late 1960s and early 1970s Iran had to reformulate its claim to the islands using a strategic argument in tune with international concerns at the time.

The Relevance of Strategy

Abu Musa, an island with a population of 600 Arabs, lies on the Arab side of a median line drawn northwest to southwest through the Gulf about 32 miles from the Arabian mainland and 40 miles from Iran. Greater Tunb (Tunb-e Bozorg) is a deserted island closer to the Iranian coast being about 15 miles from the Iranian island of Qeshm and about 40 miles from the Arabian mainland. Lesser Tunb

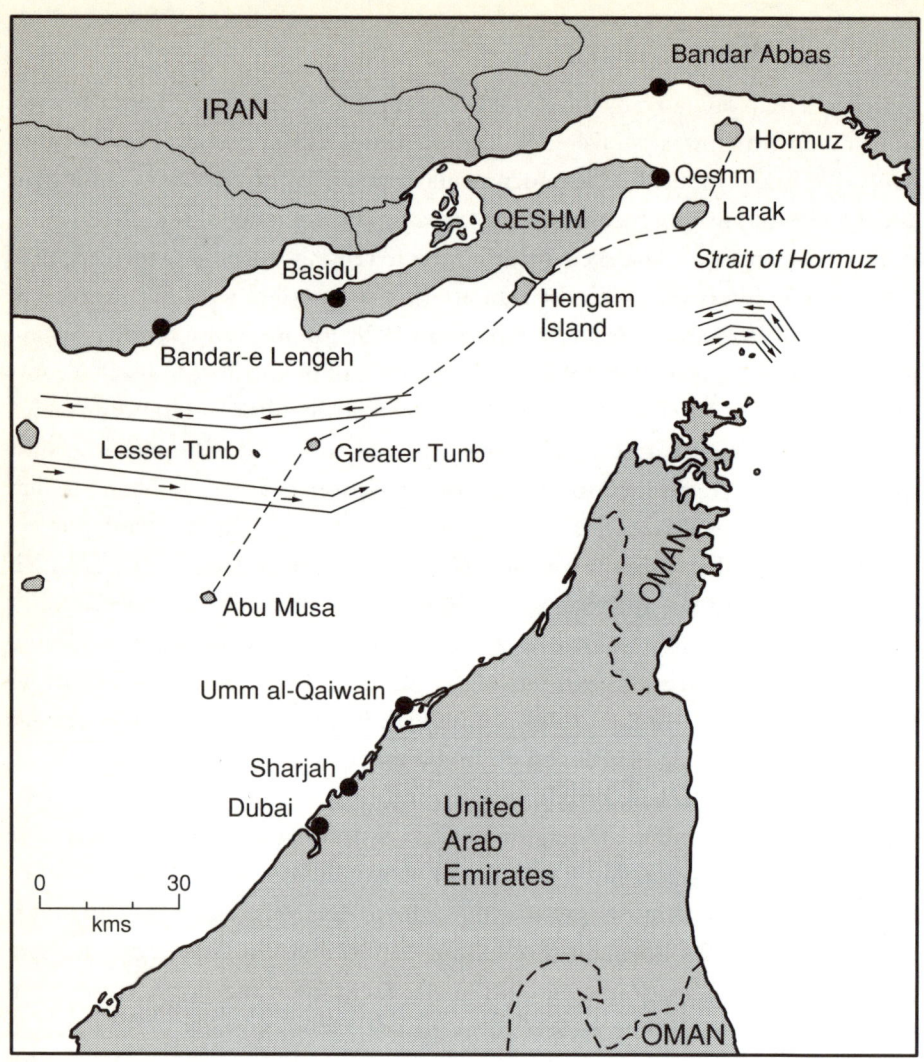

Map 2: The Strait of Hormuz: Curved Line Separating the Iranian and Arab Coasts

Source: K. McLachlan (ed.), *The Boundaries of Modern Iran*, New York: St Martin's Press, 1994.

(Tunb-e Kuchek) is another deserted island 20 miles from Qeshm and 45 miles from the Arabian mainland.[23]

The small size of these islands does not detract from their perceived political and strategic significance since the Gulf can only be entered from the Indian Ocean and the Gulf of Oman through the Strait of Hormuz. A 1979 study asserted that all vessels entering or leaving the Gulf use a route which passes near six islands, the three disputed islands – Greater Tunb, Lesser Tunb and Abu Musa – and three Iranian-owned islands – Forur, Bani Forur and Sirri.[24] Other experts refer, in addition to the three disputed islands, to the Iranian islands of Hormuz, Henjam, Qeshm and Larak as forming a 'strategically curved line' that separates the Iranian and Arab coasts. (see map 2)[25]

The strategic importance of the Strait of Hormuz increased with the growing importance of oil in the world economy, as the waterway became the 'international oil highway' or a 'global chokepoint' connecting the world's largest single site of oil reserves and production with world markets.[26] From the Iranian point of view threats to the highway could come from a number of directions, and in particular from the weakness of 'mini-states' in the Gulf region after British withdrawal.[27] The uncertainties which followed the British withdrawal from Aden and the ongoing rebellion in Dhofar from 1965 were given as examples, as was a potential disintegration of part of Pakistan. Hence the suggestion that the Shah believed that, were the islands to fall into 'the wrong hands' due to regional instabilities, they would acquire a 'nuisance value.'[28]

An additional factor in the Shah's thinking was Iran-Iraq relations which, by early 1969 had reached a new low after Iraq laid claim to the whole of the Shatt al-Arab and ordered Iranian vessels to lower the Iranian flag before entering the disputed waterway. In response, on 19 April 1969 Iran unilaterally terminated the 1937 treaty dividing the waterway between the two countries.[29] According to Peter Ramsbotham, the British ambassador to Tehran in 1971, the Shah kept reminding him that if Iraq were to take the islands 'the Iraqis could menace Iranian oil exports.'[30] In June 1971 the Shah went public with his thoughts,

> ... these islands are of considerable importance strategically and from the point of view of the region's peace and security. Their geographical position is of great military value. If a nihilist power takes over these islands it will be a source of danger for the rest of us. These islands must be in safe hands; ... their geographi-

cal and strategic position dictates that we recover them peacefully if possible, or by force if necessary.[31]

A few months earlier, the Iranian foreign minister, Ardeshir Zahedi, had stated, 'Our idea is to deter any foolish ideas and maintain stability.'[32]

With the growth of its military capability Iran's security parameters began to expand beyond the Gulf and into the Indian Ocean. Hence an argument developed that threats could also come from an international crisis in the context of east-west rivalry and a possible attempt by either power to block the strait directly or by proxy.[33] This assessment has, however, been disputed by General Hassan Toufanian who believed that modern weapons systems rendered the islands unimportant strategically.[34]

The challenges facing the parties attempting to resolve this dispute are found not only in historical archives or strategic arguments, but also in an accumulation of historical events that shaped Iran's memory and view of national territory. Here some sources speak of a perception among Iranians that their territory 'shrank throughout history.' The cases referred to are defeat in two wars with Russia in 1813 and 1828, which resulted in Persia's loss of territory in the Caucasus.[35] In addition, faced with the 1839 Persian advance into Herat, part of what is now known as Afghanistan, Britain occupied Kharg island in the Gulf and threatened the Persian mainland in order to press the Shah to evacuate Herat. This British action led the Persian *sadr-e azam*, Hajj Mirza Aghassi, to claim, in 1840, all the waters and islands of the Gulf as Persian.[36] Eventually Persia entered a war with Britain in 1856–1857 which resulted in the Persian abandonment of Herat.[37]

In February 1971 the Iranian newspaper *Kayhan* presented this argument clearly. Elaborating on a statement made by the Shah, it told its readers that

> Iran wants the islands back not because they are of military value, Iran is strong enough militarily to keep the peace in the Persian Gulf without such tactical advantages ... However, this country cannot allow its territory to be auctioned off by a colonial power. Any such infringement on Iran's sovereignty will be resolutely opposed not only by the government but by the entire nation as well.[38]

The ending of Iran's claim to Bahrain thus placed the Shah in a difficult domestic position. According to one British official, 'The Shah gave up Bahrain for the islands' which made it domestically impossible for him to make yet another compromise although at the time not many Iranians had even heard of Abu Musa.[39] Given this situation, it came as no surprise that, when asked in 1997 whether Iran had claimed the islands for historic, strategic or domestic-political reasons, former Foreign Minister Ardeshir Zahedi replied, 'all three and anything else.'[40]

Bahrain and the Islands

Whether or not the historical or strategic arguments put forward by Iran for its claim to the islands were stronger than those of the Arabs, the practical negotiating position had to take into consideration Iran's leverage on some regional issues. From January 1969, when the Shah had implied publicly that Iran was to drop its claim to Bahrain, Iranian officials had tried to link the issue of Bahrain with the islands to achieve that bargain. Shortly afterwards, on 17 February 1969 the minister of court Asadollah Alam recorded a conversation with Sir Denis Wright, the British ambassador, in his diary. 'As for Bahrain,' Alam noted, 'negotiations are already under way with a view of implementing HIM's wishes ... In strict confidence he [Wright] told me that the Islands of Tunbs are certain to be handed over to Iran. The British have warned the Sheikh of Ras al-Khaimah that the islands lie on our side of the median line, and that unless he comes to some sort of understanding with us we shall simply take them, legally or if needs be by force.' Alam then asked Wright about Abu Musa and when Wright pointed out that it lay below the median line, Alam replied 'we are sufficiently powerful to disregard the line.'[41]

Wright has later said that he believed Britain should allow Iran to take the islands as he thought the Shah would inevitably secure them anyway,[42] but this was hardly London's policy at the time.[43] If Alam's account is accurate, it might be argued that in 1969 Wright was using his diplomatic skills with the Iranian government by telling its officials that he was on their side while expressing concern that Iran's confrontational policy might lead to trouble with the Arabs, hence falling in line with London's policy.

The approach, however, did not seem to yield results. Later in their 17 February conversation Wright warned that Iranian policy in the Gulf 'may lead to trouble with the Arabs,' to which Alam responded, '... to hell with it ... What have the Arabs ever done for us? If only they would stop all this nonsense, agree to pay for the defence of the Gulf, and let us get on with the work.' 'We are prepared,' Alam added, 'to draw up a fifty year's defence agreement with them ... all in all it will be much the same as the agreement they once had with the British.'[44]

Alam's remark illustrates the failure among high-ranking Iranians to appreciate that many Gulf Arabs viewed Iran as an expansionist power with territorial ambitions in the Gulf,[45] despite the British ambassador's clear, if friendly, warning.[46]

Although in some parts of his diaries Alam records that Sir Denis offered a deal with Iran over the islands,[47] Wright himself casts great doubts over Alam's wording; rather he claims the offer came from Alam himself on 19 March 1969.[48] Alam's 19 March diary confirms that he met Sir Denis that day to discuss Bahrain and the Gulf islands, '... which he [Sir Denis] was keen to present as two distinct issues.' Wright told Alam that the Tunbs '... will be easy for [Iran] to recover but not Abu Musa, which lies too close to the Arabian peninsula.' Alam's response was that '... this didn't alter Iran's right nor entitle the Arabs to hold on to Iranian territory; territory which HIM will never abandon.' The ambassador this time tried a linkage with the proposed Arab federation suggesting that a solution to the problem of Bahrain would almost certainly encourage the establishment of a Federation of Arab Emirates, at which stage Iran might well occupy Abu Musa in the interests of joint security in the Gulf. However, this idea was rejected by the Shah[49] and Sir Denis heard little of it afterwards.[50]

In response to British reluctance to accept a deal, Iran threatened to jeopardise the process of resolving the Bahrain dispute. Alam wrote, '... we can reach no settlement in respect to Bahrain until we know the fate of the Tunbs and Abu Musa. In that case, he [Wright] declared, we have all been wasting our time.' Alam replied 'So be it.' Sir Denis, he added, then suggested that Iran '... approach the Sheikh of Sharjah as we did the Sheikh of Ras al-Khaimah. A deal might be struck and the British would back us. I said I would pass this on to HIM but was in no position to comment myself.'[51] The threat was, however, no more than a tactical move on Iran's part to pressure Britain and progress in resolving the Bahrain dispute was not interrupted. Nevertheless, London became increasingly concerned about the effect the island dispute might have on the process and Anthony Acland argued that, for the time being, Iran should not be pressed to make a deal on this front: 'It seems to us,' he noted, 'that our aims are most likely to be met by keeping our heads as low as possible on the island.'[52]

Nevertheless, following their 23 March meeting, Alam was under the impression that, '... the ambassador seemed more inclined than he was the other day to link any solution for Bahrain to proposals over the islands.' Wright hinted, according to Alam, that 'if Iran were to back the creation of an Arab Federation in the Emirates, then we might be called upon to occupy the islands on the Federation's behalf, without any fear of a backlash from the Arabs.' But Alam, who did not seem convinced by this scenario, replied 'Quite frankly I have lost any confidence in your forecasts ... six years ago ... you yourself Mr Ambassador told me that for at least another twenty years you were bound to the Sheikhs by the firmest of commitments ... yet it has taken only five years since then for Britain to announce her withdrawal from the Persian Gulf.'[53]

Iran's official position on Bahrain and the Federation was outlined by Ardeshir Zahedi on 27 May during a visit to Tehran by the British foreign secretary, Michael Stewart: '... of course you all know what the Shah said in India, Iran will not use military force to change the choice of the Bahraini people whatever this choice may be. However, we will not sit back and do nothing if we are faced with a *fait accompli*.'[54] Zahedi later explained that the *fait accompli* Iran rejected was for Bahrain to be part of another country such as Saudi Arabia, or for the island to be handed to the emirates.[55] On the Federation the Iranian foreign minister said, '... we would like to see the [emirates] remain independent and stable. However, of course, we cannot agree to the incorporation of part of our territory into this Federation. Naturally, we oppose this attempt.'[56]

During his visit Stewart reiterated Britain's position on not linking the islands question to that of Bahrain, in spite of Iranian insistence. According to Denis Wright, Stewart did, however, make a vague promise to Iran of future British backing: 'The islands were not ours to give away and could not be part and parcel of a Bahrain settlement, but he promised to do what he could to deliver them ... going,' Sir Denis added, 'rather too far than was wise.' Overall, however, Wright thought that Stewart's visit was a success, as the foreign secretary displayed a benign attitude to Iran's territorial claims. 'For me,' he wrote in his memoir, 'it will be very useful to have him as an ally at home in these difficult coming weeks.'[57]

Peter Tripp, a member of the Foreign Office who attended the Shah's meeting with Stewart, recalls that the Shah made a favourable impression on the foreign secretary and some of his staff as a leader with a vision for his country who was keen to maintain regional stability. However, Tripp sheds doubts on Wright's account. He did not believe Stewart was suggesting Britain would do its best to deliver the islands to Iran, but rather that 'We would do our best to facilitate a solution.'[58]

In a Foreign Office document Stewart records that he had told the Iranians that Britain was in no position to dispose of any Arab territory. However, he came away convinced that '... the Rulers would be very well advised to give thought now to their future relationship with Iran.' He believed that the emirates were in a better position to negotiate a deal with Iran before Britain's departure as after 1971 'Iran will be the strongest power in the waters of the Gulf.'[59] The Rulers of Ras al-Khaimah and Sharjah, however, consistently refused any accommodation with Iran which relinquished their claim to sovereignty over the islands.[60]

Simultaneously, Britain was trying to help put the internal affairs of the Arab emirates in order. As its declared policy was to leave behind a viable state structure, attempts to build a federal state were not to be jeopardised by overt support for Iran on the islands issue. British pressure on the rulers was therefore naturally limited by the intersection of the island dispute and the federation plan. Hence, a look at the status of the federation may explain some aspects of the development of the island dispute.

The Problematic Federation

Hypothetically, had Iran lent support to the idea of a federation of Arab emirates, one could argue that difficulties among its members would have proved the main obstacle to its formation as a state. Early in 1969 the emirates seemed to be making progress towards completing the preliminary process of unification. The federation's Provisional Council held a meeting in Dubai in March headed by Shaikh Khalifah bin Hamad al-Thani, the Crown Prince of Qatar. The discussions focused on the practical function of the future federal state. They reached some conclusions, and advanced laws for the approval of the Supreme Council on such matters as a unified monetary system, postal services, internal Council rules and regulations, and a budget for federal institutions.[61] The next Provisional Council meeting took place nearly a month later and reached agreement over the establishment of departments of health, education, transport and information.[62]

Whatever progress the Provisional Council had made, the final decision rested with the Supreme Council of Rulers which held a meeting in Qatar in May 1969. By this time disagreements among the Rulers themselves had begun to emerge. The meeting opened with discord between Qatar and Bahrain over the agenda. Qatar presented an agenda aimed at speeding up the practical steps for setting up federal agencies, while Bahrain, supported by Abu Dhabi, argued for a more gradual and cautious evolution of the federation, focusing on achieving an agreement on the constitution and related legal issues. In the end a committee was set up to draft a new agenda which represented a compromise between the Qatari and Bahraini approaches and the meeting was able to proceed.[63]

Soon after this obstacle was overcome a number of other contentious issues came to the fore, the first of which had to do with the emirates' representation in the federation's national assembly. Should it be based on equal representation, or should the size of each emirate's population be taken into account? Bahrain, as the emirate with the largest population, suggested that the number of seats allocated to each must be proportional to the size of its population. All the smaller emirates disagreed and called for equal representation. Qatar said it would go with the majority and then gradually shifted to Bahrain's side. Abu Dhabi proposed that Bahrain should be allocated six seats while the other eight emirates retained four each, but this suggestion received very little support. Agreement was never reached.

The site of the federation capital represented another area of contention. Bahrain wanted Abu Dhabi to be a temporary capital until an agreement could be reached on a permanent site. Abu Dhabi agreed, while Qatar did not oppose the proposal but argued that the temporary capital should be named only after agreement was reached on a permanent one which should be built between two emirates. Furthermore, there was disagreement over the ratification of laws proposed by the Provisional Council. Again Bahrain and Abu Dhabi favoured more time and deliberations.

These disagreements overshadowed what progress the Supreme Council had made with regard to agreement on the federation having a president and a vice-president; the replacement of the Provisional Council with a thirteen-member Council of Ministers; a federal flag; the formation of a committee of legal advisers to draft a constitution within a month, and the choice of Egyptian lawyer Wahid Rafat as a legal consultant following the death of Sanhuri Pasha.[64]

On 21 October the Supreme Council met for the fifth time in Abu Dhabi. By then the federal constitution was a pressing issue, and two drafts had emerged. The first was by the committee of legal advisers, which drew up a 'provisional' constitution in order to overcome disagreement on issues which might face the federation in the long term while allowing it to function in the short term; the second was by Wahid Rafat who favoured a 'permanent' constitution. A third version was later drafted by Qatar's legal adviser Hassan Kamil.[65] Surprisingly, the constitution was never discussed thoroughly during the rulers' meeting; rather the issue was left to deliberations at committee level and the rulers' discussions focused on the unfinished business of the last meeting.

Initially the meeting seemed to be heading toward a resolution of all outstanding issues as an agreement was reached on naming Shaikh Zayid of Abu Dhabi as the Federation's president and Shaikh Rashid of Dubai as vice-president, with Shaikh Khalifah, the Crown Prince of Qatar, as prime minister. Bahrain came to agree on equal representation in the National Assembly. However, when the issue of the establishment of the Council of Ministers came up disagreement emerged. Bahrain argued that each emirate should nominate three of its citizens for ministerial posts and then the Supreme Council approve the appointment of one or more candidates, while Ras al-Khaimah preferred informal discussion among the rulers for appointing ministers. Abu Dhabi supported the Bahraini viewpoint, while Dubai, Ajman, Fujairah and Umm al-Qaiwain favoured the Ras al-Khaimah option, and Qatar was non-committal.[66]

For the last two days of the meeting the rulers held closed sessions, and reportedly sharp disagreements erupted.[67] Little is known about the exact causes of these conflicts, but at a certain point the British political agent in Abu Dhabi, James Treadwell, entered the hall and read a message from the political resident in the Gulf, Sir Stewart Crawford: 'I know that some difficulties have arisen at the conference. My government will be extremely disappointed if these difficulties cannot be overcome. I believe that the failure of the meeting would also be most unwelcome to other Arab countries whose future support for the Gulf [emirates] is important.'[68] Crawford's words failed to save the day as the participants did not sign a final communiqué indicating agreements reached. They could only concur on a joint statement saying that time had run out to discuss all items on the agenda, and that another round of talks would take place within the next two weeks.[69] The Supreme Council was never to meet again. Indeed it was a meeting of the deputy rulers in August 1970 which dealt the final blow to efforts to establish a federation of nine. The meeting was primarily set to discuss drafts of the constitution. During the proceedings Bahrain revived its original opposition to equal representation in the National Assembly, and the dispute over the federation's capital and the emirates' share in the federal budget also resurfaced. The participants were unable to agree on the voting system of the Supreme Council (consensus or a two-thirds majority that included the big four).[70]

An argument could be made that Bahrain began to change its position on the idea of the federation after the Iranian claim to the island was resolved in May 1970, and went through the motions of joining a federation as protection against an Iranian move against it. However, the available evidence does not confirm either argument. Rather it indicates that confidence in the federation was fading in the months leading to the August 1970 deputies' meeting. Both Bahrain and Qatar began to prepare for independence with the announcement of a twelve-member Cabinet in Bahrain on 19 January 1970, and Qatar's subsequent proclamation of a 'provisional constitution' which, although referring to the 'United Arab Emirates,' emphasised the sovereignty of Qatar. On 29 May 1970 the Ruler of Qatar nominated seven men to form Qatar's first cabinet.[71]

With the trials and tribulations of the federation in mind Iran continued bilateral contacts with the separate rulers. The Crown Prince of Abu Dhabi visited Tehran in April 1969, the Ruler of Ras al-Khaimah in December 1969, the Ruler of Sharjah in January 1970, Shaikh Zayid of Abu Dhabi and Shaikh Rashid of Dubai in May 1970.[72] During these visits Iranian statements never referred to the islands dispute or opposition to the federation and stressed future co-operation among regional players. Statements issued in between these visits, which were critical of the federation, were seen by Foreign Minister Zahedi as part of the media campaign against Britain, the perceived architect of the federation.[73]

The Prospect of a British U-Turn

In his 26 March 1969 diary entry Alam noted that he had mentioned to the Shah complaints he received from the US Ambassador. The Shah had given an interview to the *New York Times* in which he announced 'his determination to prevent the US Navy, which had a small presence in Bahrain, from replacing Britain as Bahrain's protector.' The Shah had told Alam that '... he had meant exactly what he said and that the Americans should take careful note of our opposition to foreign intervention in the Gulf. America must be made to realise that we are an independent sovereign power and will make way for no one.'[74] Some days later, at a meeting with US officials, the Shah declared that '... it was in America's own interest to pull out [of the Gulf] as soon as the British have withdrawn; this, he claimed, was the most logical way of preventing the Russians from acquiring influence.'[75]

Such opposition to external power intervention in Gulf affairs was rising at a time when some members of the British Conservative Party were arguing for a reconsideration of Labour's decision to withdraw from the Gulf. This led the Shah to tell Alam on 27 March that, '... the British have no desire to see the entire Gulf dominated by Iran.'[76]

Iran was by no means the only Gulf power opposed to external intervention. Iraq was equally hostile to Britain. The Iraqi journal *An-Nur* saw the possibility of a Conservative reversal of the Labour government's decision as an attempt to preserve British imperialism. The paper was also critical of the concept of a political vacuum in the Gulf, claiming that it was used to maintain imperialist control in the area.[77] Relationships between Iran and Iraq were, however, fast deteriorating after Iran's April 1969 cancellation of their 1937 border treaty concerning the Shatt al-Arab in protest at measures taken by Iraq, particularly an Iraqi attempt to check the papers of ships moving up the waterway. On one occasion the Shah is reported to have declared, 'It looks as if the Iraqi leader is taking up the imperialist and colonialist heritage of Great Britain. We did not accept British colonialism and can accept Iraqi colonialism still less.'[78] Hence, common opposition to Britain's presence in the Gulf did not lead to an Iran-Iraq rapprochement.

In March Edward Heath, leader of the Conservative Party, had decided to tour the Gulf states. Heath's interest in Middle East affairs can be traced back to the early 1960s when he served at the Foreign Office as a cabinet minister with responsibilities that included the Gulf. It was Heath who signed the 1961 agreement which brought an end to Britain's special relations with Kuwait, '... it was from this time,' Douglas Hurd, then Political Secretary to Heath, argued, 'that his fascination with the Gulf can be dated.'[79] Heath had a strong belief in the stabilising role Britain played in the Gulf, and this was the source of his vociferous opposition to Labour's decision to withdraw. But by the time the leader of the opposition was briefed by members of the Foreign Office prior to this trip, the Foreign Office was a strong advocate of withdrawal. Hurd recalled that 'Heath exploded in the face of Geoffrey Arthur' and accused the Foreign Office of 'feebleness and bad faith.' Hurd added, 'We were clearly set for a stormy ride.'[80]

Heath, accompanied by Hurd and his parliamentary private secretary, Tony Kershaw, arrived in the Gulf in April. His thirteen-day visit was to cover Iran,

Kuwait, Bahrain, Oman, all the main Trucial States, Saudi Arabia, Egypt and Israel. The first stop was Tehran where he was unable to meet the Shah due to the latter's absence in America for General Dwight Eisenhower's funeral. The meeting was thus rescheduled.[81]

During their first visit to Tehran the British delegation was entertained lavishly by Prime Minister Hoveida and Foreign Minister Zahedi, during which Heath's assistant was struck by the Iranians '… lack of regard for Gulf rulers, and their determination that Iran should be the dominant military power around her own shores.'[82] This added a sense of intricacy to the task of mediating in Gulf affairs. A trip to Kuwait followed, which made it even more difficult for Heath to defend his views on Britain's role in the Gulf back home. The Kuwaitis, although expressing sympathy with Britain, believed that, as the intention to withdraw had been announced, a reversal of the decision would cause resentment in the region as a whole. The only support for a continued British presence came from some of the Trucial States.[83]

Heath eventually met the Shah without the presence of his assistants. According to Douglas Hurd, after the meeting Heath said that the Shah was '… ambiguous on the question of British presence.'[84] However, Heath made an unexpected statement in Athens indicating that he '… did not accept the view that the Shah of Iran would resent a reversal of the British decision to pull out by 1971.'[85]

The sense of surprise was strongest in Iran. Alam wrote, 'This is nonsense; HIM is adamant that he told Heath no such thing, but on the contrary advised an immediate withdrawal.'[86] Sir Denis Wright also confirms the Shah's denial that he had told Heath Iran would accept a continued British presence; the Shah told the British ambassador that the leader of the British opposition 'might have mixed up the Shah's acceptance of a British presence in the Gulf of Oman with presence in the Persian Gulf.'[87]

Whatever version of this story is correct, there was little doubt that most regional players wanted Britain out, a situation about which Hurd displayed no illusions when he wrote in his diary on 25 April, 'We are isolated from every one on this, and can only persevere if there is a real change of nerve over the next few years – dubious.'[88] Heath's statement can be viewed in the context of domestic political rivalry with the Labour Party over foreign policy issues in the approach to a general election.

The Labour Party meanwhile confirmed its intention to implement the decision taken by the Wilson government in 1968. In May 1969 Michael Stewart visited Iran on the occasion of the CENTO ministerial council's 16th session. Stewart told a press conference that after its withdrawal Britain would not be committed by the present treaties to defend the Gulf emirates and stressed that British troops would leave as planned. He insisted that a general election result in Britain would not affect that plan, 'Even if we suppose – and this is a hypothetical case – that the withdrawal would not take place by 1971, it will happen a few years after that because the world has changed and so has the British role east of Suez.'[89] At the same time Zahedi reiterated Iran's rejection of external intervention in the Gulf, repeating the idea that the security of the Gulf lies with the surrounding countries, and that Iran's security and economy depends on the region.[90] Later Zahedi declared, 'we are powerful enough to defend the entire Persian Gulf and we will not allow England to leave by the door and come back by the window.'[91]

Simultaneously *Ettela'at* sought to clarify the Shah's position and reassure the world that Iran was not implying the Gulf would become a 'closed sea,' but rather supporting the principle of free international navigation. The newspaper went on to say that the Shah meant '... foreign powers need not interfere to defend the security of the Persian Gulf. For Iran and Saudi Arabia have agreed in principle to defend the security of the Persian Gulf, free shipping in the Gulf and the rights of the [Shaikhdoms] against any possible threat.'[92]

The Conservatives in Downing Street

The real test for a possible change in Britain's decision to withdraw came after the Conservative victory in the British general elections on 18 June 1970. The Conservative election manifesto had criticised Labour's decision to withdraw from the Gulf for breaking promises to allies and exposing British interests and friends 'to unacceptable risks.' However, faced with the complex realities in the region which emerged after Heath's trip in the spring of 1969, the manifesto stopped short of committing the party to a reversal of Labour's decision. Instead it called for reconsideration of Britain's security role east of Suez, not through a unilateral British commitment, but through a five power defence system to include Commonwealth allies Australia, New Zealand, Malaysia and Singapore. It also called for further discussions with Gulf leaders.[93]

Advocates of reversing the decision were said to include Heath, Reginald

Maudling and Julian Amery. According to Douglas Hurd this was the dominant trend in the party,[94] although some diplomats continued to be sceptical about the Heath government being able to turn back the clock.[95] Shortly after the British elections, Iranian prime minister Amir Abbas Hoveida stated,

> In my view the present government is quite aware of the fact that from the historical standpoint, conditions conducive to British military presence in the Persian Gulf have disappeared forever. The British cannot ignore the legitimate right and aspirations of the people of the region for freedom and progress. Indeed, it is inconceivable in our time to turn the clock back to colonialism. In any event, the Persian Gulf is not a British legacy. Should some Persian Gulf emirates intend to invite Britain to remain in the region they should come out and say so frankly and officially.[96]

The Shah, on the other hand, said that it was not for Britain to decide whether to leave the Gulf. He expressed the view that foreign presence is governed by international law, in reference to Article 51 of the UN Charter, and that the era of colonialism was over.[97]

With the Shah's position in mind the new British foreign secretary, Sir Alec Douglas-Home, met him in Brussels on 10 July 1970 where he had made a stop to visit his dentist.[98] According to Foreign Office thinking the trip was designed to flatter the Shah's ego, and Antony Acland believed the 'aristocratic and honourable' Home would get along well with the Iranian monarch.[99] The meeting proved crucial for the new Conservative government's Gulf policy. Amir Khosrow Afshar has said that his 'friends at the Foreign Office' had told him beforehand that they had convinced Home of the merits of the Labour government's decision to pull out of the Gulf by the end of 1971.[100] For his own part, Denis Wright recalls that when the Shah showed strong opposition to Britain extending its presence in the Gulf, Home came to the conclusion that withdrawal was inevitable and told Britain's local representatives to put more pressure on the shaikhs to come to an agreement with Iran.[101] Whichever version of the narrative is correct, there can be little doubt that Home was thinking along the same lines as the Shah on the subject of continued military presence. On returning to London Home began to indicate that the Conservative government would not reverse Labour policy. Iran, Saudi Arabia and the Rulers of the Gulf emirates must, he said, be consulted before the new British government decided on its approach to the Gulf.[102]

The final decision, however, needed consensus in the Cabinet. On his way back to London from Brussels Wright recorded that he was '... feeling that my journey had been worthwhile and that the FO were taking a very sensible line on the Gulf (i.e. withdrawal and need to accommodate the Shah over the islands) though I doubt whether my view was shared by those in charge of Arab interests [in the FO]. I also hoped that the foreign secretary could get it across to the prime minister and his colleagues in the Cabinet.'[103]

Upon his return, on 23 July, Home briefed cabinet ministers on the discussions he had held with the Shah. According to Home the Shah had outlined his position on two main issues: future relations with the federation, and British presence in the Gulf. On the first issue the Shah said that now Bahrain was settled he had no objections to the federation provided there was a satisfactory agreement on the island dispute. Secondly, although the Shah was opposed to the continuation of Britain's treaties with the emirates, he did not object to the federation entering a defence agreement with Britain, or to Britain retaining an indirect presence through CENTO 'under which joint naval exercises could be organised with Iran.' The prime minister seemed in tune with the Shah's line of thinking. In summing up the discussion Heath stated, 'our objective in the Gulf area would be to secure a progressive reduction of our expenditure while encouraging and assisting the local rulers to shoulder their own responsibility.' Heath, as the Cabinet noted with approval, stopped short of explicitly confirming the Labour Government's decision to withdraw from the Gulf.[104]

Alam records that the Shah was delighted with his meeting with Home[105] which the Iranian press hailed as a victory that '... had a decisive effect on the Conservative government's view of the future of the Persian Gulf and British military forces in the region.' Some members of the Iranian press believed that the British government had '... adopted a milder tone concerning the Persian Gulf issue and the presence of British forces in the region,' and that a reversal of the British decision was now unlikely.[106]

Back to the Islands

Throughout the period when speculation was circulating about a possible change in the British decision to withdraw from the Gulf Iran's position over the islands, as can be seen from the diaries of Asadollah Alam, remained constant. On 27 May 1969 Alam wrote,

> The British continue to drag their feet in respect of restoring our islands of Tunbs and Abu Musa. As I told him [Michael Stewart], he must be well aware that Britain had gained unlawful possession of these islands and handed them as a blighted inheritance to the Shaikhs of Sharjah and Ras al-Khaimah whom his government now supports against Iran. We can see no sense in this policy, since Iran is set to become the Emirates' sole protector once the British withdraw.[107]

On 9 November Denis Wright met Alam and confirmed Britain's consistent line of argument: 'We are bound by our commitments to the shaikhs of Sharjah and Ras al-Khaimah,' said Wright, 'but we will nevertheless encourage them to reach some sort of accommodation with Iran, provided always that you confine yourselves to an occupation based on mutual agreement or a lease, and do not insist on pressing a claim to occupy the islands by legal right.' The Shah was outraged, '... he's talking out of his ears ... The islands belong to us.'[108] Moreover, when the Ruler of Ras al-Khaimah visited Iran, Alam noted, on 20 December, that he saw no chance of a settlement.[109] Three days later, the Shah privately expressed his dissatisfaction 'over negotiations with the Shaikh of Ras al-Khaimah.'[110]

Alam noted a meeting with Sir Denis Wright on 29 May 1970, 'With regard to the islands I warned him that his country would forfeit all credibility if there were no new initiatives soon.' In response, Alam claims, Wright asked, 'Why ... were we so insistent on the question of legal sovereignty over the islands? Far simpler for us just to occupy them.'[111] Sir Denis denies he ever said this to Alam, and his own diaries show that the meeting was not a formal audience but a casual conversation on horseback when out riding with the Iranian court minister, as he habitually did on Fridays.[112] British records confirm only one part of Alam's account, namely that Sir Denis believed that an agreement on the islands was possible '... if the question of sovereignty was fudged.'[113]

Had Britain offered a solution to the island dispute along the lines Alam suggested some easing of Anglo-Iranian tensions over the issue might have been expected. In fact, Iran began to sound more belligerent. On 13 July 1970 Alam noted that he had said to Wright, '... there can be no way forward until the issue of the islands has been resolved. If the British refuse to act, then it is we that shall be forced to make the running by resorting to military occupation.' Wright had replied that military action would cause more harm than good to Iran, but this did not alter Alam's position and he pointed to the Shah's domestic political considerations, mainly public perception of the handling of Iranian foreign policy.[114] This was an argument Britain had heard before when negotiating with Iran over the future of Bahrain.

By the end of 1970 a message was conveyed to the British ambassador. In continuing Iran's hardline position on the islands in November 1970, *Ettela'at* publisher Abbas Masoudi told Wright that the Shah would take the islands before the ambassador left Tehran for retirement in 1971. Wright's response was the same: 'I kept reminding the Iranians that any attempt to take the islands while our treaties with the Rulers were in force would mean hostility between us.'[115] This, however, did not seem to alter Iran's stance. When Zahedi met Home in New York the Iranian foreign minister was clear about Iran's uncompromising position even if it lead to a deterioration in relationships with Arab countries; if an agreement was not reached, Iran would simply take the islands when Britain withdrew.[116]

Another Dispute Intervenes

As continuous efforts were made to secure Iran's right to the ownership of the Hormuz islands, another dispute blew up on the periphery, among the emirates themselves, over a claim by both Sharjah and Umm al-Qaiwain to the territorial waters surrounding the island of Abu Musa which came to involve Iran and Britain. This dispute, it is argued here, had an impact on the overall settlement.

The offshore boundaries of the emirates lent themselves to dispute. Each had a seabed running from its coastal boundary to the median line that divides Arab from Iranian waters. Within such maritime territories lay some islands, notably Abu Musa, claimed by Sharjah in what was believed to be Umm al-Qaiwain's seabed. In 1951, in order to avoid overlapping, the emirates had declared a three-mile territorial water limit for these islands, rather than the conventional twelve-mile limit adopted by Saudi Arabia, Iran and Kuwait.[117]

With this three-mile limit in mind, on 18 November 1969 Umm al-Qaiwain signed an agreement with the American oil company Occidental (Oxy), by which Oxy was granted a forty-year exclusive right to explore for oil '... within all territorial and off-shore waters' of the emirate. The British Foreign Office endorsed the agreement. Oxy had also acquired another concession off Ajman on 2 February 1969.

Tests of the area indicated '... the prospect of oil and gas in very large quantities' within what Oxy believed was its concession.[118] By early 1970 drilling had begun 9 miles from the island of Abu Musa. This time a small American consortium, a combine of Buttes Gas and Oil Company and Clayco Petroleum Corporation, was drilling within the three-mile Abu Musa territorial limit. However, on 10 September 1969 Sharjah, advised by an American international lawyer named Northcutt Eley, had declared a twelve-mile territorial boundary for Abu Musa.[119] Consequently the Oxy concession fell into the waters now claimed by Sharjah, and a dispute with Umm al-Qaiwain and Oxy erupted.[120]

To the Foreign Office, Sharjah's declaration raised the problem of offshore boundaries and territorial waters 'in acute and practical form as it might encourage other emirates to do the same, hence an overlap in water claims all over the southern Gulf.'[121] Britain's initial position, stated on 15 May 1970, was that the dispute should be referred to arbitration but that Oxy should be allowed to continue drilling until a final settlement was reached.[122] The dispute, however, had provoked Iran. Alam noted on 18 January 1970 that the Ruler of Sharjah had visited Tehran where Abbas Aram, the ex-foreign minister, had been deputed to handle negotiations with him.[123] On 22 May Alam passed on a message from the Shah to the British ambassador saying,

> ... should the Shaikhs of Sharjah and Umm al-Qawain make an attempt to drill for oil in the waters around Abu Musa. ... Iran will not baulk at military intervention. Abu Musa is ours and Britain must bear in mind that it is we who they will be up against in any attempt to support the Shaikhs. Not that any such Anglo-Iranian confrontation would be without its positive side. It would clear the decks in more ways than one. Iranian pride would be satisfied, and having defeated the British we would be in a position to force the Shaikhs to accept a solution over the islands.[124]

Wright discouraged a confrontation over Abu Musa and promised he would do '... all within his power to prevent drilling around the island.'[125] Alam subsequently made it clear to the British ambassador that Iran was not interested in the island's oil as much as using it as a military base.[126] For his own part the Shah, fearing an agreement over the islands with one of the oil companies, insisted that,

'... for us to ignore such a deal would be an implicit admission that they have a valid claim.'[127]

Britain meanwhile hastened to forestall the possibility of military action. On 1 June 1970 Wright showed Alam a cautionary letter which the British government had sent to the Rulers of Umm al-Qaiwain and Ajman. It entailed, at least by Alam's account, three main points:

1. A third party be invited to settle differences between Ajman and Umm al-Qaiwain.
2. No drilling in areas claimed by Sharjah.
3. Caution be exercised by all parties, bearing in mind Iranian interests in the region.

Alam added that Wright had said, '... by playing up the disagreement between the Shaikhs we intend to bring drilling to a halt without the need for armed intervention by Iran. In the meantime we have reminded them all that Britain will withdraw from the Gulf over the coming twelve months, whereafter the Emirates will be left on their own to deal with Iran.'[128] However, according to Julian Walker, the British political agent in Dubai in 1971, Britain did not adopt the policy outlined in Alam's record, but rather continued trying to reduce differences among the Emirates.[129]

The situation threatened to lead to a political crisis between Iran and Britain. Sir Stewart Crawford, the political resident in Bahrain, instructed John Coles, then assistant political agent in Dubai, to go aboard a Royal Navy frigate carrying orders to Oxy to halt drilling and move the company's oil rig out of disputed waters. Oxy complied and an immediate political crisis was averted.[130]

An official British statement at the time confirmed the impression that Iranian pressure was the driving force behind the order: 'This action does not imply acceptance of the Iranian claim, although the reassertion of Iranian threat of force was a major political factor.'[131] Acland concurs with this view, arguing that British intervention saved Britain from a probable military confrontation with Iran while British treaties with the emirates were still valid.[132]

Luce Comes to the Rescue

With no easing of the dispute between Iran and the Gulf Arabs, and the efforts to form an Arab federation showing no signs of progress by mid-1970, some in the Foreign Office believed that the Gulf required exceptional attention, the normal machinery in the Arabian Department needed to be enhanced. The addition took the form of a British special envoy to the Gulf who had the flexibility to travel and ponder the affairs of the region. Antony Acland recommended Sir William Luce for the task, and Douglas-Home approved the suggestion.[133]

Luce was a retired career diplomat whose familiarity with the Gulf dated back to 1961 when he had served as Political Resident in Bahrain. He had also served as governor of Aden (1956–1960) and as advisor to the governor general of Sudan on constitutional and foreign affairs (1953–1956). In the last two mentioned posts Britain's power was in decline, and Luce, therefore, could be seen as an 'end of empire expert.' Some who worked closely with him argue that in addition to his expertise in the area he had a reputation for strong leadership combined with charm and skill in negotiations.[134]

Before Luce was appointed special envoy he had expressed views about the Gulf regional order which were not different from those championed by the Foreign Office at the time. In an article published in 1967 Luce came over as an ardent supporter of British presence in the Gulf and was critical of the Labour government's decision to abandon Aden.[135] After the decision to withdraw from the Gulf was announced in 1968 Luce moderated his view. Although he was critical of the fact that the decision was taken without prior consultation with the rulers and regarded it as '... morally wrong, unwise and unnecessary,' Luce recognised that the change of policy was '... one of timing and method rather than principle,' and that Britain's efforts ought to focus on encouraging an understanding between Iran and the Arabs, particularly Saudi Arabia, and supporting the union of the Gulf Arab emirates.[136]

Luce was sent to the Gulf in August 1970, stayed there until September, and visited the area again in October and in January–February 1971. He had full powers to explore new options, but decisions rested with the Cabinet.[137]

During his visits to Tehran Luce would normally meet the Shah, and often Zahedi and Amir Khosrow Afshar would attend the meetings.[138] According to Acland the Luce mission worked as follows:

He would go round in the area and meet leaders, and very often have a one to one meeting with leaders. Then he would dictate reports to his secretary which were sent to the Foreign Office. If the Foreign Office saw a need to comment it would do so and this would be sent to Luce. When Luce arrived in London he would present a final report and discuss it with Home and me. Unless there were new developments Home would not normally take Sir William's reports to Cabinet.[139]

In September 1970 Luce left Tehran after meeting the Shah and other officials, but was silent about the outcome of his trip. He hoped the British government would announce its final decision in two or three months.[140] Zahedi likewise made no comments, confining himself to describing the talks with Luce as 'useful' and a reiteration of Iran's opposition to external intervention in the Gulf.[141] Alam recorded in his diary entry for 22 September that the Shah insisted that foreign powers must leave the area before a bilateral treaty between the emirates and Britain could be considered.[142]

In the first months of the mission, no fresh initiative was made by Britain's special envoy who refrained from making statements implying that he had specific ideas in mind. He described his talks with regional leaders as friendly and expressed optimism about the formation of the federation.[143] In other words this was a period of gathering views and reflection before venturing into specific proposals for conflict resolution.

Containing Iran

Like other British officials in previous years, Sir William's task in the Gulf was not made easy by Iran. Some time before his appointment, Iran had launched a diplomatic and media campaign to make it clear that the new reality in the Gulf called for Britain's departure. The Ruler of Qatar, Shaikh Ahmed al-Thani,[144] visited Iran in April 1970 and while he was there the media took pains to stress Iranian cooperation with the coastal Gulf states after British withdrawal and spoke of the shaikhdoms as equal partners.[145] Omar Saqqaf, the Saudi foreign minister, visited the country a few days later followed, in May, by Shaikh Zayid of Abu Dhabi.[146] During Shaikh Zayid's three-day stay the Iranian media took the opportunity to claim that the Gulf states rejected external intervention. Iran also eased its hardline rejection of the Federation depicting it '... as the first step the Persian Gulf Rulers have taken for their defence.' *Ettela'at* claimed, '... as a sign of respect for Iran the Rulers postponed serious decisions until the Bahrain issue had been resolved. Now that this issue has been removed, thanks to Iran's courageous and principled action, the creation of the Persian Gulf Federation will naturally become a more serious consideration.'[147] Two-way contacts between Iran and Bahrain had, as we have seen, already been established. On 23 May Iran dispatched three trade and goodwill missions to Bahrain[148] and in June the Bahraini prime minister, Shaikh Khalifah bin Salman, headed a six-man delegation to Tehran.

Meanwhile, the Shah publicly maintained that Iran was the only power in the Gulf capable of guarding its peace in the future, and occasionally stressed cooperation with the small emirates.[149] He also said in a July interview that Iran did not see why any government or nation in the Persian Gulf should want British troops to stay in the area, thereby maintaining the symbols of colonialism.[150] Close to Luce's own arrival in the region the Iranian media intensified their campaign with Tehran radio stating, 'No doubt the British foreign secretary's special envoy will observe that the people of the region in general wish the area free from foreign political influences. Everyone wants the British [Labour] government's decision to be properly and completely implemented.'[151]

To some British diplomats such statements represented Iranian muscle flexing.[152] But the political tide in the region seemed to have turned in Iran's favour. The Kuwaiti foreign minister publicly stated, 'We have informed the British government that under no circumstances will we accept the continued presence of British military forces in the Persian Gulf,'[153] and in mid-July Shaikh Zayid ended a trip to Kuwait with a communiqué saying agreement had been reached on mutual relations including Gulf issues. At around the same time Zahedi and the Saudi minister for foreign affairs, Omar al-Saqqaf, met and stressed that, '... both Iran and Saudi Arabia want Britain to withdraw its forces from the area.'[154]

In another move to gather more Arab support for its policy in the Gulf, in the summer of 1970 Iran resumed diplomatic relations with Egypt. The long-standing animosity between the Shah and President Nasser had begun to fade following the 1967 war,[155] but according to Amir Khosrow Afshar what really broke the ice between the two countries were comments the Egyptian vice-president, Anwar Sadat, had made during the Islamic summit held in Morocco in 1969. The fluent Persian speaking Sadat referred to Reza Shah as a great leader in modern Islamic history who stood firmly against imperialism.[156] To some in Iran a strong mutual interest underlay such statements: Egypt needed Iranian support in the Arab-Israeli conflict,[157] while Iran needed Egypt to gain Arab support for its Gulf policy. Afshar recalls that talks with Egypt began through various channels, but the actual normalisation with Egypt took place only after the death of Nasser in September 1970.[158] According to one assessment, the normalisation between Iran and Egypt left Iraq as the main 'trouble-maker' in the Gulf.[159]

By October 1970 the Shah could afford a more conciliatory posture. In his speech at the opening of the Iranian parliament he referred proudly to the resolution of the Iranian claim to Bahrain: 'As you know, an overwhelming majority of the Bahrainis opted for independence. We accepted this as we had promised. As a result, the Bahrainis today are perhaps one of the closest friends of Iran, instead of enemies.' The Bahrain policy, the Shah went on in a message to Gulf Rulers:

> ... is representative of Iran's general policy in the Persian Gulf. Apart from the islands belonging to Iran, we in the Persian Gulf covet no territory. Nor do we cast a greedy eye on anyone's wealth. On the contrary, we have extended our hand in friendship to the largest as well as the smallest country in the region. We are ready to offer any assistance we can afford to anyone who asks for it without any strings attached.[160]

The notion that Iran adopted an aggressive approach in the Gulf as a result of US support and arms build-up requires some modification. Iranian assertiveness of supremacy over the Gulf was reflected in increasing media hostility to outside forces, a firm and non-negotiable claim to total sovereignty over the islands, and belligerent threats to Britain over allowing the emirates to give oil concessions around the island of Abu Musa. The Iranian rejection of a federation which incorporated the islands stood firm.

Nevertheless, Iran relied on pragmatic manoeuvres which allowed it to take such positions. Anti-British statements served to guard against the uncertainty of the new Conservative government's approach to the Gulf at a time when the country was assured of full American backing. Nor, above all, did Iran let the island issue hinder co-operation with Britain in other areas, most notably on Bahrain.

Bahrain was also used by Iran to enhance good relations with countries such as Saudi Arabia and Kuwait and encourage them to take a similar position to Iran's with regard to British influence in the region. Iran also used the Bahrain settlement to demonstrate its policy of restraint and tolerance of small neighbours, and to improve the Rulers of the Gulf emirates understanding of its intentions. Lastly, Iran made a breakthrough in the Arab circle by improving relations with Egypt which meant that there could be little chance of a unified regional position against Iran.

The years 1969 and 1970 can, therefore, be seen as the period in which Iran was preparing for the settlement which came a year later. Iran had to compete with Britain and the two emirates, Ras al-Khaimah and Sharjah, with claims to the islands. The success of Iran's diplomatic moves during the two years prior to the final settlement is a question for the following chapter.

6

The Final Year

The date set by the British government to end its military presence in the Gulf and terminate treaties committing Britain to the defence of the Gulf Arab emirates was 31 December 1971. The goal of leaving behind a stable regional structure, set in 1968, was to meet its final test in 1971.

The impending deadline can be seen either as an incentive to speed up a settlement, or as an arbitrarily set date which added time pressure to what would otherwise have been patient diplomatic efforts to resolve outstanding disputes. Whatever the effect of the deadline, it arguably worked against Britain. The previous two years had exposed the limits of British influence on regional players, in particular in the dispute over Bahrain and the Hormuz islands. The US had, in addition, confirmed its position of no direct involvement in regional affairs, and developed a strategic doctrine that favoured regional autonomy. Above all Iran's self-confidence had reached a new high.

The year 1971 began with Iran brokering an agreement between OPEC countries and international oil companies led by British Petroleum by which the oil companies accepted that the price of Marker Crude oil (Arabian light) would increase from 98 cents to 1.27 dollars a barrel.[1] Although successful confrontation with the oil companies was first achieved by Libya in 1970, Iranian officials did not fail to stress that what was to be known as the Tehran agreement was a personal victory for the Shah and not without consequence for Iran's regional posture.

To Alam, '... the whole thing was a triumph and confirmed us in unrivalled leadership of the entire Gulf.'[2]

With that in mind the final year of British presence was the ultimate test for power relations in the Gulf region. It was also an opportunity to achieve a comprehensive settlement of regional disputes. At the twilight of Pax-Britannica and the dawn of the era of Iran as the main power in the Gulf, Iran's immediate concern was to capture the two Tunb islands and the island of Abu Musa before the end of the year. The way Iran pursued its claim, and the manner in which Pax-Britannica ended, reflected the main characteristics of the newly emerging regional order.

The Choice Narrowed to One

In 1970 Iranian officials were passing messages to Britain that their government would resort to force if the Tunb and Abu Musa islands were not handed to Iran. Towards the end of the year Iran went public on the strategy. In November Foreign Minister Ardeshir Zahedi declared, 'These islands have been ours and they are going to be ours. There is no compromise. Look at the Chinese communists in Aden. If these islands go all our interests will be damaged.'[3] On the other hand, Zahedi later stated that if the island dispute were resolved Iran was prepared to give economic aid to the emirates, and that support for the federation hinged on that issue.[4] By 1971 the Shah himself was explicit in saying that Iran would use force, if necessary, to recapture the islands.[5]

Britain received this news with dismay. On 19 February 1971 Sir Denis Wright wrote:

> The Shah is determined to seize them [the islands] by force if we can't arrange some settlement with the Shaikhs concerned before we leave the Gulf. This looks almost impossible despite all our efforts: On Saturday it was clear that the Shah's attitude had hardened so that the sort of compromise settlement we were trying for is not going to work. Our hope now is that he won't seize the islands while we are still bound by our treaty, if he does we'll be in a state of war with our ally.[6]

From that time onwards one could argue that Britain was convinced of Iran's unwavering will to seize the islands, and its efforts centred on how to prevent a confrontation. In a conversation with the Crown Prince of Ras al-Khaimah, Luce affirmed that the 'Shah was not bluffing.' He urged compromise with Iran over the Tunbs arguing that 'half a loaf for Ras al-Khaimah was better than no bread.'[7] According to Zahedi the US, USSR and France also knew of Iranian intentions,[8] but for Britain to accommodate Iran it had to gain Arab consent to a settlement. On the Arab side, although the belief had been expressed that the dispute could only be settled peacefully, the rulers of Sharjah and Ras al-Khaimah stood fast on their claim to sovereignty over the islands and made this clear at every opportunity.[9]

The Emirates' Landscape

By the end of 1970 the shape of the proposed federation was emerging more clearly with reports that Bahrain might decide to leave, and that Qatar might follow.[10] The British government was privately willing to support a union of seven if Bahrain and Qatar were to seek independence.[11] In February Sir William Luce arrived in Tehran and told journalists that, '... the differences that existed between the Gulf Shaikhdoms on the formation of a federation have diminished,' and the question of British troop withdrawal [will] soon be addressed.'[12]

This change of mind over the Labour government's decision to withdraw from the Gulf was confirmed by discussions Luce held with regional players who received his conclusion 'calmly and without surprise.'[13] However, Luce believed that something might be done to reassure the rulers of the Trucial States that Britain still had some role preserving the security of the region, though to avoid widespread condemnation Britain could only offer 'token' military support.[14] These ideas were reflected in a statement to the House of Commons by Sir Alec Douglas-Home on 1 March 1971 which, after giving '... very careful consideration to the future relationship between Britain and the Gulf states,' and after consulting with Gulf rulers, said Britain was fully behind the development of a Union of Arab Emirates. Britain was prepared to offer the following:

1. A Treaty of Friendship containing an undertaking to consult together in time of need, to replace the existing treaties between Britain and all nine emirates which would be terminated by the end of 1971.
2. Handing over of the Trucial Oman Scouts to form the nucleus of a Union Army.

3. British assistance in training Union security forces.
4. Regular training exercises involving British army and air force units.
5. Regular visits to the area by ships of the Royal Navy.[15]

Although Home did not admit to confirming Labour's decision to withdraw by the end of 1971 the message was implicit. As *The Economist* remarked, '... the foreign secretary dressed up his statement to appease some of his party's backbenchers.'[16] To Douglas Hurd, however, the decision did not cause significant dissent within the party, as by that time British military presence in the Gulf was not 'a major political issue.'[17]

After a period of stalemate in high-level negotiations on the Federation following the deputy rulers' meeting in October 1970, a last attempt, initiated by Saudi Arabia and Kuwait, was made to revive the idea of a federation of nine. In January 1971 a delegation headed by Prince Nawaf bin Abdul Aziz, an adviser to King Faisal, and the Kuwaiti foreign minister, Shaikh Sabah al-Ahmad al-Sabah, toured the Gulf emirates. According to the available documents the Saudi-Kuwaiti mission tried to find technical legal solutions to outstanding disputes. No political or diplomatic pressure was applied on the rulers. Two drafts of recommendations were made. The first before the rulers' comments were received, and the second afterwards.[18] In the end the Saudi-Kuwaiti mission realised that the shattered consensus was impossible to restore.

While the Saudi-Kuwaiti delegations pursued their attempts at mediation Bahrain continued toward independence. On 17 June 1971 Bahrain signed a continental shelf agreement with Iran, and six days later Zahedi visited the island. Later the rulers were privately informed that Bahrain would 'go it alone.' It was not until 14 August that the declaration of independence was announced; Qatar followed suit on 1 September.

Qatar's declaration of independence made Dubai hesitate about joining the Federation. Thus Abu Dhabi prepared for the failure of the Federation by forming its first cabinet on 1 July, and a fifty-member National Assembly.[19] The chances for successful formation of the Federation now hinged, it seemed, on an agreement between Abu Dhabi and Dubai, the largest of the emirates left. Subsequently an agreement was reached between Shaikh Zayid of Abu Dhabi and Shaikh Rashid of Dubai during the summer of 1971.[20] On 10 July the seven rulers of the Trucial States met in Abu Dhabi and reached an agreement on a revised but 'provisional' constitution. On 18 July a communiqué was issued announcing the formation of the United Arab Emirates.

The only Emirate which did not sign the agreement was Ras al-Khaimah. The reasons for its hesitation were not announced officially, but some argue that the Emirate was not willing to compromise on the issue of representation.[21] Also there were rumours that Union Oil of California had made a promising oil strike which might give Ras al-Khaimah the economic viability needed to survive as an independent state.[22] In any event, Ras al-Khaimah's reluctance to sign up to the Federation had no impact on its claim to the Tunb islands, nor did the declaration of the federation of the United Arab Emirates change Iran's claim to the Tunbs and Abu Musa.[23]

Iran Prepares to Use Force

As far back as June 1970 the British political agent had presented Shaikh Saqar of Ras al-Khaimah with a tentative proposal to settle the Tunb islands dispute. It included the following points:

1. An agreement to resolve the legal status of the islands which accommodated claims made by both parties.
2. Deployment of Iranian troops on the islands by 1 January 1972.
3. Ras al-Khaimah's government agencies would remain on the islands with no outside intervention [in their functions].
4. Ras al-Khaimah's flag would continue to fly over the Tunbs.
5. Ras al-Khaimah would retain the rights to all offshore oil and minerals around the islands.
6. An agreement on a median line that separated Iranian from emirates' territorial waters.
7. Iran would grant Ras al-Khaimah [an unspecified sum in] financial aid.
8. Iran would supply Ras al-Khaimah with [an unspecified quantity of] arms.[24]

Almost a year later on his way home via the Gulf, on 27 April 1971, Sir Denis Wright told the Ruler of Ras al-Khaimah that if a settlement were not reached the Shah would seize the islands by force; if it were then the Emirate would benefit financially. On 29 April Sir Denis conveyed the same message to the Ruler of

Sharjah, Shaikh Khalid, but got no response. Earlier he had written in a letter home that '... the Persians will do all they can to prevent the [formation of the] UAE until they have the islands.'²⁵ Such proposals for a settlement were to face a serious obstacle, posed not by the Shah, but by the Ruler of Ras al-Khaimah, Shaikh Saqar bin Mohammed al-Qasimi.

Frail-looking and small in stature, Shaikh Saqar is not a man who can easily settle for a compromise. In an interview with the author he spoke of the rightful protection of what he saw as his Emirate's land as equal to the protection of personal dignity and pride; he perceived the conflicting claims over the Tunbs as a struggle between right and wrong, justice and injustice.²⁶ Above all, he believed he was a man of destiny who would prevail in the end. It was, quite evidently, such thinking that led historian J. B. Kelly to describe him as 'the Bonaparte of the Trucial Coast.'²⁷ Consequently, in dealing with British officials over the Tunbs dispute, Shaikh Saqar instantly rejected what was proposed, and insisted, like the Shah, that the other side should recognise his sovereignty over the islands before he would sit at the negotiating table.²⁸

Sir Denis Wright's diplomatic career in Iran ended on 21 April 1971. At his last audience he felt that he had achieved partial success over the islands dispute. He believed he had '... moved HIM quite a bit and got him to agree not to force the sovereignty issue for the time being. Maybe this will provide a way out.'²⁹ Nevertheless, Iran's hostile attitude toward Britain hardened. In May 1971 Iran protested British military sorties over Iranian warships and islands in the Gulf. The protest was delivered to the chargé d'affaires at the Tehran embassy, Donald Murray, who, in an unprecedented threat, was told that Iranian warships had an order to fire on 'buzzing' British aircraft.³⁰ To some British representatives in the Gulf this was merely Iran's way of demonstrating its leadership of the region.³¹

The anti-British spin on the news continued in the Iranian press. *Kayhan* said of the impending declaration of Bahraini and Qatari independence that it was a snub to Britain and colonialism, and that the two countries would enjoy the support of the people and government of Iran. The paper wrote, 'The victory of Bahrain and Qatar in achieving independence once again proves that imperialism can no longer impose its will, even on the smaller states.'³² On the other hand, some parts of the Iranian media were arguing that the island dispute was set up by Britain as an excuse to enter the Gulf and exploit regional problems. An editorial in *Ettela'at* saw it as an attempt by Britain to leave behind a problem which would ensure its continued intervention, 'This is what they have done in other places when they had to withdraw.'[33] *Peygham-e Emruz* saw the island disputes as, '... a trap with attractive appearance, but a pitfall laid to divert the attention of the Arab and Islamic world from the most important catastrophe of Islamic history, the fall of Jerusalem.'[34]

For his own part, Foreign Minister Zahedi restated Iran's rejection of external power intervention in the Gulf.[35] In an interview in Bahrain Zahedi gave the following answer to a question on the future of the Iranian claim to the islands:

> This is not a claim. It is a fact that these islands in the Persian Gulf have been and are part of Iran, and they will continue to be so. These islands were occupied by British troops nearly 75 years ago but now that the British are leaving the area they should be returned to Iran; that is, to their original owner. Of course, Iran will do its best to solve this problem by peaceful means, but if it is not successful in this attempt then it will use any step necessary to regain these islands. We cannot allow part of our country's territory to be detached. Likewise, we believe that once the area is emptied of British troops, no one in this area will have the right to inherit from imperialism.[36]

In the summer of 1971 senior Iranian officials reiterated Iran's position that if the islands were not returned peacefully military action would be taken. In a speech to a gathering of local citizens at Bandar Abbas airport Prime Minister Hoveida asserted Iran's historical and legitimate rights in the Gulf and said Iran would use 'whatever means necessary' to regain them.[37] The Shah reiterated the warning in response to an Iranian journalist who asked about a comment made by Sir William Luce that Iran would use force to regain the islands: '... what Luce has said is true. The islands belong to us. I hope the issue will be resolved by peaceful means. But I must again stress that we are determined to regain what is ours. I cannot sit here watching my country being auctioned and handed over to the ruler of another country.'[38]

With a hint of pessimism some British diplomats in the Gulf saw such comments as a statement of the obvious.[39] In the United States, according to Richard Murphy, the island dispute did not even come to the attention of senior officials in the Nixon administration. There was no US effort to resolve it, and 'It was seen as a bit of unfinished British business.'[40] Britain, then, followed the arduous route of a negotiated settlement between Iran and the rulers of the emirates.

The Encounter with Shaikh Saqar

After meeting the Shah in May 1971 Sir William Luce visited the Trucial States. In his meeting with Shaikh Saqar of Ras al-Khaimah, he conveyed Iran's firm demand for sovereignty over the islands, the position of Iran being that it would allow Ras al-Khaimah to have a police presence on the Tunbs for only a year. In exchange Iran once more offered the Emirate financial aid, and recognised the federation and the median line dividing Iranian-Arab waters. In response Shaikh Saqar asked for time to consult with other Trucial rulers, members of his family and notables of Ras al-Khaimah.[41] Two days later he told Julian Walker that there was no change in Ras al-Khaimah's original claim of sovereignty over the Tunbs and expressed his wish that Britain should concentrate on helping to establish the federation rather than trying to 'appease Iran.'[42]

At another meeting with Julian Walker, Shaikh Saqar stressed in addition that support of the federation should precede resolution of the islands issue.[43] It might thus be argued that Ras al-Khaimah tried to use the idea of participation in an Arab federation to strengthen its position against Iran and Britain. Amir Khosrow Afshar, the Iranian deputy minister of foreign affairs, believed that the notion that Iran should recognise the federation before the island dispute was resolved was an Arab ploy designed to make Iran appear as an aggressor against a sovereign state; Iran was compelled – if force were needed – to act before the emirates gained international recognition.[44] Britain, however, seems not to have lent support to the Shaikh's idea, and it appears that he threatened to seek support from other countries, not ruling out even the Soviet Union.[45]

In September 1971 another meeting was held between Luce and Shaikh Saqar. Luce continued to stress that the Shah would accept nothing less than full sovereignty over the islands and repeated the Iranian line saying that, if the matter was not resolved peacefully, Iran would simply take the islands by force. In abandoning a position Britain had sought to defend for over a hundred years, Luce argued that his government could not enforce a settlement as it was playing the role of 'a mediator' rather than taking sides. Luce added that time was running out and at that point mentioned a detailed proposal drafted by the Shah and his ambassador to London, Amir Khosrow Afshar, as well as a draft series of pledges to be signed by the rulers separately committing them to the terms of the agreement.[46] According to Ras al-Khaimah archives, the Iranian proposal included the following:

1. The landing of Iranian troops on the islands.
2. Twelve months after the landing of troops the Emirate's officials and police force would be withdrawn and the Emirate's flag would be removed.
3. During these twelve months the number of Emirate officials and the police force on the islands would not be increased.
4. Terms regulating the conduct of Iranian troops and officials on the islands would be agreed with the Emirate's administration at a later stage.
5. For eighteen months, beginning from the landing of Iranian troops, no public statements would be made by Emirate officials relating to the question of sovereignty over the island.
6. Iran would compensate residents on the islands in case of any damage to their property during the first three years of Iranian military presence.
7. All Rulers of the proposed federation would pledge not to take or support actions which might change the settlement agreed upon, and in exchange Iran would support the federation.
8. All pledges would be made to the British government in its capacity as the government responsible for the foreign relations of the Emirates. The British government would secretly pass on the exchange of pledges between Iran and the Emirates and would support the agreement.
9. Iran would give financial support to the Emirate. The financial aid on offer consisted of 750,000 pounds to be paid to the Emirate in two instalments on 21 April and 21 October.
10. The agreement would be valid for nine years starting 21 April 1972, and would be reviewed at the end of the eighth year by the Iranian government and the Emirate.[47]

On 12 September Luce and Shaikh Saqar held another meeting where the shaikh rejected the Iranian proposal which, to him, gave less to his emirate than the offer presented by Britain back in 1970, an offer Ras al-Khaimah had refused to accept. The new proposal, he said, was merely of financial help to the emirate. Shaikh Saqar then expressed his belief in Arab support, but Sir William responded that it was not a worthwhile option as King Faisal had told him that Saudi Arabia did not want to play an active role in the dispute, and Egypt was now on friendly terms with Iran. Nevertheless, Shaikh Saqar refused to compromise his position of full sovereignty over the Tunbs[48] and at best offered to rent the islands to Iran.[49]

One wonders about the origin of Shaikh Saqar's persistent stance in these negotiations. A possible interpretation is that the financial gains to be had from incorporating the Tunb islands as part of Ras al-Khaimah could have been larger than the financial assistance offered by Iran since by 1971 there was speculation that oil might be struck off the Tunbs shores. Such speculation was strengthened by the fact that Iran, as Shaikh Khalid bin Saqar, the Crown Prince of Ras al-Khaimah, mentioned to British officials, had given oil concessions to foreign companies around the Iranian Gulf coast.[50] But of equal importance to an understanding of Ras al-Khaimah's position are a set of cultural considerations which some British officials seem to have had difficulty dealing with. Among these was Shaikh Saqar's belief that protection of land is an act of dignity which could not be compromised. When the Ruler of Ras al-Khaimah told Julian Walker, the political agent in Dubai, that he could not give up his land, Walker asked, 'Even if this land is desert?' Shaikh Saqar replied 'Yes' and went on to explain that 'To relinquish the islands is impossible; history will not forgive me for that.'[51]

An even starker contrast between what British officials were trying to achieve and how some locals saw the situation appears in the following conversation between Shaikh Saqar and Sir William Luce when the latter reminded the Shaikh of the Shah's military might:

Saqar: 'God will send one who is even stronger than him.'
Luce: 'Do you mean the Russians?'
Saqar: 'God knows.'
Luce: 'China?'
Saqar: 'God knows.'[52]

Shaikh Saqar was not referring to a specific international power in military-strategic terms; rather he was expressing a general religious belief in the supreme power of God over the material power of mankind. But his convictions were not to affect Iran's intention to seize the islands, if possible by consent and if necessary by force. Shaikh Saqar's position led Britain to direct its efforts from then on toward an accommodation between Iran and the Gulf Arabs over another disputed island, Abu Musa, where Shaikh Saqar's cousin Shaikh Khalid bin Mohammed al-Qasimi, the Ruler of Sharjah, showed a willingness to negotiate in order to avoid the use of force against him.[53]

A Last Minute Deal with Sharjah

Peter Ramsbotham, the newly appointed British ambassador to Iran, recalls driving with Sir William Luce to see the Shah at his Caspian palace once or twice a week during the summer of 1971 to discuss a possible solution to the islands dispute.[54] To the Shah, one could argue, the islands of Abu Musa and the Tunbs represented two distinct cases. The Tunbs are close to the Iranian coast, on its side of the median line, and are regarded as strategically important for the control of the Strait of Hormuz. Abu Musa, on the other had, is south of the median line and closer to the Arab side; hence Iran could present a weaker legal case for title over the island. According to Julian Walker, negotiations started sometime during that summer on the future of Abu Musa, after the Shah had told Sir William that Iran would not insist on resolving the issue of sovereignty over the island provided Iranian troops could be stationed there. Intense negotiations between Iran, Britain and Sharjah went on for weeks and it was not until mid-November that the Ruler of Sharjah agreed to a deal with Iran.[55]

Before negotiations began Shaikh Khalid bin Mohammed al-Qasimi sent a memorandum to all Arab leaders in which he pleaded for Arab support to counter the Iranian claim to Abu Musa. The Lebanese newspaper *al-Anwar* published the text of this memorandum which was circulated on 24 August 1971. It reveals that Shaikh Khalid stressed Sharjah's rightful ownership of the island and claimed that some British officials had acknowledged that fact. For its own part, Iran had proved inflexible over the issue of sovereignty but said it was willing to negotiate according to the following conditions:

1. Iran would be able to land troops on the island with no opposition from the Ruler of Sharjah.
2. Once Iranian troops had landed on the island Sharjah would withdraw its police force.
3. Sovereignty over the island would not be contested for two years, following which Iran's sovereign rights would be recognised.
4. Iran would give generous annual aid to Sharjah and a percentage of the island's oil revenue.
5. Iran would be willing to sign an agreement over financial aid but not sovereignty over the island.

Finally the memorandum claims that the Shah threatened to seize the island by force if an agreement was not reached before the end of 1971.

The Ruler of Sharjah refused to accept the Iranian claim of sovereignty but at the same time rejected the use of force and was willing to negotiate in order to find a way to settle the dispute peacefully. According to *al-Anwar* only four unnamed Arab countries responded to Shaikh Khalid's memorandum; the content of their response is unknown.[56]

The rhetoric on both sides, however, was not to stifle negotiations seeking a practical accommodation of the parties' demands. According to Julian Walker, when the negotiations got underway they centred on a division of the island. In the end an 'administrative line' which divided Abu Musa into two sections was agreed: Iran was to control the northern section, while the southern section remained under Sharjah. The northern section included the hills Iran insisted on controlling to secure strategic domination of the island, while the southern included the island's village, a water well, palm trees, graves, an old jetty used by the British Oxide mining company, and company housing.[57] (see map 3)

After a meeting with the new Iranian foreign minister, Abbas Ali Khalatbari, Luce declared that Britain and Iran had 'sorted out their differences.'[58] On 29 November the agreement was announced with a prelude stating that neither Iran nor Sharjah would give up its claim to Abu Musa or recognise the other's claim. Against this background the two sides agreed on the following:

1. Iranian troops would be stationed in part of the island, and in this area the Iranian flag would be flown and Iran would exercise full jurisdiction.
2. Sharjah would retain jurisdiction over the rest of the island including the existing Sharjah police post.
3. Both Iran and Sharjah would recognise a twelve-mile limit of territorial waters round the island, and agreed that the present concessionaire, Buttes Gas and Oil, would continue oil exploration both on the island and offshore.
4. Revenues accruing from oil exploration would be shared equally between Iran and Sharjah.
5. Iran would also give 1,500,000 pounds a year to Sharjah in aid until Sharjah's annual revenues from oil deposits reached 3,000,000 pounds a year.
6. Iranian and Sharjah nationals would have equal fishing rights in the island's territorial waters.[59]

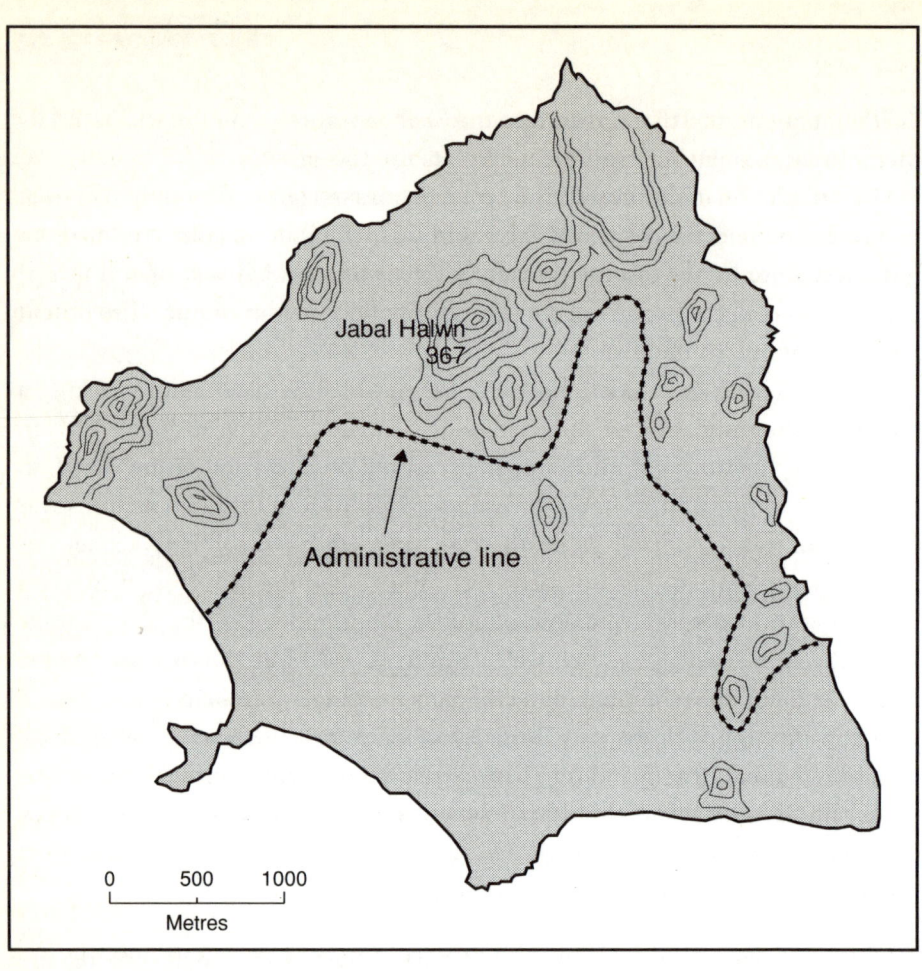

Map 3: Abu Musa: 1971 Administrative Line Dividing the Northern (Iranian) and Southern (Sharjah) Sectors

It might be argued that this agreement was doomed from the outset. Firstly, the Memorandum of Understanding did not resolve the question of sovereignty over the island, nor did it outline a method for a future settlement. Secondly, it appears to have been interpreted differently by each side. The Ruler of Sharjah stated that it was temporary and was an instrument for preventing bloodshed, while the Shah continued to reject Sharjah's claim of sovereignty over Abu Musa.[60] The Iranian prime minister told the Majlis:

> I deem it necessary to point out here, however, that His Imperial Majesty's government has in no conceivable way relinquished or will relinquish its incontestable sovereignty and right of control over the whole of Abu Musa island. Thus, the presence of local agents in part of Abu Musa should in no way be regarded as conflicting with this policy. Another point is that the Imperial Government, in order to prove its absolute goodwill in solving this issue by peaceful means, has brought an oil agreement which had been previously concluded with Sharjah and an oil company into line with recent regulations of the Organisation of Petroleum Exporting Countries so that it can be acceptable to Iran. Iran has further agreed that should oil be found the revenue from it will be equally divided between Iran and Sharjah to help the progress of our brothers in Sharjah. In addition, Iran will provide financial and technical aid to further social and development progress in Sharjah.[61]

Policy-makers on both sides were well aware of the shortcomings of the Memorandum of Understanding,[62] but the different views of its significance did not alarm them. The public statements made at the time were not a sign of misunderstanding; both parties felt that they were a way of reassuring public opinion on their own side that their perceived national interests had not been jeopardised.

The memorandum served the immediate interests of Iran and Sharjah well. For Iran it guaranteed military control of Abu Musa and a share in its oil. For Sharjah an agreement with the Gulf's most powerful country, which had Britain's blessing, legitimised a twelve-mile territorial water claimed by Umm al-Qaiwain and Occidental, and guaranteed its oil company, Buttes-Clayco, the right to prospect for oil. In addition it gave the Emirate financial assistance badly needed at the time.[63] In other words the Iran-Sharjah Memorandum of Understanding was a way of reaching a *modus vivendi* which lasted until the early 1990s.

Despite the signature of this memorandum, the Ruler of Ras al-Khaimah continued to stand firm on its previous position, and when he learnt of the understanding expressed his discontent with his cousin's decision.[64] A final failed attempt to resolve the dispute came when Sir Geoffrey Arthur met Shaikh Saqar in the last days of December 1971 to try once more to get a compromise, but found him as insistent as ever on his position.[65]

Meanwhile Iran rejected solutions proposed by the Arab side. The Kuwaiti foreign minister, Shaikh Sabah al-Ahmad al-Sabah, revealed to the Lebanese newspaper *An Nahar* that Iran had dismissed two Arab proposals for solving the islands dispute. The first was to lease the islands to Iran for ninety-nine years on condition that Iran recognise Arab sovereignty over them. The second was to station joint Arab and Iranian forces on the islands.[66] The Kuwaiti permanent representative at the UN, Abdullah Bishara, added a third proposal: demilitarisation of the islands while Arab sovereignty over them remained.[67] The Shah, however, would have none of it.

In early November *The Guardian* speculated that on his return to London Sir William Luce would back Iran's claim.[68] This report is not, however, confirmed by available British documents. Amir Khosrow Afshar's assessment is that Luce strongly argued the Arab case when he first arrived in Tehran in 1970. He hoped Iran's position on the islands might change leading to a compromise acceptable to both parties, as in the case of Bahrain, but gradually came to the view that Iran would not yield this time and tried to convince the Arabs to come to terms.[69]

Another argument is that the question should not be seen from the perspective adopted by Luce; rather it was a matter of the lack of options available to Britain at the time. Many British officials were convinced by then that it was a question of when, and not whether, the Shah would move on the Tunbs.[70] Accordingly the British ambassador to Tehran, Peter Ramsbotham, has recalled hinting to the Shah that he should be ready to move in to the island the day Britain left the Gulf in order to avert a direct confrontation with Britain. When asked in an interview, Ramsbotham could not remember whether he received instructions from the Foreign Office to that effect but added that he would at least have checked with London as it was inconceivable that he would act against British policy.[71] According to Afshar, no British official said explicitly that Iran would take the islands, but the understanding with Britain was implicit as by 1971 no objections were voiced on a possible Iranian move on the islands.[72] On 18 November the foreign secretary told the Cabinet that the failure to reach agreement over the Tunbs 'made it virtually certain that the Shah would take control of the islands in his own time'.[73]

Military Takeover

Admiral Rasa'i, who was the commander of the Iranian Navy from 1965–1975, remembers that the preparation for landing on the islands began in early December. The operation was conducted in complete secrecy, and the Shah told the commander that only he, the Shah himself and the British ambassador knew of the plan. Ships were brought from Bandar Abbas on the pretence of a naval exercise and only a week before the landing did the Shah give the precise time of the mission to the admiral, who then informed his subordinates. It was to be 30 December, and only at 12.00 am was the commander to order the force to advance and effect a landing at 6.50 am.[74] On that day Prime Minister Hoveida announced the news in the Majlis.[75]

The Iranian force was between 3,000 and 4,000 strong with helicopters and hovercraft, against eight to thirteen members of the Ras al-Khaimah police who showed some resistance but in the end were no match for the Iranians. A few were wounded and, according to Julian Walker, one man was killed.[76] According to another source Iran announced that local police had opened fire on Iranian troops, killing a naval officer and two soldiers and wounding another; Iranian troops returned fire, killing four island policemen and injuring five others.[77]

In 1973 the editor of *Ettela'at*, revealed that,

> ... regarding the two Tunbs neither Iran nor Britain considered the consent of the Shaikh of Ras al-Khaimah necessary. For this reason the negotiations between Iran and Britain concluded that Iran could regain its two islands after the British withdrawal. But as Iran wished to regain its islands at the time of the British presence, it did so a day before the British departure.'[78]

Julian Walker could not confirm that Britain had any knowledge of the timing of Iranian troop landings on the Tunbs and says that he only heard about it through the Ras al-Khaimah police force, although Britain knew the timing of the arrival of Iranian forces on Abu Musa, as the Ruler of Sharjah's brother, was there to greet them.

Walker personally believes the Iranian action to have been a blatant use of force against a 'just cause' of the Emirates. However, he suggests it suited Britain that Iran made its move a day before the termination of Britain's treaties with the individual emirates since it was inconceivable that Britain would enter a war with Iran on its last day in the Gulf,[79] Afshar also believes that had Iran moved on the islands after the declaration of the UAE it would have placed 'other Arab countries, particularly Saudi Arabia, in an awkward position.' They would have been forced to take a position for or against Iran, which would have led to further tensions among Gulf states. It was far simpler to present the Iranian move as a rejection of Britain's colonial heritage.[80]

When he announced the news to the House of Commons, Joseph Godber, the minister of state at the Foreign Office, expressed his 'regret' but confirmed Walker's view by stating that it was neither 'possible nor practicable' for Britain to do anything about Iran's action.[81] In reporting to Cabinet about the consequences of the Iranian move Godber said, 'our own troops should not intervene and plans for their withdrawal could not be allowed to stand.' In general there were, he continued, reasonable hopes for stability in the Gulf area.[82] Alec Douglas-Home announced the news to the House of Commons and expressed his 'regret.' Nevertheless, the overall record of British policy in the Gulf between 1968 and 1971 seemed to satisfy him. Referring to the creation of the UAE and the independence of Bahrain and Qatar he said:

> These are solid noteworthy achievements, on which can be built co-operation for the future, both between the Arab states themselves and, I hope, between them and Iran. The situation now achieved represents a reasonable and acceptable basis for the security and future stability of that area.[83]

To the US the Iranian take-over of the islands was no more than a problem that should be worked out among regional players. Richard Murphy confirmed that the US was never asked, nor did it ask, to get involved in the issue,[84] and Henry Kissinger has said that the island issue never came to his attention during his service at the White House.[85]

Arab reaction came in various strengths. Iraq severed diplomatic relations with Britain and a protest rally was organised in Baghdad. In Kuwait, Syria, Libya, North Yemen, South Yemen, Sudan and Egypt, there was strong condemnation of the occupation of the islands, while Qatar, Bahrain, Jordan, Lebanon and Saudi Arabia expressed regret or surprise.[86] Although Saudi Arabia had privately supported Ras al-Khaimah's claim to the Tunbs,[87] once Iran moved militarily there was little the Saudi government could do to alter its position. In reporting some of the strongest reactions Tehran Radio said, 'The Imperial colours are now flying at the mouth of the Persian Gulf. Imperial armed forces are now established on the Greater and Lesser Tunb and Abu Musa islands. No power on earth can turn Iran back.'[88]

A number of Arab states, namely Algeria, Libya, South Yemen (in addition to the Ruler of Ras al-Khaimah) went to the UN in an attempt to raise the issue before the Security Council.[89] Here, Rouhollah Ramazani believes, Iran's attempt to befriend Egypt paid off as Egypt refused to join these Arab states in their complaint. Furthermore, owing to help from Egypt during an Arab League emergency session on 5–7 December, Iraq's proposal for a rupture of diplomatic relations with Iran failed.[90]

In a meeting with Sir Geoffrey Arthur on 1 December 1971 the man who had most to lose from Iran's action, Shaikh Saqar, expressed the view that it was 'an insult to Britain'; Sir Geoffrey had nothing to say except to reveal that the Shah had told him three years earlier of his intention to seize the islands. Sir Geoffrey offered no future protection to the Emirate.[91] Ras al-Khaimah eventually joined the federation on 10 February 1972.[92]

Public reaction was hostile to Iran in Ras al-Khaimah and Sharjah. Iranian banks and other institutions were targets of stone-throwing, and the Deputy Ruler of Sharjah, who had greeted the Iranian troops on Abu Musa, was shot and wounded.[93] When these reports reached London Antony Acland recalled telling Sir William Luce, 'This looks serious.' The end of empire expert answered, 'I have seen this before, it will die down.'[94] He was right.

There was a greater degree of consistency between Iranian public statements and action during the final year of British presence in the Gulf than at any time in the past. This was matched by a clarity in Iran's objectives, principally the securing of the two Tunb islands and Abu Musa, and an ability to achieve declared goals with minimal costs.

Iran's capacity to achieve its objectives can be explained in a number of ways. Crude analysis of military power has some merit, especially if Iranian military power is compared with that of the Gulf Arab states. Military retaliation was hardly contemplated, if at all, by Iran's Arab neighbours. Iran's power during a period of military expansion and firm US support for the Iranian state as the new guardian of the Gulf was considerable.

The regional political environment can also explain the relative ease of Iran's seizure of the islands. Iran's attempts to improve relations with key Arab states, principally Saudi Arabia and Egypt, reduced the chances of a hostile reaction to its military move by these two countries, although they continued to disapprove of the takeover of the islands. That left Iraq and some remotely located states, such as Libya and Algeria, to lead the way in a futile attempt to gather regional and international support for the isolation of Iran.

The most significant factor was the change of Britain's role from Gulf hegemon to mediator. Britain's efforts focused on carrying messages between the Shah and the Rulers of the Arab side of the Gulf, but Britain failed to enforce any solution. This applied equally to the militarily strong Shah and to the resilient Ruler of the small Emirate of Ras al-Khaimah. Hence the settlement of the islands question truly reflected the balance of power among regional players. The British acquiescence in Iran's action thus was not so much the result of an Anglo-Iranian deal as a reflection of lack of options on the part of Britain. However, the act committed by Iran in Britain's final moment in the Gulf put a major dent in almost one hundred and fifty years of British imperial presence.

Epilogue

The central argument of this book has been that a focus on the role of regional powers in the Gulf in the years 1968–1971 offers a better explanation of the period than viewing the Gulf in terms of outside power domination or rivalry. The local balance of power naturally leads to emphasis on Iran's role in the transition from imperial domination to regional autonomy. Iran had witnessed a steady increase in its military and economic power from the mid-1960s. However, the timing of its emergence as a regional power was somewhat unexpected and Iran had very little experience in handling regional affairs or of dealing with much smaller political entities with much less power.

Although the British Empire was in gradual decline after the end of the Second World War, the British presence in the oil-rich Gulf was seen in terms of a new British role in the post-war world. The Labour government elected in 1964 emphasised that role, and the Wilson government saw a connection between a British world role and warm relations with the United States, which was at the time embroiled in the Vietnam war.

American support for Britain's remaining role in global strategy manifested itself on the economic front, specifically in support for the weakening pound. The connection was implicit, but was made explicit by US officials as Britain announced its withdrawal from Aden and an end to the British presence in the Gulf was expected to follow. The Wilson government assured both the US and Arab Rulers that it had no intention of abandoning the Gulf. Soon after these assurances were made economic difficulties at home forced the Labour government to make savings in all sectors of the domestic economy. To gain party support for the new budget the government had to cut military spending and made symbolic reductions in foreign defence expenditure, including commitments in the Gulf.

On 16 February 1968 Harold Wilson told parliament that Britain would terminate its treaty commitments in the Gulf by the end of 1971. The decision opened a Pandora's box in the Gulf. A whole set of questions were raised which Britain gave itself little time to address. These questions were either of a long-term nature, such as constructing a regional security structure and finding rules for co-existence among regional players, or of immediate concern such as territorial disputes. In practice, both the short British deadline and Iran's priorities placed territorial disputes at the top of the Gulf agenda.

Iranian lack of preparation to tackle Gulf questions was demonstrated during the first year of British withdrawal when its relations with Gulf Rulers were handled through a process of trial and error. At first Iran adopted an uncompromising stance in its disputes with Britain and the Gulf Arabs, reflected in both its rhetoric and its policy positions. The immediate result was a deterioration in its relations with all its Arab neighbours. The issue of Bahrain presented Iran with the most pressing difficulty. Although the claim to Bahrain dated back to the 19th century, it was not until Britain announced its decision to withdraw that the future of the island was thrown into doubt, and Iran could vigorously press its claim.

Bahrain's proximity to the Arab shore and its close historical relations with the Arabian Peninsula meant that the Iranian demand led to strained relations with Saudi Arabia. At the same time, Saudi-Iranian relations were witnessing difficulties as a result of an ongoing dispute over the division of offshore oil reserves in the mid-Gulf waters. Foreign policy decision-making in Iran was centralised in the person of the Shah. The conduct of Iranian policy in both the Bahrain dispute and the division of the disputed waters with Saudi Arabia best demonstrates this claim.

In early 1968 the Shah was quick to notice that Iran was isolated in the region. Thus, achieving a working relationship with Saudi Arabia was essential if Iran was to have an effective regional role. The Shah began sending private messages to the US and the Saudis indicating that he had no interest in Bahrain and that he was merely looking for a face-saving formula to let go of the Iranian claim. Soon after, political will on both sides ensured that Iran and Saudi Arabia were able to reach an agreement over the disputed Gulf waters, and, after accepting a British proposal suggesting that the status of Bahrain should be resolved through the good offices of the UN secretary-general, in January 1969 the Shah took his close aides by surprise by announcing that Iran would not press its claim to Bahrain if the people of Bahrain wished to be independent.

With the Bahrain question nearing resolution and Saudi-Iranian relations mended, Iran focused on its claim to the islands of Tunb and Abu Musa. There has been speculation about a secret deal between Britain and Iran by which Iran would relinquish Bahrain in exchange for the islands. The sources indicate that Iran did indeed press for such a deal, but no evidence has come to light which suggests that Britain accepted it. This remains a question historians will debate in years to come as more sources are revealed. In practice, for strategic and domestic-political reasons, Iran acted as if such a deal existed.

As the island issue became Iran's primary focus in the Gulf, the country's international position underwent changes caused by the advent of the Nixon administration in 1969. Nixon had a greater interest in international affairs than many of his predecessors, and more than any post-war US president he recognised the key role to be played by Iran in cold war rivalry. Such recognition was not confined to the president, but was shared by some of his top advisers.

Nixon's keen interest in foreign policy led him to attempt a reform of the decision-making process in order that the White House, and hence the president, might have a larger role in setting and choosing policy options. Close relations between the Shah and members of the Nixon administration helped Iran become America's main Gulf ally. At the time the US was advocating the need for its allies to be able to defend themselves against regional threats without external help, a policy which came to be known as the Nixon doctrine. The result of such policy was increased arms sales to Iran and the promise of more weapons on unprecedented credit terms.

While the US intensified security relations with Iran, Iran did not see itself as an American protégé. Rather, the policy implications of increased arms transactions were that Iran began to take a more militarised approach to Gulf politics. Although most weapons purchased in the late 1960s and early 1970s were not delivered until at least the mid-1970s, there was a psychological dimension to arms sales that led Iran to conduct policy as if these weapons were in full operation.

With the reduction of British forces in the Gulf, the military task of capturing territory from either Ras al-Khaimah or Sharjah was relatively simple and did not require a large-scale operation. Iran's growing feeling of security and increased fighting capacity, however, reinforced the belief that the answer to the long-term question of regional security rested with Iran as the ultimate guardian of the Gulf.

Nevertheless, Iran was a conservative power and apart from the disputed islands its territorial ambitions did not go beyond its national boundaries. In short, Iran tried to maintain a status quo which favoured its perceived national interests. Iran's preparations for British departure from the Gulf demonstrated a degree of pragmatism in Iranian diplomacy. It attempted to befriend Gulf Arab countries, mainly Saudi Arabia, Kuwait and Bahrain; it resumed diplomatic relations with Egypt following the death of President Nasser; and, while opposing the formation of the Gulf Arab federation, Iran's opposition centred on the prospect of the emirates continuing their claim to the islands. Thus, bilateral contacts continued between Iran and the Rulers of the emirates throughout the period. Iraq, with its claim to the Shatt al-Arab, was the only country Iran could not come to terms with.

Whatever political gains Iran achieved in the Arab world, with the impending British departure the islands dispute became a central issue in Arab-Iranian relations. The Gulf Arabs did not possess the necessary force to counter Iran, and the US displayed a lack of interest in inter-Gulf disputes. As far as America was concerned Britain had conveniently played the role of protector of Western interests in the Gulf throughout the post-War period, and with British retreat the US was willing to support Iran to assume that role.

Britain was the only party trying to broker a solution. However, throughout the 19th century and for the best part of the 20th century when the Gulf was part of the British imperial order no sustained effort had been made to settle the islands dispute with Iran. Such efforts were only made at a time when British power was at its lowest. In other words, when Britain was able to influence a settlement, it would not; when it sought to resolve the island dispute in 1971, it could not.

The British special envoy to the Gulf, Sir William Luce, achieved an agreement between Iran and Sharjah regarding the island of Abu Musa which satisfied Iran's security concerns and Sharjah's financial needs, but failed to persuade either the Shah or the Ruler of Ras al-Khaimah to come to a settlement over the Tunb islands. In the end Britain acquiesced in Iran's take-over of the Tunbs. Such acquiescence does not suggest Anglo-Iranian collusion, but rather reflects Britain's lack of options. Iran ended the period of British withdrawal with a solution on its own terms. The Tunb islands were to become part of Iran, and a period of Iranian supremacy in the Gulf was ushered in.

One could claim that British weakness, America's unwillingness to take over from Britain and Iran's rapidly increasing power, represent structural changes which led to Iranian domination of the Gulf region. But equally true is that the nature of Iran's interaction with both the Arab side and international powers concerned was influenced either by individual factors such as the Shah's personal relations with heads of states and his own assessment of Iran's security role, or by the forces of Iranian nationalism which coloured perception of national interests and an expanded regional role.

In general Iran adopted an approach based on *Realpolitik* in the Gulf similar to that adopted by Britain for over a hundred and fifty years. The idea of a single power upholding regional order remained the main underlying assumption of Gulf security. The period of transition from external domination to regional autonomy and the emergence of new states made little difference to that assumption. The main difference was that upholding the interests of the Persian side of the Gulf became the order of the day. In the final analysis, the Pax Britannica gave way to a Pax Iranica.

Notes

Preface

1. John C. Campbell, 'The Superpowers in the Persian Gulf Region' in Abbas Amirie (ed.), *The Persian Gulf and the Indian Ocean in International Politics*, (1975), p. 49.

2. For example see Glen Balfour-Paul, *The End of Empire in the Middle East: Britain's Relinquishment of Power in Her Last Three Arab Dependencies* (Cambridge: Cambridge University Press, 1991); J. B. Kelly, *Arabia, the Gulf and the West: A Critical View of the Arabs and their Oil Policy*, (London: Weidenfeld and Nicholson, 1980).

3. A notable exception is the treatment of the subject by Rouhollah K. Ramazani, *Iran's Foreign Policy, 1941–1973: A Study of Foreign Policy in Modernizing Nations*, (Charlottesville: University Press of Virginia, 1975), and S. Chubin and S. Zabih, *The Foreign Relations of Iran: A Developing State in a Zone of Great-Powers Conflict*, (Berkeley: University of California Press, 1974). Also C. D. Carr's use of the concept of 'reverse influence' to demonstrate the influence Iran practised on the US in the area of arms transactions, see C. D. Carr, 'US Arms Transfer to Iran: 1948–1972,' PhD thesis, LSE, (1980).

4. Campbell, 'The Superpowers in the Persian Gulf Region' p. 40.

5. See Chubin and Zabih, *The Foreign Relations of Iran*, pp. 11–17. The same point was stressed by Dr Reza Ghasemi, member of the Iranian Foreign Ministry department dealing with Gulf issues 1969–1975, then ambassador to Kuwait 1975–1977. Dr Ghasemi's

answer came in the shape of a written response to questions by the author received in April 1997.

Chapter 1: The Historical Background

1. R. Ramazani, *The Persian Gulf: Iran's Role* (Charlottesville: University Press of Virginia, 1972), p. 11.

2. Ibid., p. 12.

3. For the domestic instabilities that followed the death of Nader Shah see Peter Avery (ed.), *The Cambridge History of Iran, Vol. 7: From Nadir Shah to the Islamic Republic*, (Cambridge: Cambridge University Press, 1991), pp. 56–62.

4. Richard Schofield (ed.), *Territorial Foundations of the Gulf States*, (London: UCL Press, 1994), p. 35.

5. Balfour-Paul, *The End of Empire in the Middle East*, p. 98. Although the British Foreign Office and some historians often describe the Qasimi interception of British trade as piracy, the description is strongly contested by some Arab historians such as the present Ruler of Sharjah, Shaikh Sultan Al Qasimi. See Al-Qasimi, Muhammad, *The Myth of Arab Piracy in the Gulf*, (London: Croom Helm, 1986).

6. For text of the 1820 agreement see PRO/FO, 93/137/5a. Also see Muhammad Morsy Abdullah, *The United Arab Emirates: A Modern History*, (London: Croom Helm, 1978), p. 23.

7. Balfour-Paul, *The End of Empire in the Middle East*, p. 100.

8. Schofield (ed.), *Territorial Foundations of the Gulf States*, p. 35.

9. Balfour-Paul, *The End of Empire in the Middle East*, p. 101. To Glen Balfour-Paul, with the signing of these agreements the Gulf emirates occupied a 'curious' legal status in the British Empire as they could not be defined as protectorates or colonies. For details on the legal distinction between a protectorate and a colony see Balfour-Paul, *The End of Empire in the Middle East*, pp. 101–3.

10. As evidence of this policy see the text of the first Anglo-Saudi treaty in 1915 which stated that 'Bin Saud undertakes, as his fathers did before him, to refrain from all aggression on, or interference with the territories of Kuwait, Bahrain, and the Shaikhs of Qatar and the Oman Coast,' PRO/FO, 93/137/1. The same principle was reinstated in the Jeddah treaty of 1927.

11. Balfour-Paul, *The End of Empire in the Middle East*, p. 105.

12. Ramazani, *The Persian Gulf*, pp. 23–4.

13. John F. Standish, *Persia and the Gulf: Retrospect and Prospect*, (London: Curzon, 1998), pp. 170–3.

14. Anthony Verrier, *Through the Looking Glass: British Foreign Policy in an Age of Illusion*, (London: Cape, 1983), Introduction.
15. Ramazani, *The Persian Gulf*, pp. 20–1.
16. William Roger Louis, *The British Empire in the Middle East, 1945–1951: Arab Nationalism, the United States, and Post-War Imperialism*, (Oxford: Oxford University Press, 1984), p. 15.
17. Verrier, *Through the Looking Glass*, p. 53.
18. Louis, *The British Empire in the Middle East*, p. 28.
19. Ibid., p. 15.
20. Ibid., p. 33. According to Philip Darby facilities at the Canal Zone were valued between £500–700 million, see Philip Darby, *British Defence Policy East of Suez: 1947–1968*, (London: Oxford University Press for the Royal Institute of International Affairs, 1993), p. 36.
21. Verrier, *Through the Looking Glass*, p. 56.
22. Darby, *British Defence Policy East of Suez*, p. 85.
23. Louis, *The British Empire in the Middle East*, p. 188.
24. Ibid., pp. 8–9.
25. Moiara de Moraes Ruehsen, 'The Advent of American Hegemony in the Persian Gulf, 1953–1956,' PhD thesis, John Hopkins University, (1992), p. 272.
26. Ibid., p. 18.
27. Ibid., p. 222.
28. Ibid., p. 121.
29. Robert Stookey, *America and the Arab States: An Uneasy Encounter*, (New York, London: Wiley, 1975), p. 142.
30. Ramazani, *Iran's Foreign Policy*, p. 267.
31. Verrier, *Through the Looking Glass*, pp. 155–6.
32. Darby, *British Defence Policy East of Suez*, p. 99. It is noteworthy that in an article published in 1987 Nixon suggested that both he and President Eisenhower thought the position the US took during the Suez Crisis was a 'major foreign policy mistake' which weakened British will in the Middle East in the coming years. See Richard Nixon, 'My Debt to Macmillan,' in *The Times*, 28 January 1987.
33. Darby, *British Defence Policy East of Suez*, pp. 130–1.
34. Verrier, *Through the Looking Glass*, p. 175.
35. Darby, *British Defence Policy East of Suez*, pp. 107–8.
36. Balfour-Paul, *The End of Empire in the Middle East*, p. 68.
37. Darby, *British Defence Policy East of Suez*, p. 210.
38. Verrier, *Through the Looking Glass*, p. 171.
39. Ibid.

40. PRO/FO, 371/156670, from the British Residency to London, 22 November 1961.

41. Shahram Chubin, 'Iran and the Persian Gulf: Iranian Policy and the Arab States, 1959–1967,' PhD. thesis, Columbia University, (1969), pp. 11–17.

42. Ibid., p. 39.

43. Ibid., pp. 46–7.

44. PRO/FO, 371/168832, from Tehran to London, 11 December1962.

45. PRO/FO, 371/168632, from Tehran to London, 4 February 1963.

46. PRO/FO, 371/175715, from FO to Tehran, 4 September 1964.

47. PRO/FO, 371/140794, from Tehran to London, 4 November 1959.

48. PRO/FO, 371/164187, from, Tehran to London, 22 May 1962.

49. PRO/FO, 371/168626, from Tehran to London, 12 October 1963.

50. PRO/FO, 371/168626, from Tehran to London, 14 December 1963.

51. PRO/FO, 371/168626, from Tehran to London, 21 December 1963.

52. PRO/FO, 371/174709, 10 March 1964. This confirmation of Britain's long-held position came after the Iranian government protested about exploration around the island of Abu Musa by the Ruler of Sharjah's oil concessionaire.

Chapter 2: The 16 January Decision

1. James Callaghan, *Time and Chance*, (London: Collins, 1987), p. 169.

2. Domestic economic measures included an attempt to reduce imports by imposing a 15 per cent surcharge on a wide range of manufactured goods, restriction of consumer spending by imposing an across the board increase of 2.5 per cent in personal income taxes, and a 7 pence a gallon increase in domestic duties on oil and gas. But in spite of these measures imports continued to rise. See National Security Files (NSF): CIA staff memorandum No. 26–65 (18b), 1 July 1965, 'United Kingdom, Tredex (Burke Trend),' box 215, Country File, the United Kingdom, LBJ library.

3. Denis Healey, *The Time of My Life*, (London: Penguin, 1990), pp. 280–1.

4. In the beginning the US suggested to Britain a 'joint venture' in the Far East with the aim of getting Britain to make a 'substantial contribution' to the US war effort in Vietnam in return for US help to Britain in Malaysia. See NSF, memo, 'What the US wishes to achieve,' from George Ball to the President (05), 5 December 1956, 'UK PM Wilson visit (1),' box 213, Country File, the United Kingdom, LBJ Library. Although Britain expressed willingness to help the US in Vietnam, at least one US official had a realistic view of limits to British help, '… they have a vision of ships steaming around the Indian Ocean, not of men getting killed in Vietnamese jungles. Yet British sacrifice is just what we need most.'

NSF, White House memo to the President (34a), 4 December 1965, 'UK PM Wilson visit (1),' Country File, United Kingdom, LBJ Library.

5. *The Times*, 17 January 1968.

6. Harold Wilson, *The Labour Government 1964–1970: A Personal Record*, (London: Weidenfeld and Nicolson, 1971), p. 42.

7. House of Commons debate, 19 March 1965, Col. 1547.

8. Wilson, *The Labour Government*, p. 212.

9. House of Commons debate 19 December 1965, Col. 424–425.

10. Interview with Lord Healey, the House of Lords, 4 July 1995.

11. Healey, *The Time of My Life*, p. 279.

12. Wilson, *The Labour Government*, p. 212.

13. Darby, *British Defence Policy East of Suez*, p. 283.

14. Callaghan, *Time and Chance*, p. 169.

15. Christopher Mayhew, *Britain's Role Tomorrow*, (London: Hutchinson, 1976), p. 131. Mayhew was the British First Lord of the Admiralty 1964–1966.

16. Ibid.

17. PRO/CAB, 129/120 C(65)49, Memorandum by the Secretary of State for Foreign Affairs, 24 March 1965. In a Cabinet meeting six days later members of the Cabinet seemed to agree on the idea of 'a gradual and orderly [British] withdrawal from the Middle East'; however, no time frame was given for such withdrawal nor was there any indication that it would take place in the short or medium term. See PRO/CAB, 128/39, Cabinet meeting, 30 March 1965.

18. The reassurance to the Americans was given during Wilson's first visit to Washington on 7–8 December 1964. The joint communiqué stated, '… the President and the Prime Minister reaffirmed their determination to continue to contribute to the maintenance of peace and stability in the Middle East and the Far East.' See NSF: The White House, text of joint communiqué (67), 'United Kingdom PM Wilson visit (II),' box 213, Country File, the United Kingdom, LBJ Library. However, one emerges from reading the US records of Wilson's 1964 visit with the impression that east of Suez questions, or even economic issues, were not a priority in the bilateral discussions. Most of the discussions centred on European security, policies within NATO and the role of Britain's nuclear weapons. This impression is confirmed by Harold Wilson's own record, see Wilson, *The Labour Government*, p. 48. East of Suez became a priority issue at a later stage.

19. Callaghan, *Time and Chance*, p. 175–6; and NSF, CIA staff memorandum Nos 26–65 (18b), 1 July 1965, 'UK, Tredex (Burke Trend),' box 215, Country File, the United Kingdom, LBJ Library.

20. Callaghan, *Time and Chance*, p. 190.

21. At least one US official, National Security Council Staff member Francis M. Bator,

saw an implicit connection. See NSF, The Callaghan visit (45a), 25 June 1965, 'Vol. VI,' box 208, Country File, the United Kingdom, LBJ Library.

22. Callaghan, *Time and Chance*, p. 176.

23. The idea of setting political conditions was contemplated in Washington and even recommended to the president, but there is no evidence that the idea was put to the British government. See NSF. Sterling crisis (6), 6 August 1965, 'UK, Tredex (Burke Trend),' box 215, Country File, the United Kingdom, LBJ Library.

24. Statement of the Defence Estimates, February 1965, Cmnd. 2592.

25. Gregory Gause, 'British and American Policies in the Persian Gulf, 1968–1973,' *Review of International Studies*, Vol. 11 (October 1985).

26. Ibid.

27. Humphrey Trevelyan, *The Middle East in Revolution*, (London: Macmillan, 1970), pp. 209–10. A number of conferences were held in London to achieve a peaceful settlement to the Aden civil war. For details see Balfour-Paul, *The End of Empire in the Middle East*, pp. 49–96.

28. Quoted in Balfour-Paul, *The End of Empire in the Middle East*, p. 85.

29. Mayhew, *Britain's Role Tomorrow*, pp. 134–5.

30. Statement of the Defence Estimates, February/1966, Cmnd. 2901.

31. Wilson, *The Labour Government*, p. 212.

32. Ibid.

33. Ibid.

34. Ibid., p. 213. The decision to cancel the CVA 01 carrier caused the resignation of Christopher Mayhew, the First Lord of the Admiralty 1964–1966, as he believed the White Paper tried to achieve an impossible balance. To Mayhew the choice was between maintaining an overseas presence backed by sufficient military support or total withdrawal. See Mayhew, *Britain's Role Tomorrow*, pp. 131–53.

35. Statement of the Defence Estimates, February 1966.

36. Statement of the Defence Estimates (supplementary statement), July 1967, Cmnd. 3357.

37. Balfour-Paul, *The End of Empire in the Middle East*, p. 86. This expansion could be viewed in the context of a Joint Intelligence Committee recommendation in December 1965. As it was feared that Arab rulers in the Gulf might see withdrawal from Aden as a sign of British weakness and might then seek an understanding with Nasser, the Committee recommended that Britain should back its declared intention to remain in the Gulf by physical evidence. The Committee also recommended that the British base in Cyprus be maintained to reassure the Shah of British commitment to CENTO. See PRO/CAB, 148/49, Cabinet Joint Intelligence Committee, 'The Effects in the Middle East and Africa of an

Early Announcement of British Withdrawal from South Arabia in 1967 or 1968,' 17 December 1965.

38. *The Times*, 3 February 1966.

39. *The Times*, 1 July 1966.

40. This point is also made by Philip Darby, see Darby, *British Defence Policy East of Suez*, p. 304.

41. Going by Gulf Arab rulers' reaction to Britain's decision to withdraw from the Gulf as discussed later in this chapter, one could argue the contrary, that there was a feeling that Britain should stay for the foreseeable future.

42. Sir William Luce, 'Britain's Withdrawal From the Middle East and the Persian Gulf,' *Royal United Service Institution Journal*, vol. 114, no. 653 (March 1969), p. 7.

43. Ibid., p. 8.

44. Statement of the Defence Estimates (supplementary statement), July 1967.

45. Healey, *The Time of My Life*, p. 293.

46. Ibid.

47. Interview with Lord Healey.

48. Richard Crossman, *The Crossman Diaries*, edited by A. Howard, (1991) p. 264.

49. Darby, *British Defence Policy East of Suez*, pp. 310–11.

50. House of Commons debate, 20 July 1966, Col. 631–632.

51. Statement of the Defence Estimates, February 1967, Cmnd. 3203.

52. Wilson, *The Labour Government*, p. 376.

53. Ibid., p. 377.

54. Ibid.

55. House of Commons debate, 14 April 1967, Col.245–246.

56. House of Commons debate, 12 June 1967, Col. 2482.

57. Ibid.

58. Callaghan, *Time and Chance*, p. 211.

59. NSF, Memorandum from Dean Rusk to the President (1a), 17/12/1967, 'UK PM Visit Briefing Book,' box 215, Country File, the United Kingdom, LBJ Library.

60. NSF: Telegram from US Ambassador in London to the State Department (20), 9 September 1956, 'Vol. VI,' box 208, Country File, the United Kingdom, LBJ Library.

61. NSF: (224a), 'Vol. VII, Visit of PM Wilson Dec 15–19 1965,' box 209, Country File, the United Kingdom, LBJ Library.

62. NSF: Position Paper (3j), 27/1/66, 'UK defense review,' box 215, Country File, the United Kingdom, LBJ Library.

63. NSF: Telegram from US Ambassador in London to Rusk (7), 18 April 1967, 'Vol. X,' box 210, Country File, the United Kingdom, LBJ Library.

64. NSF: Memorandum from Rusk to the President (5), 3 May 1967, 'UK Visit of PM Wilson,' box 216, Country File, the United Kingdom, LBJ Library.

65. Callaghan, *Time and Chance*, p. 211.

66. NSF: Telegram, text of message to Foreign Secretary Brown from Secretary Rusk (70), Undated/1967, 'UK Vol. XI,' box 211, Country File, The United Kingdom, LBJ Library.

67. NSF: Letter from LBJ to PM Wilson (144a), Undated/1967, 'UK Vol. XII,' box 211, Country File, the United Kingdom, LBJ Library.

68. NSF: Meeting between Secretaries McNamara and Healey (13a), 10 May 1967, 'UK Vol. XI,' box 211, Country File, The United Kingdom, LBJ Library.

69. Statement of the Defence Estimate (supplementary statement), July 1967.

70. Ibid., and Healey, *The Time of My Life*, p. 239.

71. Statement of the Defence Estimate (supplementary statement), July 1967.

72. House of Commons debate, 28 February 1967, Col. 305.

73. Interview with Sir Denis Wright, British Ambassador to Iran 1963–1971, 7 June 1995, at his home in Haddenham, Buckinghamshire.

74. In some British official and academic circles there were concerns regarding the stability of the Gulf Arab states. Potential sources of instability included local conflicts over territorial claims, political fragmentation, spread of revolutionary groups and Russian penetration. See Luce, Lecture (1969). Also D. C. Watt, 'The Decision to Withdraw from the Gulf,' *Political Quarterly*, (July–September 1968).

75. Wilson, *The Labour Government*, p. 459, and Callaghan, *Time and Chance*, pp. 214–16.

76. Gause, 'British and American Policies in the Persian Gulf,' p. 251.

77. Wilson, *The Labour Government*, pp. 479–80.

78. Ibid.

79. Crossman, *Diaries*, p. 436.

80. Ibid., pp. 441–2.

81. NSF: Memorandum for the President from the Under Secretary of State (213), 11 January 1968, 'Vol. XIII,' box 212, Country File, the United Kingdom, LBJ Library.

82. NSF: Letter from LBJ to Wilson (213), 12 January 1968, 'Vol. XIII,' box 212, Country File, the United Kingdom, LBJ Library.

83. Crossman, *Diaries*, p. 443.

84. Ibid.

85. House of Commons debate, 16 January 1968, Col. 1583.

86. Statement of the Defence Estimates, January 1968, Cmnd. 3540.

87. House of Commons debate, 16 January 1968, Col. 1584.

88. House of Commons debate, 16 January 1968, Col. 1619–20.

89. According to British government estimates the budget cost of stationing troops in the Gulf was £12 million. See Statement of the Defence Estimates, February/1967. According to one scholar the balance of payments effect of the Gulf military presence was around £60 million, see Gause, 'British and American Policies in the Persian Gulf,' p. 252. This can be compared with the relatively high budget cost of maintaining the Aden Base of £100 million, in House of Commons debate, 14 March 1965, Col. 1611

90. House of Commons debate, 16 January 1968, Col. 1592.

91. House of Commons debate, 16 January 1968, Col. 1594, and 18 January Col. 1069.

92. House of Commons debate, 17 January 1968, Col. 1859.

93. Ibid.

94. See Healey's reaction in *The Times*, 17 January 1968.

95. House of Commons debate, 25 March 1968, Col.1046–1052.

96. *Daily Telegraph*, 17 January 1968.

97. A 'Special Committee of the National Security Council' was established by President Johnson on 7 June 1967, to co-ordinate handling of the Middle East crisis during and after the Arab-Israeli war. The Special Committee ended its formal work in August 1967, but the US records give the impression that Arab-Israeli conflict questions dominated Middle East policy debates for the rest of 1967.

98. *The Times*, 19 January 1968.

99. *The Times*, 22 January 1968.

100. Interview with Lord Healey.

101. House of Commons debate, 25 January 1968, Col. 278.

102. *The Daily Telegraph*, 15 February 1968.

103. Interview with Lord Healey.

104. Ramazani, *Iran's Foreign Policy*, pp. 312–15.

105. PRO/FO, 371/180784, Telegram from the British Embassy in Tehran to the Foreign Office, 28 October 1965.

106. National Security Archives (NSA), CIA memorandum 'The Shah and His Policies,' 5 June 1967, 003108 (Dels 1988).

107. Chubin and Zabih, *The Foreign Relations of Iran*, pp. 118–24.

108. Telephone conversation with Ambassador Theodore Eliot, country director for Iran at the State Department 1966–1969, 3 October 1995.

109. NSF, White House memorandum, From Walt Rostow to LBJ (256), 'Vol. II,' box 136, Country File, Iran, LBJ Library.

110. NSA, CIA memorandum 'The Shah and his policies,' 5 June 1967.

111. NSA, CIA memorandum 'The Shah's increasing assurance,' 7 May 1968, 002493 (Dels 1988).

112. This impression was confirmed by Ambassador Eliot in a telephone conversation.

113. NSF, Memorandum from Rostow to LBJ (245), 17 May 1967, 'Vol. II,' box 136, Country File, Iran, LBJ Library.
114. Ibid.
115. NSA, CIA memorandum 'The Shah and his policies,' 5 June 1967.
116. See Y. Alexander and A. Nanes, *The United States and Iran: A Documentary History*, (Frederick, MD: Athletic Books, 1980), pp. 368–9.
117. NSF, White House Memorandum (241), Undated, 'Vol. II,' box 136, Country File, Iran, LBJ Library.
118. NSA, CIA memorandum 'The Shah and his policies,' 5 June 1967.
119. Telephone conversation with Eliot.
120. Ibid.
121. NSA, CIA memorandum 'The Shah and his policies,' 5 June 1967.
122. NSF, White House memorandum from the Vice President to the President (23), 30 August 1967,' Vol. II,' Box 4, The Vice President, LBJ Library.
123. NSA, CIA memorandum 'The Shah and his policies,' 5 June 1967.
124. NSA: 'Visit of the Shah of Iran August 22–24 1967' paper on suggested topic of conversation, 15 August 1967, 001767 (Dels 1982).
125. The Shah said to the US Vice President, ' ... as the UK gradually leaves the Persian Gulf area, the only Free World partners able to fill that vacuum are Iran and Saudi Arabia,' see NSA, 'White House memorandum' from the VP to LBJ on meeting with the Shah, 30/Aug/1967 (Dels 1989). That idea was later seconded by members of the State Department, see NSA, 'Briefing memorandum' from Stuart W. Rockwell to the Secretary of State, 7 June 1968, 001415 (Dels 1993).
126. NSF, White House memorandum of conversation between H. Wriggins and Ambassador Khosro Khosravani of Iran (258a), 26 July 1966, 'Vol. II,' box 136, Country File, Iran, LBJ Library.
127. Interview with Sir Denis Wright, 9 May 1995.
128. Interview with Amir Khosrow Afshar, Iranian Deputy Minister of Foreign Affairs 1965–1969, 14 June 1995.
129. *Kayhan*, 'Britain and the Gulf Rulers Sign Security Accord,' 16 November 1967.
130. *The Daily Telegraph*, 18 January 1968.
131. SWB, Tehran Home Service, 13 March 1968.

Chapter 3: From Gunboat Diplomacy to Compromise

1. SWB, Baghdad Home Service in Arabic, 6 March 1968.
2. SWB, Tehran in Arabic, 28 May 1968.

3. *Ettela'at*, 26 February 1968.

4. FBIS, Tehran *Ayandegan*, 17 September 1968. This dispute had far reaching effects on Iranian-Arab relations. In the context of reporting on Iran's relations with Kuwait the British ambassador to Iran wrote to the Foreign Office in 1965 saying that the Iranian prime minister, '... seemed to be suggesting that, if only we could persuade the Kuwaitis to stop talking about the 'Arabian Gulf,' everything would be all right.' See PRO/FO, 371/180784, Telegram from the British Embassy in Tehran to the Foreign Office, 6 April 1965. It was also claimed that the Iranian government instructed all Iranian banks to refuse to handle any documents which refer to the 'Arabian Gulf.' See PRO/FO, 371/180784, Telegram from the British Embassy in Tehran to the Foreign Office, 27 May 1965.

5. FBIS, Tehran Domestic Service in Persian, 29 January 1968.

6. Interview with Sir Denis Wright, Haddenham, Buckinghamshire, 9 June 1996.

7. *Daily Telegraph*, 9 January 1968.

8. Interview with Ardeshir Zahedi, the Iranian foreign minister 1967–1971, Montreux, 13 September 1996.

9. Saudi Arabian Royal Court Archives (SARCA): Telegram from the Saudi Ambassador in Tehran to King Faisal, 12 February 1968.

10. Interview with Frank Brenchley, assistant under-secretary at the Foreign Office in 1968, London, 13 June 1996. Brenchley could not confirm that a specific proposal was made to Saudi Arabia at the time. However, British Government records reveal that Goronway Roberts told King Faisal '... that the Shah was most ready to co-operate in a system if defence for the Gulf in which no country dominated another,' see PRO/FO, 8/47, 'Record of meeting between the Minister of State For Foreign Affairs and King Faisal of Saudi Arabia at Riyadh airport,' 10 January 1968.

11. Balfour-Paul, *The End of Empire in the Middle East*, pp. 111–12. Some argue that the 1965 meeting was directly inspired by Britain, see Chubin, 'Iran and the Persian Gulf,' p. 120, while others argue that British influence was indirect: as events in Aden developed, particularly Britain's promise for independence of the South Arabian Federation, this stimulated the Gulf Rulers' enthusiasm for a federation, see Balfour-Paul, *The End of Empire in the Middle East*, p. 122.

12. Interview with Sir Julian Bullard, the British Political Agent in Dubai in 1968, All Souls College, Oxford, 11 June 1996.

13. The former view was expressed by Bullard and the latter by Brenchley.

14. Statement of Defence Expenditure, Feb. 1968, Cmnd. 3927. But according to Frank Brenchley the federation was not thought of as an alternative security structure after British departure so much as a system to provide economic viability to the smaller shaikhdoms and improve their chances of international political recognition.

15. *Financial Times*, 10 January 1968.

16. FBIS, Tehran Domestic Service in Persian, 27 January 1968.

17. SWB, Tehran Home Service in Persian, excerpts from the Shah's replies to the publisher of *Iran Tribune*, 24 May 1968.

18. Interview with Brenchley.

19. Interview with Bullard.

20. Interview with Afshar, London, 14 June 1995.

21. SARCA: Telegram from Saudi Ambassador in Tehran to King Faisal, 20 January 1968.

22. *Observer*, 21 January 1968. Five days later the Iranian Embassy in London denied such reports, see *The Observer*, 26 January 1968.

23. *Times*, 18 January 1968.

24. *Al Riyadh*, 18 January 1968.

25. PRO/FO, 8/518/42, from Bahrain to London, 19 January 1968.

26. Interview with Sir Anthony Parsons, British Political Agent in Bahrain 1965–1969, Devon, 10 June 1996. On the other hand Sir Stewart Crawford believed that by proposing to join the federation Bahrain would avoid an immediate change in its international status, thus '… giving more time for the Government of Iran and Bahrain to find a *modus vivendi*,' see PRO/FO, 8/11/59459, from Bahrain to London, 27 April 1968.

27. SARCA: Telegram from the Saudi Embassy in Bangkok to the Foreign Ministry, 27 January 1968.

28. Interview with Afshar, London, 24 May 1996.

29. NSF: Telegram from the US Ambassador in Tehran to Rusk (76), 30 January 1968, 'Iran Cables Vol. II 66–69 [1 of 2],' box 136, Country File, Iran, LBJ Library.

30. SARCA: Telegram from Saudi Ambassador in Tehran to King Faisal, 1 February 1968.

31. SARCA: Telegram from Foreign Ministry to King Faisal, 31 January 1968.

32. SARCA: Rashad Pharon meeting with Fertash, 1 February 1968.

33. SARCA: Telegram from King Faisal to Saudi Ambassador in Tehran, 29 January 1968.

34. SARCA: Telegram from King Faisal to Saudi Ambassador in Tehran, 31 January 1968.

35. SARCA: Telegram from Saudi Ambassador in Tehran to King Faisal, 6 February 1968.

36. *Middle East Economic Survey*, Vol. XI, no. 43, 23 August 1968, p. 4. The rig incident took place on 1 February, but was leaked to the press a week later. No armed clash was reported, but the US expressed disappointment that the matter was handled in that fashion, see NSF: Telegram from US ambassador in Tehran to Rusk (70), 1 February 1968, 'Iran Cables Vol. II, 66–69 [1 of 2],' box 136, Country File, Iran, LBJ Library.

37. Interview with Herman Eilts, US Ambassador to Saudi Arabia 1965–1970, Boston, Mass, 19 May 1997. According to Eilts the Iranian government did not order the seizure of the rig and blamed the admiral in charge who ordered the act. He was subsequently removed from his post.

38. NSF: Telegram from US Ambassador in Tehran to Rusk (70), 1 February 1968, 'Iran Cables Vol. II 66–69 [1 of 2],' box 136, Country File, Iran, LBJ Library.

39. *The Times*, 23 January 1968.

40. Frauke Heard-Bey, *From Trucial States to United Arab Emirates*, (London: Longman, 1982), p. 341.

41. SWB, Kuwait Home Service in Arabic, 27 February 1968.

42. Riad Al-Rayyes, *Watha'iq al Khaleej Al Arabi* (Arab Gulf Documents), (London: Riad El Rayyes, 1986), pp. 26–9. Heard-Bey reveals that the agreement was based on a Qatari draft. However, there were noticeable differences between the Qatari draft and the final agreement. Qatar envisaged a smaller number of participants in the federation, with the smaller shaikhdoms (Sharjah, Ajman, Umm al-Qaiwain, Fujairah and Ras al-Khaimah) forming a union among themselves to be known as the 'United Arab Coastal Emirates,' thus producing a federation of four shaikhdoms with comparable population size and economic resources. That idea was rejected overwhelmingly by the other Emirates. Also the draft outlined procedures for settling disputes among the member states, which was dropped in the final agreement in order to '… avoid reference to such disputes and to assume a sense of cohesion from the outset.' Moreover, the Federal Council was intended to resemble a parliament in the draft, but in the agreement it was to operate under the close supervision of the Supreme Council. Finally, the functions of the Federal Court were only specified in the draft. See Heard-Bey, *From Trucial States*, pp. 343–4.

43. Riad Al Rayyes, *Watha'ik al-Khalij al-Arabi*, p. 28.

44. SWB, Iranian statement on the Gulf, 2 April 1968.

45. Eric Jensen, 'The Secretary-General's Use of Good Offices and the Question of Bahrain,' *Millennium: Journal of International Studies*, vol. 14, no. 3, (Winter 1985), pp. 336–7.

46. *The Times*, 16 July 1968.

47. Jensen, 'The Secretary-General's Use of Good Offices,' p. 337.

48. Interview with Parsons.

49. NSF: Telegram from US Ambassador in Tehran to State Department (69), 1 February 1968, 'Iran Cables Vol. II 66–69 [1 of 2],' box 136, Country File, Iran, LBJ Library.

50. J. I. Charney and L. M. Alexander (eds), *International Maritime Boundaries*, vol. II, (Dordrecht, Boston and London: Martinus Nijhoff, 1993), p. 1520.

51. R. Young, 'Equitable Solution for Offshore Boundaries; The 1968 Saudi Arabian-Iran Agreement, *The American Journal of International Law*, vol. 64, (1979), pp. 153–5.

52. Charney and Alexander, *International Maritime Boundaries*, vol. II, p. 1521.

53. *MEES*, Vol. XI, no. 43, 23 August 1968, p. 4.

54. Ibid.

55. SARCA: Meeting between Yamani and Iranian delegation, 21 February 1968. The same document reveals that during Yamani's visit to Tehran in November 1967 the idea of a joint venture was put forward but King Faisal rejected it because Iran had recognised certain areas to be Saudi in 1965.

56. SARCA: Undated document; but the content suggests that the conversation might have taken place during Yamani's visit to Iran in February 1968.

57. NSF: Telegram from Rusk to US Ambassador to Tehran (157), 28 February 1968, 'Iran Cables Vol. II, 66–69 [2 of 2],' box 136, Country File, Iran, LBJ Library.

58. NSF: Telegram from Rusk to US Ambassador in Tehran (160), 3 February 1968, 'Iran Cables Vol. II 66–69 [2 of 2],' box 136, Country File, Iran, LBJ Library.

59. SARCA: Telegram from Saudi Ambassador in Tehran to King Faisal, 12 February 1968.

60. Interview with Parsons.

61. Interview with Afshar.

62. Interview with Wright. It could be argued that events in the Middle East in the late 1950s, notably the Iraqi coup and the rise of the Nasser challenge, might have delayed attempts to resolve the Bahrain issue.

63. Sir Denis Wright's memoirs, unpublished manuscript, p. 415.

64. NSF: Shah-Rostow meeting (62), 9 February 1968, 'Iran Cables Vol. II 66–69 [1 of 2],' box 136, Country File, Iran, LBJ Library. After the meeting with the Shah, Rostow told the Saudi and Kuwaiti ambassadors that he did not discuss any 'Gulf security' issues with the Shah, and that his visit was by invitation from the Iranian ambassador to Washington. See SARCA: Telegram from Saudi Ambassador in Tehran to King Faisal.

65. Interview with Armin Meyer, US Ambassador to Iran 1965–1969,Washington D.C., 16 May 1997.

66. NSF: Shah-Rostow meeting (62), 9 February 1968, 'Iran Cables Vol. II 66–69 [1 of 2],' box 136, Country File, Iran, LBJ Library.

67. NSF: Telegram from US Ambassador in Tehran to Rusk (55), 15 March 1968, 'Iran Cables Vol. II 66–69 [1 of 2],' box 136, Country File, Iran, LBJ Library.

68. NSF: Telegram from US Ambassador in Tehran to Rusk (180), 15 March 1968, 'Iran Cables Vol. II 66–69 [2 of 2],' box 136, Country File, Iran, LBJ Library.

69. PRO/FO, 26/59510/167, from Tehran to London, 7 April 1968. Sir Denis Wright's prompt rejection of the Shah's proposal is not a surprising as the Foreign Office had been opposed to such a deal prior to the British ambassador's meeting with the Shah, see PRO/FO, 8/25/59510, from London to Tehran, 12 March 1968.

70. NSF: Telegram from US Ambassador in Tehran to Rusk (41), 20 April 1968, 'Iran Cables Vol. II 66–69 [1 of 2],' box 136, Country File, Iran, LBJ Library.

71. SARCA: Telegram from Saudi Ambassador in Tehran to King Faisal, 3 April 1968.

74. NSF: Telegram from US Ambassador in Tehran to Rusk (41), 20 April 1968, 'Iran Cables Vol. II 66–69 [1 of 2],' box 136, Country File, Iran, LBJ Library.

72. *Ettela'at*, 7 May 1968.

73. *Ettela'at*, 11 May 1968.

74. NSF: Telegram from US Ambassador in Tehran to Rusk (32), 11 May 1968, 'Iran Cables Vol. II 66–69 [1 of 2],' box 136, Country File, Iran, LBJ Library.

75. Interview with Zahedi.

76. SARCA: Memorandum from Foreign Ministry to King Faisal, 14 April 1968. Here again we face the problem of gaps in the Saudi archival sources, as there is no evidence of exchanges preceding the US Ambassador's suggestion that the climate was right to resolve Saudi-Iranian differences.

77. Interview with Eilts.

78. NSF: Telegram from US Ambassador in Tehran to Rusk (53), 20 April 1968, 'Iran Cables Vol. II 66–69 [1 of 2],' box 136, Country File, Iran, LBJ Library.

79. Interview with Maroof al-Dawalibi, Adviser to King Faisal in 1968, Riyadh, 9 April 1996.

80. Interview with Wright.

81. Interview with Parsons.

82. SARCA: Telegram from Saudi Ambassador in Tehran to King Faisal, 13 May 1968.

83. SARCA: Telegram from Saudi Ambassador in Tehran to King Faisal, 17 May 1968.

84. Interview with Zahedi.

85. NSF: Telegram from US Ambassador in Tehran to Rusk (54), 20 March 1968, 'Iran Cables Vol. II 66–69 [1 of 2],' box, 136, Country File, Iran, LBJ Library.

86. NSF: Telegram from Rusk to US Ambassador in Tehran (139), 18 May 1968, 'Iran Cables Vol. II 66–69 [2 of 2],' box, 136, Country File, Iran, LBJ Library.

87. NSF: Memorandum from Foster to Rostow (222), 21 May 1968, 'Iran memos Vol. II 66–69,' box 136, Country File, Iran, LBJ Library.

88. Young, 'Equitable Solution for Offshore Boundaries,' p. 155.

89. SARCA: Letter from King Faisal to the Shah, 16 August 1968.

90. SARCA: A technical definition of 'oil reserves' is 'estimated quantities of all liquids defined as crude oil, which geological and engineering data demonstrated with reasonable certainty to be recoverable in future years from known reservoirs under existing economic and operating conditions,' See *Energy Information Administration/International Energy Annual* (1993), p. 157. While the 'oil in place' can be defined as 'the amount of

crude oil that is estimated to exist in a reservoir and that has not been produced,' see *A Dictionary of Petroleum Terms*, second edition (1979), p. 76.

91. Interview with Zahedi.

92. SARCA: Telegram from Saudi Ambassador in Tehran to Foreign Ministry, 19 August 1968.

93. *MEES*, Vol. XI, no. 43, 23 August 1968, p. 4.

94. SARCA: Telegram from Saudi Ambassador in Tehran to Foreign Ministry, 22 September 1968.

95. Sir Denis Wright, unpublished memoirs, p. 420.

96. Interview with Wright.

97. FBIS, Tehran, *Kayhan International* in English, 10 May 1968.

98. Heard-Bey, *From Trucial States*, p. 345.

99. SWB, Tehran Home Service in Persian, 27 May 1968.

100. SWB, Kuwait Home Service in Arabic, 7 July 1968.

101. *The Times*, 8 July 1968.

102. SWB, Tehran Home Service, 8 July 1968.

103. SWB, Tehran Home Service in Persian, text of *Ayandegan* editorial entitled 'The Persian Gulf neighbours,' 18 August 1968. According to British sources talks between the Ruler and the Shah did not refer to any territorial disputes, '... but kept to a more general discussion of [the Shah] policy in the area,' see PRO/FO, 28/59510/327, from the Political Agency, Trucial States, Dubai, to London, 31 August 1968.

104. PRO/FO, 8/960/23, from Dubai to London, 30 October 1968).

105. *New York Times*, 17 September 1968.

106. *The Times*, 8 August 1968.

107. *Ettela'at*, 24 July 1968.

108. One explanation offered by Zahedi for this disjunction between Iran's public line and actual policy was that the Iranian wish to compromise over Bahrain should not be taken for granted, in case the dispute should end in a manner which would not save face for the Shah or would strengthen the position of any of the Arab countries (e.g. make Bahrain part of Saudi Arabia, Kuwait or the federation).

109. NSF: Telegram from US Ambassador in Tehran to Rusk (25), 30 July 1968, 'Iran Cables Vol. II 66–69 [1 of 2],' box 136, Country File, Iran, LBJ Library. Meyer told the author in an interview on 16 May 1997 that he discouraged the Security Council option as he believed that public debate of the issue would 'complicate matters,' and the US did not know how the USSR would react.

110. Ibid.

111. NSF: Telegram from Rusk to US Ambassador in Tehran (136), 2 August1968, 'Iran Cables Vol. II 66–69 [2 of 2],' box 136, Country File, Iran, LBJ Library.

112. NSF: Telegram from US Ambassador in Tehran to Rusk (23), 4 August 1968, 'Iran Cables Vol. II 66–69 [1 of 2],' box 136, Country File, Iran, LBJ Library.

113. Interview with Wright.

114. Interview with Parsons. For more on Parson's comments to the Foreign Office see PRO/FO, 8/519/46, from Bahrain to London, 19 July 1968.

115. PRO/FO, 28/59510/284, from Tehran to London, 6 August 1968.

116. Jensen, 'The Secretary-General's Use of Good Offices,' p. 339.

117. PRO/FO, 28/59520/348, from Bahrain to London, 23 September 1968.

118. Interview with Afshar.

119. Jensen, 'The Secretary-General's Use of Good Offices,' p. 330.

120. Interview with Afshar.

121. SARCA: Telegram from Saudi Ambassador in Tehran to King Faisal, 18 October 1968.

122. *Ettela'at*, 9 November 1968.

123. *The Times*, 15 November 1968.

124. *Ettela'at*, 13 November 1968.

125. Interview with Zahedi.

126. NSF: Telegram from US Ambassador in Tehran to Rusk (10), 14 December 1968, 'Iran Cables Vol. II 66–69 [1 of 2],' box 136, Country File, Iran, LBJ Library.

127. Wright, unpublished memoirs, p. 422.

128. PRO/FO, 8/939/72, from Tehran to London, 24 December 1968.

129. Transcript of BBC Radio programme no: 6R/44/B658/G, 'Peaceful Solutions,' producer: Keith Hindell, 6–7 April 1986.

130. Wright, unpublished memoirs, pp. 422–3. The British records confirm Sir Denis's account of this meeting and reveal that what the Shah cared about was to see a clear expression of the 'will of the people of Bahrain' and not merely 'the sounding of one or two shaikhs or community leader.' Also the Shah wanted to be rid of the Bahrain issue 'quickly and once and for all.' See PRO/FO, 8/960/72, From Tehran to London, 24 December 1969. In two separate interviews with the author Afshar argued, and Zahedi agreed, that the idea of referring the dispute to the UN had been Iranian not British, and that Henry Rollar, a Belgian lawyer, was advising the Iranian government to find a way out through the UN before Wright made his suggestion. The fact that the Shah had asked the US ambassador for a legal study, including referring the dispute to the US, supports that view. But no records were found of specific suggestions made by Rollar or the US Embassy. Sir Anthony Parsons, on the other hand, has supported Wright's record. No documentary evidence has been found to suggest that the idea of using the UN secretary-general's good offices came from anywhere other than the British Foreign Office in late 1968.

131. PRO/FO, 8/939/75, from Tehran to London, 28 December 1968.

132. This applies to Zahedi, Afshar, Wright, Meyer and Parsons. According to British sources Aram was also not aware of the Shah's intention to relinquish the claim to Bahrain, see PRO/FO, 8/960/W3, from Tehran to London, 20 February 1969.

133. FBIS, Tehran Domestic Service in Persian, 14 January 1969.

134. Interview with Zahedi. It is noteworthy that Sir Denis was under the impression that the Iranian press were not prepared for the New Delhi statement, see PRO/FO, 8/940/133, Tehran to London, 15 January 1969.

135. Hussain Al-Baharna, 'The Fact-Finding Mission of the United Nations Secretary-General and the Settlement of the Bahrain-Iran Dispute, May 1970,' *International and Comparative Law Quarterly*, vol. 22, (July 1973), p. 544.

136. Jensen, 'The Secretary-General's Use of Good Offices,' p. 339.

137. PRO/FO, PRO/FO, 8/1365/153, from Zurich to London, 6 February 1970.

138. *Daily Telegraph*, 18 August 1969.

139. *The Times*, 18 September 1969.

140. Jensen, 'The Secretary-General's Use of Good Offices,' pp. 339–40.

141. PRO/FO, 8/1364/99, London to Brussels, 4 February 1970. For specific objections and changes recommended by the Foreign Office see PRO/FO, 8/1365/124, from London to Bahrain.

142. Interview with Sir Denis Wright, Haddenham, 7 June 1995. By that time Afshar was ambassador to United Kingdom but on the Shah's instructions was still heavily involved in Gulf matters.

143. *Daily Telegraph*, 25 March 1970. For the text of the Permanent Representatives of Iran and Britain's letters to the UN Secretary-General regarding the use of the Secretary-General's good offices see Keesing's Contemporary Archives, 23998, 23–30 May 1970.

144. Keesing's Contemporary Archives, 23998, 23–30 May 1970.

145. Jensen, 'The Secretary-General's Use of Good Offices,' p. 346.

146. Ibid., p. 340.

147. SWB, Text of the Iranian Foreign Minister to the Majlis, Tehran Home Service in Persian, 29 March 1970. Zahedi had also made it clear that Iran opposed the idea of Bahrain becoming part of an Arab federation a month prior to his Majlis speech, see SWB, Tehran Home Service in Persian, 23 February 1970.

148. Asadullah Alam, *The Shah and I*, (London: I. B. Tauris, 1991), p. 142.

149. *Sunday Times*, 29 March 1970.

150. *Daily Telegraph*, 30 March 1970.

151. Jensen, 'The Secretary-General's Use of Good Offices,' p. 341.

152. Ibid., pp. 341–2.

153. Transcript of BBC Radio programme no: 6R/44/B658/G, 'Peaceful Solutions,' producer: Keith Hindell, 6–7 April 1986.

154. UN Documents, Security Council, S/9772, 30 April 1970. For a list of these organisations see the same document.

155. Ibid.

156. Jensen, 'The Secretary-General's Use of Good Offices,' p. 342.

157. UN Documents, Security Council, Res. 278 of 11 May 1970. For the proceedings of the Security Council meeting see UN Documents, Security Council Fifteen Hundred and Thirty-Sixth Meeting, held in New York, Monday at 3 p.m.,11 May 1970.

158. FBIS, Tehran Domestic Service in Persian, 23 May 1970.

159. SWB, Tehran Home Service in Persian, 3 April 1970.

160. See *Ettela'at*, 12 May 1970.

Chapter 4: The Nixon Doctrine: Iran and the Gulf

1. Interview with Ardeshir Zahedi, Montreux, Switzerland, 18 November 1997.

2. His Imperial Majesty Mohammed Reza Shah Pahlavi Shahanshah of Iran, *Mission For My Country*, (London: Hutchinson 1960), p. 296.

3. Interview with Armin Meyer, Washington D.C., 16 April 1997.

4. Telegram, from the Secretary of State to the US Ambassador in Tehran, 2 November 1968, folder: 'CO 68 Iran,' Box 37, Subject files, WHCF, Nixon Presidential materials staff, National Archives.

5. Letter from President-elect Nixon to the Shah, 1 December 1969, folder: 'CO 68 Iran,' Box 37, Subject files, WHCF, Nixon Presidential materials staff, National Archives.

6. NSA: memorandum from Stuart W. Rockwell to Dean Rusk, 7 June 1968 (00684), (Dels 1983).

7. 'Foreign Military Sales,' hearing before the committee on Foreign Relations, United States Senate, Nineteenth Congress, second session, S 3092, 20 July 1968, p. 12.

8. Interviews with Meyer and Herman Eilts, Boston, Mass, 19 May 1997.

9. Robert Litwak, *Détente and the Nixon Doctrine: American Foreign Policy and the Pursuit of Stability, 1969–1976*, (Cambridge: Cambridge University Press, 1984), p. 1. For Nixon's recognition of the newly emerging multi-polar international system see Richard Nixon, 'US Foreign Policy for the 1970s: A New Strategy for Peace,' A Report of Congress, in Department of State *Bulletin*, 9 March 1970, p. 273.

10. Richard Nixon, *In the Arena: A Memoir of Victory, Defeat, and Renewal*, (London: Simon and Schuster, 1990), p. 331.

11. Interview with Harold Saunders, senior member of the NSC covering the Near East and South Asia 1967–1974, Washington D.C., 23 May 1997.

12. Henry Kissinger, *The White House Years*, (London: Weidenfeld and Nicolson, 1979), p. 39.

13. Henry Kissinger, *A World Restored*, (London: Victor Gollancz, 1973), p. 327.

14. Henry Kissinger, 'Bureaucracy and Policy Making: the Effect of Insiders and Outsiders on the Policy Process,' *Bureaucracy, Politics and Strategy*, Security Studies Paper No. 17, University of California, LA, 1968, p. 5.

15. Ibid., p. 3. However, according to one observer the NSC employed 120 permanent staff members by the year 1972 which was more than double the pre-Nixon years. See John P. Leacacos 'Kissinger's Apparat,' *Foreign Policy*, Vol. 5, Winter 1971–1972, p. 3.

16. Litwak, *Détente and the Nixon Doctrine*, p. 64.

17. Richard Nixon, *The Memoirs of Richard Nixon*, (London: Sidgwick and Jackson, 1978), p. 340.

18. 'The National Security Council System: Responsibilities of the Department of State,' in Department of State *Bulletin*, 24 February 1969, p. 163.

19. Peter Rodman, 'The NSC System: Why It's Here to Stay,' *Foreign Service Journal*, February 1992, pp. 24–5.

20. Interview with Saunders.

21. Kissinger, *The White House Years*, pp. 38–9.

22. Litwak, *Détente and the Nixon Doctrine*, p. 64.

23. Ibid., p. 67.

24. Kissinger, *The White House Years*, p. 42.

25. Ibid., pp. 42–5.

26. Litwak, *Détente and the Nixon Doctrine*, pp. 68–70.

27. Ibid.

28. Kissinger, *The White House Years*, p. 47.

29. Department of State *Bulletin*, 24 February 1969, p. 163.

30. In Litwak, *Détente and the Nixon Doctrine*, p. 71.

31. Interview with Michael Van Dusen. From 1973 Van Dusen served as a member of staff in a number of Congressional committees dealing with the Middle East. In 1977 he became staff director for the house subcommittee on Europe and the Middle East chaired by Lee Hamilton, Congress, Washington D.C., 22 May 1997. The Nixon administration at the time was able to invoke the principle of 'executive privilege' to avoid some high ranking officials having to testify before Congress, see Litwak, *Détente and the Nixon Doctrine*, p. 71.

32. In an interview with the author Kissinger stated that the idea was not thought of by Nixon, rather it came from Eisenhower in a conversation with Nixon while the former was in hospital in 1968. Interview with Henry Kissinger, New York, 3 June 1997. Nixon, how-

ever, recorded that it was Kissinger who suggested reforming the national security apparatus, see Nixon, *Memoirs*, p. 341.

33. Interview with Alfred Atherton, member of the Bureau for Near East and South Asian Affairs 1966–1970, and assistant to Joseph Sisco in 1970 for the Arab-Israeli conflict, Washington D.C., 29 May 1997.

34. Interview with Atherton. These informal channels of communication between the State Department and the NSC are confirmed by an outside observer, see Leacacos, 'Kissinger's Apparat,' p. 6.

35. Department of State *Bulletin*, 24 February 1969, p. 164.

36. To Litwak some characterised the new NSC structure as 'a closed "two-man" system,' *Detente and the Nixon Doctrine*, pp. 71–2.

37. Interview with Kissinger. Some even questioned whether the new NSC system would function effectively without Henry Kissinger, see Leacacos, 'Kissinger's Apparat,' p. 4.

38. Kissinger, *The White House Years*, p. 40.

39. Interview with Richard Helms, deputy director and then director of the CIA 1965–1973, former ambassador to Iran 1973–1976, Washington D.C., 2 June 1997.

40. Kissinger, *The White House Years*, p. 223.

41. Ibid.

42. See US President, Public Papers of Presidents of the United States: Richard Nixon 'Informal Remarks in Guam With Newsmen 25 July 1969,' p. 549.

43. Interview with Peter Rodman, member of NSC 1969–1977, Nixon Center for Peace and Freedom, Washington D.C., 15 May 1997, and see 'The Nixon Doctrine: A Progress Report,' Department of State *Bulletin*, 8 February 1971, p. 161.

44. Kissinger, *The White House Years*, p. 223.

45. Ibid., p. 224. For the administration's effort to elaborate statements on the Guam statement see Nixon, 'US Foreign Policy for the 1970s: A New Strategy for Peace,' pp. 273–332, and Richard Nixon, 'US Foreign Policy for the 1970s: Building for Peace,' A Report of Congress, Department of State *Bulletin*, 22 March 1971, pp. 341–432.

46. Richard Nixon, 'US Foreign Policy for the 1970s: A New Strategy for Peace,' in Department of State *Bulletin*, 18 February 1970, p. 276.

47. 'The Nixon Doctrine: A Progress Report,' in Department of State *Bulletin*, 8 February 1971, p. 161.

48. Interview with Rodman. Kissinger also confirmed that view to the author.

49. Nixon, 'US Foreign Policy for the 1970s: A New Strategy for Peace,' p. 276.

50. Nixon, 'US Foreign Policy: Building for Peace,' p. 344.

51. Nixon, 'US Foreign Policy for the 1970s: A New Strategy for Peace,' p. 27.

52. Interview with Saunders.

53. Interview with Richard Murphy, director of Arabian Peninsula affairs, US State

Department 1969–1971. Washington D.C., 27 May 1997. Murphy added that during his period as Arabian affairs director he received only one telephone call during a weekend, when Sultan Qabus of Oman overthrew his father to take power on 28 July 1970. Alfred Atherton, who was working on the Arab-Israeli conflict at the State Department at the time, confirmed Murphy's impression and added that the State Department's primary focus was on the Arab-Israeli issue.

54. Hussein Sirriyeh, *US Policy in the Gulf 1968–1977: Aftermath of British Withdrawal*, (London: Ithaca, 1984), p. 62.

55. Interview with Kissinger. Some argue that the long time Kissinger spent with the president and his preoccupation with Vietnam, China and the issue of arms control with the Soviet Union left little time for attention to other issues. See I. M. Destler, 'Can One Man Do,' in *Foreign Policy*, Vol. 5, (Winter 1971–1972), pp. 37–8.

56. For example Michael T. Klare argues that the contents of the memorandum could be 'reconstructed' from a 1969 related study by Georgetown University's Center for Strategic and International Studies titled 'The Gulf: Implications of British withdrawal' as its finding, it is claimed, was parallel to the Nixon administration's thinking at the time. See Klare, *American Arms Supermarket*, (Austin: University of Texas Press, 1984), pp. 112–13. Also statements made by US officials before Congressional Committees shed some light on the contents of NSSM 66, see Sirriyeh, *US Policy in the Gulf*, pp. 58–61.

57. Interview with Saunders.

58. Interview with Rodman. According to Noyes had the US attempted to replace Britain such a role would not only have been resented by radical Arab states, but would have been unacceptable to 'Saudi Arabia's and Iran's growing sense of national stature,' see James H. Noyes, *The Clouded Lens, Persian Gulf Security and U.S. Policy*, 2nd ed. (Stanford: Hoover University Press, 1982), p. 55.

59. See Klare, *American Arms Supermarket*, p. 114.

60. It is unclear where this term originated as members of the US government did not use it in the early stages, and it is arguable that in came either from journalistic jargon or was invoked by outside observers.

61. Richard Helms in an interview with the author confirmed that the Shah felt this way at the time.

62. Klare, *American Arms Supermarket*, p. 115.

63. This opinion was expressed by William Quandt, former member of the NSC, in Sirriyeh, *US Policy in the Gulf*, p. 63. Also see Ali Sadeghi, 'United States and the Persian Gulf 1969–1978: Implementing the Nixon Doctrine.' PhD thesis, London School of Economics and Political Science (1988), pp. 154–60.

64. Interview with Rodman.

65. Interview with Saunders.

66. Interviews with Kissinger and Helms.
67. Mohammad Reza Shah Pahlavi, *Mission For My Country*, p. 313.
68. Kissinger, *The White House Years*, p. 1262.
69. Interview with Helms. And see NSA, CIA report, 'National Intelligence Estimate: Iran' 1 October 1969, (000610), (Dels 1986).
70. Telegram, from the Secretary of State to the US Ambassador in Tehran, 25 April 1969, folder: 'CO 68 Iran,' Box 37, Subject files, WHCF, Nixon Presidential materials staff, National Archives.
71. For the State Department draft of the communiqué see memorandum, from Theodore Eliot, Executive Secretary, to Henry Kissinger, 11 October 1969, folder: 'CO 68 Iran,' Box 37, Subject files, WHCF, Nixon Presidential materials staff, National Archives.
72. *Daily Telegraph*, 22 October 1969.
73. *New York Times*, 24 October 1969.
74. For reasons behind the consortium refusal see Memorandum from Peter M. Flanigan to Henry Kissinger, 23 January 1970, folder 'CO 68 Iran,' Box 37, Subject files, WHCF, Nixon Presidential materials staff, National Archives.
75. Alam, *The Shah and I*, p. 95.
76. FBIS, *Kayhan* International in English, 7 October 1969.
77. FBIS, *Kayhan* International in English, 15 October 1969.
78. FBIS, Tehran Radio Domestic Service in Persian, 30 September 1970.
79. 'U.S. Military Sales to Iran: A Staff Report to the Subcommittee of Foreign Assistance of The Committee on Foreign Relations,' United States Senate, 94th Congress, 2nd Session, July 1976, p. 4.
80. In Sirriyeh, *US Policy in the Gulf*, p. 90.
81. 'US Military Sales to Iran,' p. 4.
82. Mohammed Ayoob, 'The Dynamics of Iran's Foreign Policy,' *Institute for Defence Studies and Analysis Journal*, Vol. 3, 1970, pp. 249–350.
83. Stockholm International Peace Research Institute (SIPRI), 'The Arms Trade With the Third World,' (1971), p. 842.
84. NSA: National Intelligence Estimate 'Iran's International Position,' 3 September 1970, (000611), (Dels 1986).
85. The Import-Export Bank guaranteed that Iran had the funds to pay for these weapon purchases; in other words it was an insurance policy, but it was never called upon as Iran did not run out of cash during those years.
86. Interview with Atherton.
87. C. D. Carr, 'US Arms Transfer to Iran: 1948–1972,' PhD thesis, London School of Economics and Political Science, (1980), p. 297.
88. According to one source this was particularly true in the case of the sale of F-14s

and F-15s, see Sadeghi, p. 172. For presidential power over the bureaucracy see Carr, 'US Arms Transfer to Iran: 1948–1972,' p. 20, pp. 285–6 and p. 298. According to Carr the main difference between the Johnson and the Nixon administration's approach to arms sales to Iran was that in the former it was the bureaucracy that loosened the control on arms sales, while in the latter the president himself pushed for increased sales to Iran, see pp. 300–2.

89. Kissinger, *The White House Years,* pp. 1263–4.

90. Nevertheless, Toufanian stated in an interview with the author that the USSR at the time was also prepared to sell Iran sophisticated weapons but the Shah chose not to buy. Interview with General Hassan Toufanian, Virginia, 6 June 1997. General Toufanian served as the head of Iranian Military Industry Organisation during the early 1970s and deputy minister of war from 1975–1979. In 1968 the US naval presence consisted of two destroyers and a tender based in Bahrain, and no plans were made for its enlargement. According to one account the US and the USSR both had a presence in the Indian Ocean, but neither could claim naval supremacy in the Persian Gulf, see John C. Campbell, 'The Superpowers in the Persian Gulf Region,' p. 46.

91. Interview with Admiral Rasa'i, Iranian navy commander, 1965–1975. Virginia, 6 June 1997.

92. For incidents in the Shatt al-Arab from 1959 onwards see Chubin, 'Iran and the Persian Gulf,' pp. 12–27.

93. Interview with Toufanian. For the evolution of Soviet-Iraqi military relationship see Shahram Chubin, *Security in the Persian Gulf: the Role of Outside Powers*, (Aldershot: Gower, 1982), pp. 79–89.

94. Interview with Rasa'i. According to Noyes, by 1969 this development of the Iranian navy proved sufficient to deter Iraq from attempting to block ships flying Iran's flag from passing through waters claimed by Iraq. See Noyes, *The Clouded Lens*, p. 33.

95. Interview with Toufanian. See also SIPRI, 'The Arms Trade With the Third World,' p. 842.

96. *The Military Balance*, 1969–1970, p. 60, and 1971–1972, p. 117.

97. Interview with Toufanian. It is also said that the Shah was knowledgeable about air warfare and that he was a regular reader of 'Aviation Weekly,' see 'US Military Sales to Iran,' p. 7.

98. *The Military Balance*, 1968–1969, p. 58.

99. Interview with Toufanian.

100. 'US Military Sales to Iran,' p. 7.

101. Interview with Henry Precht, US counselor in Tehran, 1972–1976, Washington D.C., 12 June 1997.

102. See *Foreign Military Sales: Hearing Before the Committee on Foreign Relations*, United States Senate, Ninetieth Congress, second session no S.3092, 20 June 1968. According to

James Bill, Senator William Fulbright, chairman of the Senate Committee of Foreign Relations, was particularly critical of the sale of advanced weapons to Iran as he wrote to the President in October 1966 the he was 'disturbed' by the sale of the F-4s, see James Bill, *The Eagle and the Lion: The Tragedy of American-Iranian Relations*, (London: Yale University Press,1988), p. 172.

103. Interview with Rodman.

104. For details of Mansfield's proposal see Congressional Record, Senate Resolution 929–Submission of a Senate Resolution relating to substantial reduction of US forces stationed in Europe, 1 December 1969, p. 36147.

105. Interview with Van Dusen. As a proof of Mansfield's orientation towards Asia, Van Dusen argued, he was appointed US Ambassador to Japan. For Mansfield's views on Asia see Congressional Records, Senate, Perspective on Asia-the Mansfield Report, 22 September 1969, pp. 26511–6.

106. Interview with Seth Tillman, consultant at the Senate Committee on Foreign Relations under Senator L.W. Fulbright 1964–1974, Georgetown University, Washington D.C., 10 June 1997.

107. Interview with Van Dusen.

108. Interview with Tillman.

109. Interview with Van Dusen.

110. Ibid. However, this form of lobbying Congress was only effective until the Congressional reforms of 1974 and the mushrooming of House subcommittees. Lawmakers then began to take a more assertive role in foreign policy, and the power of senior members of Congress was largely constrained. For more on the end of the 'seniority system' in Congress see Hedrick Smith, *The Power Game: How Washington Works*, (London: Collins, 1989) pp. 20–30.

111. *International Herald Tribune*, 23 May 1968.

112. *The Military Balance*, 1970–1971, p. 70.

113. *Guardian*, 6 May 1970.

114. *The Military Balance*, 1971–1972, p. 70.

115. *The Military Balance*, 1972–1973, p. 72.

116. *Strategic Survey*, IISS, 1971, p. 40.

117. *The Military Balance*, 1972–1973, p. 72.

118. *Strategic Survey*, 1971, p. 40.

119. *New York Times*, 25 June 1971.

120. Ibid.

121. Klare, *American Arms Supermarket*, p. 116.

122. Ibid., p. 109, and SIPRI 'The Arms Trade With the Third World,' p. 841.

123. *Daily Express*, 20 December 1971.

124. 'U.S. Military Sales to Iran,' p. 41.
125. This view was expressed by Congressman Gerry E. Studds, in Klare, *American Arms Supermarket*, p. 108.
126. Interview with Rodman.
127. 'U.S. Military Sales to Iran,' pp. 52–3.
128. Interview with Kissinger.

Chapter 5: The Insoluble Disputes

1. Interview with Antony Acland, Eton College, Windsor, 17 February 1997.
2. Wright, memoirs, p. 431. However these press statements were seen by Acland as made for public opinion to compensate for Iran giving up Bahrain.
3. Pirouz Mojtahedzadeh, 'Perspectives of the Territorial History of the Tonbs and Abu Musa,' in H. Amir-Ahmadi (ed.) *Small Islands, Big Politics*, (London: Macmillan, 1996) pp. 34–41
4. Schofield (ed.), *Territorial Foundations of the Gulf States*, p. 35.
5. J. B. Kelly, *Britain and the Persian Gulf*, (Oxford: Oxford University Press, 1968), p. 20.
6. Schofield (ed.), *Territorial Foundations of the Gulf States*, p. 35.
7. Ibid.
8. Ibid., p. 36.
9. Ibid., p. 37.
10. Ibid., pp. 35–6.
11. Morsy Abdullah, *The United Arab Emirates*, pp. 222–3. Morsy Abdullah points out the ownership of the island was also in dispute between the Qawasim of Lingeh and the Qawasim of the Trucial emirates, pp. 236–43.
12. Morsy Abdullah, *The United Arab Emirates*, pp. 230–1.
13. Schofield (ed.), *Territorial Foundations of the Gulf States*, p. 35.
14. Morsy Abdullah, *The United Arab Emirates*, pp. 31–2.
15. Ibid. For background on the 1892 treaty see ibid., pp. 23–7.
16. Guive Mirfendereski, 'The Ownership of the Tonb Islands: A Legal Analysis,' in Houshang Amir-Ahmadi (ed.), *Small Islands Big Politics*, (London: Macmillan, 1966), pp. 126–7.
17. Denis Wright, *The English Among the Persians*, (London: Heinemann, 1977), p. 68.
18. Schofield (ed.), *Territorial Foundations of the Gulf States*, p. 36.
19. Ibid., p. 37. For more details of incidents around the island in the inter-war years see Morsy Abdullah, *The United Arab Emirates*, pp. 255–73.

20. PRO/FO, 371/16070, 27 September 1932.

21. Schofield (ed.), *Territorial Foundations of the Gulf States*, p. 38.

22. Ibid.

23. R. K. Ramazani, *International Straits of the World: The Persian Gulf and The Strait of Hormuz*, (Alphen ann der Rijn: Sijthoff & Noordhaff, 1979), p. 2. Also Schofield (ed.), *Territorial Foundations of the Gulf States*, p. 34.

24. Ramazani, *International Straits of the World*, p. 4.

25. Mojtahedzadeh, 'Perspectives of the Territorial History of the Tonbs and Abu Musa,' pp. 32–3.

26. Ramazani, *International Straits of the World*, p. 23.

27. Ibid., p. 27.

28. Chubin and Zabih point out that in the view of some observers, the Shah's attitude was influenced by the attack on an oil tanker bound for Eilat in Israel in June 1971 '... by the Popular Front for the Liberation of Palestine from a motor launch off Perim island in the narrow channel of waters known as Bab el-Mandab,' see Chubin and Zabih, *The Foreign Relations of Iran*, p. 223.

29. During the 1960s Iran had been arguing that Iraq was violating the treaty. For the Iranian argument see Ali Sadeghi, 'United States and the Persian Gulf 1969–1978: Implementing the Nixon Doctrine,' PhD thesis, LSE, pp. 127–8.

30. Interview with Peter Ramsbotham, British ambassador to Iran 1971–1974, London, 11 March 1997.

31. SWB, excerpts from an *Ettela'at* editorial, Tehran Home Service, 27 June 1971.

32. In *Middle East Journal*, Vol. 25 (2), 1971, chronology, Iran, 12 November 1970, pp. 234–5.

33. For different scenarios for the rise of conflict over the Strait of Hormuz see Ramazani pp. 89–94. The Iranian Commander of the Navy, Admiral Farajullah Rasa'i agreed with this assessment in an interview with the author; he particularly expressed concern about Iraq and South Yemen. Interview with Rasa'i, Virginia, 6 June 1997.

34. Interview with Toufanian.

35. H. Amir-Ahmadi (ed.) *Small Islands, Big Politics*, (London: Macmillan, 1996), pp. 4–5.

36. Mojtahedzadeh, 'Perspectives of the Territorial History of the Tonbs and Abu Musa,' p. 41.

37. Amir-Ahmadi (ed.), *Small Islands, Big Politics*, pp. 4–5, and also Wright, *The English Among the Persians*, pp. 58–9.

38. FBIS, *Kayhan* International in English, 'Editorial: A Matter of Principle,' 20 February 1971.

39. Government of Ras al-Khaimah Documents (GRD), meeting with Sir William Luce,

30 October 1971. This is a point that Sir Denis Wright made to Afshar, with which the latter did not seem to disagree. See PRO/FO, 8/960/90, from Tehran to London, 29 January 1969.

40. Interview with Ardeshir Zahedi, Montreux, 18 November 1997.

41. Alam, *The Shah and I*, p. 34. In fact at the Foreign Office the idea of a median line between Saudi Arabia and Iran, drawn on mainland basis, was discussed as a possible guide, if not a determinant of other offshore boundary disputes in the southern part of the Gulf. See PRO/FO, 8/960/19, from London to Jeddah, 30 October 1968. Some in London also saw such a median line as a means to save face for the rulers if they were to yield to Iranian demands, see PRO/FO, 8/961/197, from London to Bahrain, 27 November 1969.

42. Interview with Wright.

43. Interview with Acland. In fact some at the Foreign Office believed that the Shah was playing the Bahrain card to pressure Britain in order of maximise his gain in the lower Gulf. See PRO/FO, 28/59520/349, from London to Tehran, 2 August 1968.

44. Alam, *The Shah and I*, p. 34.

45. Interview with Shaikh Saqar bin Mohammed al-Qasimi, the Ruler of Ras al-Khaimah, Ras al-Khaimah, 7 April 1997. In an interview with the author Ardeshir Zahedi said such perceptions were caused by President Nasser's anti-Iranian propaganda.

46. Alam, *The Shah and I*, p. 34. This Iranian perception could have been caused by the large gap between the capabilities of the Arab emirates and Iran. To give an example of such a gap, Peter Tripp, a member of the Arabian Department at the Foreign Office 1969–70, recalled visiting the Gulf in 1969 and made an interesting comparison between the glamorous palaces and lifestyle of the Iranian monarch and the primitive, humble surroundings of the Arab emirates at the time. Interview with Tripp, London, 31 January 1997.

47. According to Alam these offers were made in the months of February and March 1969, see *The Shah and I*, pp. 34–45.

48. Interview with Wright.

49. Alam, *The Shah and I*, p. 43.

50. Wright, unpublished memoirs, p. 424. Sir Denis was not the only British official to deny a linkage. Every other British official interviewed by the author did so.

51. Alam, *The Shah and I*, pp. 44–5.

52. PRO/FO, 8/960/W3, 20 February 1969.

53. Ibid., p. 45. But Sir Denis says now that what Alam recorded on 23 March was quite untrue.

54. SWB, Tehran Home Service, 27 May 1969.

55. Interview with Zahedi.

56. SWB, Tehran Home Service, 27 May 1969.

57. Wright, unpublished memoirs, p. 430.

58. Interview with Tripp. Afshar also doubts Wright's record on what Stewart said to the Shah. Interview with Afshar.

59. PRO/FO, 8/961/134, from London to Bahrain, 13 June 1969.

60. For the position of the Ruler of Ras al-Khaimah see PRO/FO, 8/962/209, from Dubai to London, 29 December 1969, and PRO/FO, 8/960/2, from Dubai to London, 14 October 1968. For Sharjah's view see PRO/FO, 960/116, from Dubai to London, 2 April 1969.

61. El Rayyes, Minutes of the Third Provisional Council Meeting, 4 March 1969, pp. 217–39.

62. Ibid., minutes of the Fourth Provisional Council meeting, 1 April 1969, pp. 261–84.

63. Ibid., minutes of the Supreme Council's fourth meeting, 10–14 May 1969, pp. 301–9.

64. Ibid., pp. 310–43.

65. Ibid., p. 474. For details on discussion of the committee of legal advisors see pp. 482–99.

66. Ibid., Minutes of the Supreme Council's fifth meeting, 21–25 October 1969, pp. 411–38.

67. Heard-Bey, *From Trucial States*, p. 352.

68. SWB, Cairo 'Voice of the Arabs' in Arabic, 27 October 1969.

69. El Rayyes, *Watha'ik al Khalij al-Arabi*, p. 439. In reaction to the British Political Resident's message the Rulers of Qatar and Ras al-Khaimah walked out while Treadwell was reading the Political Resident's message. They claimed that Britain was imposing the federation. See Heard-Bey, *From Trucial States*, p. 353. It is noteworthy that although the meeting failed to produce an agreement among the Rulers, the Iranian Royal Court continued to oppose the federation as it deplored the discussions at the Abu Dhabi conference which were '… contradictory to the state of friendship and cooperation which the Imperial Government seeks for the establishment of security, stability, and prosperity of the Persian Gulf region,' see FBIS, Tehran International Service in English, 25 October 1969.

70. El Rayyes, minutes of the Deputy Rulers, 22 August 1970, pp. 525–75.

71. Heard-Bey, *From Trucial States*, p. 354. It is noteworthy that during a visit to Iran in May 1969 Michael Stewart expressed no objection to Bahrain seeking independence, leaving a 'mini-federation,' though he expressed his preference for a 'maxi-federation,' see *The Times*, 30 May 1969. According to Sir Stewart Crawford, the British political resident in Bahrain 1966–1970, Bahrain had no intention of taking part in the federation in the first place. Interview with Sir Stewart, 27 November 1996, Henley on Thames. While Andrew Green, assistant political agent in Abu Dhabi 1970–1972, believes now that had Britain concentrated on forming a federation of seven the federation would have been established much more quickly. Interview with Andrew Green, Riyadh, 30 December 1996.

72. *Ettela'at*, 21 December 1969, 17 January 1970, 13 May 1970 and 16 May 1970.
73. Interview with Zahedi.
74. Alam, *The Shah and I*, p. 46.
75. Ibid., p. 50. But the Shah's anti-American Gulf role rhetoric did not lead to confrontation with the US, rather some saw it as confirming the Shah as the leader of the Persian Gulf. Interview with Murphy.
76. Alam, *The Shah and I*, p. 47.
77. SWB, Baghdad Home Service, 3 April 1969.
78. FBIS, Paris AFP, 25 May 1970.
79. Douglas Hurd, *An End to Promises: Sketch of a Government 1970–1974*, (London: Collins, 1979), p. 41.
80. Ibid., p. 42.
81. Ibid., pp. 42–3.
82. Ibid., p. 43.
83. Ibid.
84. Interview with Douglas Hurd, the House of Commons, London, 5 March 1997.
85. *The Times*, 10 April 1969.
86. Alam, *The Shah and I*, p. 68.
87. Interview with Wright.
88. Hurd, *An End to Promises*, p. 46.
89. *The Times*, 30 May 1969.
90. SWB, Tehran Home Service, 27 May 1969.
91. FBIS, Tehran Domestic Service, 23 July 1969.
92. SWB, Tehran Home Service, Excerpts from broadcast of *Ettela'at* article entitled: 'The Shah's Views and the Destiny of the Persian Gulf,' 12 June 1969. This line of thinking was confirmed by Labour MP Roy Roebuck after a meeting with the Shah in September 1969, see FBIS, Tehran Domestic Service, 14 September 1969.
93. Keesing's Contemporary Archives, 30 May–6 June 1970, 23011.
94. Interview with Hurd.
95. Wright, unpublished memoirs, p. 432.
96. FBIS, Tehran Domestic Service, 23 June 1970.
97. *Ettela'at*, 26 June 1970. The trend of Iranian rejection of international intervention in the Gulf was matched by a desire to isolate the Gulf from regional influence, and emphasise the Gulf as an Iranian sphere of influence. In response to Iraqi and Kuwaiti criticism of Iran's Gulf policy *Kayhan International* reported that Iran reasserted sovereignty over the islands and regarded them as 'an integral part of Iranian territory,' see FBIS, *Kayhan International*, 23 May 1970. In a television interview the Shah was critical of what he saw

as Syrian attempts to find a place in the Gulf, see SWB, The Shah French Radio and Television interview, 27 May 1970.

98. Interview with Wright.

99. Interview with Acland.

100. Interview with Afshar. In interviews with Acland and Tripp they confirmed that the Foreign Office was in favour of withdrawal.

101. Interview with Wright.

102. *Guardian*, 11 July 1970.

103. Wright, unpublished memoirs, p. 433.

104. PRO/CAB, 128/17, Cabinet meeting, 23 July 1970.

105. Alam, *The Shah and I*, p. 163.

106. SWB, Tehran Home Service, 12 July 1970. Nearly three months later Zahedi met with Douglas-Home who confirmed that 'British forces will leave the Persian Gulf on schedule.' He added that 'Iran's Persian Gulf policy is quite clear and that Britain is aware of Iran's position. I and my old friend Sir Alec have reached an understanding on this point. At any rate, Iran's policy and views in this regard have not changed,' see FBIS, Tehran Domestic Service, 9 October 1970.

107. Alam, *The Shah and I*, p. 70.

108. Ibid., p. 101.

109. Ibid., p. 113.

110. Ibid., p. 114. Shaikh Saqar also expressed dissatisfaction with the options put to him in Tehran during a meeting with Julian Bullard. See PRO/FO, 8/962/209, from Dubai to London, 29 December 1969.

111. Ibid., pp. 154–5.

112. Interview with Wright.

113. PRO/FO, 8/1307, from Sir Denis Wright to Mr Drace-Francis, 4 March 1970.

114. Alam, *The Shah and I*, pp. 163–5.

115. Wright, unpublished memoirs, pp. 434–5.

116. PRO/FO, 71/1224/44, 'Record of Conversation between the Foreign and Commonwealth Secretary and the Iranian Foreign Minister,' New York, 25 September 1970.

117. Interview with Julian Walker, the British Political Agent in Dubai 1971, London, 13 December1996.

118. Armand Hammer with Neil Lyndon, *Witness to History*, (London: Simon and Schuster, 1987), p. 363.

119. Interview with Acland. According to Heard-Bey Sharjah's declaration of a twelve mile territorial boundary for Abu Musa was not generally known until March 1970. Sir John Coles, assistant political agent in Dubai 1968–1971, confirmed this and said Britain

was not given an explanation for the time gap between the date of the decree and its announcement to Britain (Interview with Coles).

120. Interview with Acland.

121. PRO/FO, 8/1342/1, Arabian Department, 30 September 1970. This view was also shared by the British Embassy in Tehran. See PRO/FO, 8/1342/2, from Tehran to London, 30 November 1970.

122. *MEES*, No. 32, Vol. XIII, 5 June 1970.

123. Alam, *The Shah and I*, p. 125.

124. Ibid., p. 153.

125. Ibid.

126. Ibid., p. 156.

127. Ibid., p. 161.

128. Ibid., pp. 155–6.

129. Interview with Walker.

130. Interview with Sir John Coles, 11 March 1997, the Foreign Office, London. Coles, who at the time of the interview was permanent under-secretary of state, argues that the episode was not a reversal in British position on the concession. He read from a classified document that Britain signed a political agreement with each oil concession and committed itself to 'making a binding recommendation' to the Emirates for the imposition of operating limits if necessary to avoid disputes between neighbouring Emirates. Coles was assistant political agent in Dubai from 1968–1971.

131. *MEES*, 5 June 1970.

132. Interview with Acland. Armand Hammer would not give in and tried to sue the British government in US courts and the High Court in London, but without success as the US courts ruled that 'The laws of sovereign states do not provide for other sovereign states to be sued for commercial misconduct,' see Hammer, *Witness to History*, p. 368. Acland added in the same interview that in Britain the case went to the House of Lords but Oxy got no satisfactory result there either.

133. Interview with Acland. Glen Balfour-Paul also confirmed that the Luce recommendation came from the Foreign Office. Interview with Balfour-Paul, University of Exeter, 11 November 1996. It is noteworthy that Balfour-Paul is one of the few people who read the Luce reports and used them in his book *The End of Empire in the Middle East*, although he did not make reference to them in the bibliography.

134. Interview with Balfour-Paul.

135. William Luce, 'Britain in the Persian Gulf,' *The Round Table*, no. 227, July 1967, pp. 227–83.

136. William Luce, 'A Naval Force for the Gulf,' *The Round Table*, no. 326, Oct 1969, pp. 347–55.

137. Interview with Acland.
138. Interview with Wright.
139. Interview with Acland.
140. FBIS, Tehran Domestic Service, 22 September 1970.
141. SWB, Tehran Home Service, 20 September 1970.
142. Alam, *The Shah and I*, p. 170.
143. SWB, Tehran Home Service, 22 September 1970.
144. FBIS, Tehran Domestic Service, 8 April 1970.
145. SWB, Tehran Home Service, 7 April 1970.
146. SWB, Tehran Home Service, 12 April 1970 records Omar Saqaf's visit.
147. SWB, Tehran Home Service, 16 May 1970.
148. *Financial Times*, 17 June 1970.
149. *Ettela'at*, 3 June 1970.
150. FBIS, Tehran Domestic Service, 9 July 1970.
151. FBIS, Tehran Domestic Service, 27 August 1970.
152. Interview with Green.
153. SWB, Tehran Home Service, July 1970.
154. FBIS, Tehran Domestic Service, 14 July 1970.
155. Interview with Zahedi.
156. Interview with Afshar.
157. *Ettela'at*, 26 May 1970.
158. Interview with Afshar.
159. *Financial Times*, 17 June 1970.
160. SWB, 'The Shah's speech at the opening of the Majlis and Senate,' Tehran Home Service, 6 October 1970.

Chapter 6: The Final Year

1. Sir Denis Wright, 'Ten Years in Iran - Some Highlights,' *Asian Affairs*, Vol. 78, (October 1991). For details of the Tehran agreement see Anthony Sampson, *The Seven Sisters* (1975). This increase was minimal compared with the dramatic rise in oil prices later in the 1970s, but the Tehran agreement marked a turning point in oil companies' relations with OPEC countries. From there onwards companies could no longer change the price of oil without consulting oil producing countries.

2. Alam, *The Shah and I*, p. 199.

3. In *Middle East Journal*, Vol. 25 (2), 1971, chronology, Iran, 12 November 1970, pp. 234–5.

NOTES 163

4. *Ettela'at*, 27 December 1970.

5. FBIS, *Kayhan* International in English, editorial entitled: 'A Matter of Principle,' 20 February 1971.

6. Wright, unpublished memoirs, p. 435.

7. PRO/FO, 8/1553/93, from Luce to London, 23 February 1971.

8. Interview with Zahedi.

9. See Abdullah Omran Taryam, *The Establishment of the United Arab Emirates: 1905–1985*, (London: Croom-Helm, 1987), p. 180. See also PRO/FO, 8/1585/116, 'Record of a Conversation between Shaikh Mohammad bin Khalid al-Qasimi and Sir William Luce,' 31 January 1971.

10. *The Times*, 19 November 1970.

11. PRO/FO, 8/1554/7, 'Policy in the Persian Gulf,' 8 March 1971.

12. FBIS, Tehran Domestic Service, 11 February 1971.

13. PRO/FO, 8/1585/137, 'Report by Sir William Luce addressed to the Foreign Secretary,' 15 February, 1971.

14. Balfour-Paul, *The End of Empire in the Middle East*, p. 130.

15. House of Commons debate, 1 March 1971, Col. 1228.

16. *The Economist*, 6 March 1971. This point was also picked up by former Defence Secretary Denis Healey, see House of Commons debate, 1 March 1971, Col. 1229.

17. Interview with Hurd. The confirmation of British withdrawal by the Conservative government could be seen as a success for Iran's regional manoevures to prevent a change in Britain's decision to leave the Gulf, as the Conservative government's announcement was welcomed by most countries in the region. A notable exception, however, was the reaction of the Ruler of Dubai who expressed his disappointment to the London Times. See *The Times*, 3 March 1971, also see Shaikh Rashid's interview in the *Daily Telegraph*, 29 March 1971.

18. For the text of the Saudi-Kuwaiti recommendations see El Rayyes, *Watha'ik al khaleej al Arabi*, pp. 627–43.

19. Keesing's Contemporary Archives, (24843), 25 September 1971. Also see Heard-Bey, *From Trucial States*, pp. 361–2.

20. Interview with Walker.

21. Heard-Bey, *From Trucial States*, pp. 362–3.

22. Ibid., p. 369.

23. At a press conference Zahedi stated clearly that Iran's recognition and even support of the federation depended on the outcome of the islands dispute, SWB, Tehran Home Service, 24 June 1971.

24. GRD, minutes of meeting with the British Political Agent, 11 June 1970.

25. Wright, unpublished memoirs, p. 436.

26. Interview with Shaikh Saqar bin Mohammed, Ras al-Khaimah, 7 April 1997.
27. Kelly, *Arabia, the Gulf and the West*, p. 90.
28. GRD, minutes of meeting with the British Political Agent, 11 June 1970.
29. Wright, unpublished memoirs, p. 437.
30. FBIS, London REUTER, 9 May 1971.
31. Interview with Walker.
32. FBIS, Tehran Domestic Service, 14 June 1971.
33. FBIS, Tehran Domestic Service, 16 June 1971.
34. SWB, Tehran Home Service, 15 June 1971.
35. SWB, Tehran Home Service, 23 June 1971.
36. SWB, Tehran Home Service, 24 June 1971.
37. FBIS, Tehran Domestic Service, 27 June 1971.
38. Ibid.
39. Interview with Walker.

40. Interview with Murphy. Sir William Luce went to Washington in January 1971 to brief members of the State Department on developments in the Gulf. The record of that meeting indicates that informal and personal expertise on that part of the world was lacking at the highest levels of the US government. This could be partly due to the fact that the US did not have representatives in the Trucial emirates or Bahrain or Qatar from 1972 onwards. See PRO/FO, 8/1583, record of discussion on the Persian Gulf at the State Department, 13 January 1971.

41. GRD, minutes of meeting with Sir William Luce, 8 May 1971.
42. Ibid.
43. Ibid.
44. Interview with Afshar, London, 14 June 1995.
45. GRD, minutes of meeting with Sir William Luce, 7 September 1971.

46. GRD, minutes of meeting with Sir William Luce, 7 September 1971. This document contains records of two different meetings. The first took place on 7 September 1971, the second is an undated meeting between Shaikh Saqar and Julian Walker that seems to have taken place soon after the meeting with Luce.

47. GRD. On the top of each copy of the proposed pledges there is a note in Arabic saying 'Rejected' or 'Rejected by Shaikh Saqar' to prove Ras al-Khaimah's refusal to agree with the above proposal. Details of the financial offer made by Iran are given in a 'Draft letter on financial aid' preserved in this archive.

48. GRD, minutes of meeting with Sir William Luce, 12 September 1971. Shaikh Saqar had mentioned this idea in a meeting with Julian Walker and said if the Shah took the islands by force the Arab world would rise against Iran, but Walker kept reminding him that neighbouring Arab states, such as Saudi Arabia, did not possess the necessary mili-

tary force to confront Iran. GRD, 14 September 1971. Shaikh Saqar also visited Iraq in 1970 which caused some concern among Iranian and British officials, see Alam, *The Shah and I*, p. 161. According to a Saudi source after Shaikh Saqar's visit to Iraq Iranian senator Masoudi felt Iran could no longer trust him. In SARCA, minutes of meeting between Saudi ambassador to Tehran and senator Abbas Masoudi, 29 September 1971.

49. GRD, minutes of meeting with Sir William Luce, 14 September 1971.
50. GRD, minutes of meeting with Sir William Luce, 18 September 1971.
51. Ibid.
52. Ibid.
53. Interview with Afshar, 20 December 1997.
54. Interview with Ramsbotham.
55. Interview with Walker.
56. *Al Anwar*, 30 November 1971.
57. Interview with Walker.
58. Some took Luce's statement as evidence of a deal between Iran and Britain over the islands, see Amir-Ahmadi (ed.) *Small Islands, Big Politics*, p. 11, while this statement only referred to Abu Musa and not the Tunbs.
59. Keesing's Contemporary Archives (25010), 25/December–1 January 1972. According to Sir William Luce the Shah insisted on a 50–50 sharing of the oil, not because Iran needed more income, but rather because the Shah believed that had he given more than 50 per cent it could be interpreted as a sign of accepting Sharjah's title to the island, see GRD, meeting with Sir William Luce, 30 October 1971.
60. Ramazani, *International Straits of the World*, p. 74.
61. SWB, text of statement by Premier Hoveida in Majlis, Tehran Home Service, 30 November 1971.
62. Interview with Walker.
63. According to Ahmad Duraij, Umm al-Qaiwain and Ajman, who had granted Oxy an off-shore oil concession, did not come out of this empty handed as they were given an unspecified sum in financial compensation by Iran. Interview with Duraij, legal adviser to the Ruler of Umm al-Qaiwain 1970–1972, London, 17 February 1997. Nevertheless, after the declaration of the UAE, Umm al-Qaiwain issued a statement demanding the cancellation of Sharjah's agreement with Iran on Abu Musa on the grounds that the agreement was signed under duress. This statement, however, had no effect on Sharjah's position or on drilling in the disputed waters, see *MEES*, No. 6, Vol. XV, 3 December 1971. On the other hand according to Julian Walker all the Emirates declared a twelve-mile territorial water limit for their islands after the United Arab Emirates were established, and as all the other islands with the exception of Abu Musa are more than twelve miles apart there were no other overlaps. Telephone conversation with Walker, 14 November 1997.

64. Interview with Shaikh Saqar.
65. Interview with Acland.
66. *The Guardian*, 9 November 1971.
67. UN Documents, Security Council S/PV. 1610, pp. 10–14. Bishara also mentioned a series of meetings between the Kuwaiti Foreign Minister and his Iranian counterpart in Jeddah on 23–26 March 1970; in Kuwait on 4 August 1970; in Karachi on 26–28 December 1970; and in Tehran on 9–10 August 1971. Throughout these meetings, according to Bishara, the Iranian hardline stance was consistent. Acland also confirmed these proposals and the new Iranian foreign minister, Khalatbari, also confirmed that Iran had rejected the idea of leasing the Tunb islands, adding that Iran's sovereignty over these islands was not negotiable, see *Ettela'at*, 13 November 1971.
68. *Guardian*, 3 November 1971.
69. Interview with Afshar.
70. Interview with Acland. This view is also shared by Julian Walker.
71. Interview with Ramsbotham.
72. Interview with Afshar.
73. PRO/CAB, 128/49/70987, Cabinet meeting, 8 November 1971.
74. Interview with Rasa'i.
75. SWB, text of statement by Premier Hoveida in Majlis, Tehran Home Service, 30 November 1971.
76. Interview with Walker. According to Rasa'i although the operation was small the Navy had to prepare for every eventuality.
77. Keesing's Contemporary Archives (25010), 25 December 1971–1 January 1972.
78. In Ramazani, *Iran's Foreign Policy*, p. 424, Ramazani's own translation from *Ettela'at Hava'i*, 12 May 1973.
79. Interview with Walker. For the same reason Andrew Green thought it was a convenient date, interview with Green.
80. Interview with Afshar.
81. House of Commons Debate, 13 December 1971, Col. 22.
82. Keesing's Contemporary Archives (25010), 25 December 1971–1 January 1972.
83. PRO/CAB, 128/49/70987, Cabinet meeting, 2 December 1971.
84. Interview with Murphy.
85. Interview with Kissinger.
86. For reactions of individual Arab states see SWB, 1–4 December 1971.
87. GRD, minutes of a meeting with the Saudi ambassador, 12 August 1970.
88. SWB, Tehran Home Service, 1 December 1971.
89. Ramazani, *Iran's Foreign Policy*, p. 425.
90. Ibid.

91. GRD, minutes of meeting with the British Political Resident, 1 December 1971.
92. Heard-Bey, *From Trucial States*, p. 369.
93. Ibid., p. 366.
94. Interview with Acland.

Bibliography

Official Documents

Government of Ras al-Khaimah Documents, 1970–1971, Emirate of Ras al-Khaimah.
House of Commons Debates, 1965–1971.
Lyndon B. Johnson (LBJ) Library, National Security Files, Iran, U.K.
National Security Archives, U.S. declassified documents, 1967–1970, London School of Economics and Political Science (LSE): Library Collection.
Public Record Office, UK: Cabinet Meetings (CAB), 1965.
—— FO/371 and FO/372, 1932–1966.
Saudi Arabian Royal Court Archives (SARCA), 1968–1971, Royal Court, Riyadh.
Statement of the Defence Estimates, 1965–1968.
Statement of the Defence Expenditure, 1968.
UN Documents, Security Council, 1970–1971.
U.S. Congressional Records, 1968–1972.
U.S. Dept. of State, Bulletin, 1970–1971.
U.S. National Archives, Subject File, WHCF, Nixon Presidential Materials Staff, 1969–1970.

Interviews

Acland, Sir Antony, Head of Arabian Department, Foreign Office, 1970–1972. Eton College, Windsor, 17/2/1997.

Afshar, Amirkhosrow, Iranian Deputy Minister of Foreign Affairs, 1965–1969. London, 14/6/1995, 24/5/1996, 20/12/1997.

Atherton, Alfred, member of the Bureau for Near East and South Asian Affairs, 1966–1970, and Assistant to Joseph Sisco in 1970. Washington D.C., 29/5/1997.

Balfour-Paul, Glen, Political Resident, Persian Gulf 1966. University of Exeter, 11/11/1996.

Brenchley, Frank, Head of Arabian Department, Foreign Office, 1963–1967. London, 13/6/1996.

Bullard, Sir Julian, British Political Agent in Dubai in 1968. Oxford, 11/6/1996.

Coles, Sir John, Assistant Political Agent, Trucial States (Dubai) 1968–1971. London, Foreign Office, 11/3/1997.

Crawford, Sir Stewart, British Political Resident in Bahrain, 1966–1970. Henley on Thames, 27/11/1996.

Al-Dawalibi, Maroof, Adviser to King Faisal in 1968. Riyadh, 9/4/1996.

Duraij, Ahmad, Legal Adviser to the Ruler of Umm al-Qawain, 1970–1972. London, 17/2/1997.

Eliot, Theodore, Country Director of Iran at the State Department 1966–1969. Washington D.C., 3/10/1995.

Eilts, Herman, US Ambassador in Saudi Arabia, 1965–1970. Boston, Mass., 19/5/1997.

Ghassemi, Reza, Iranian Ambassador to Kuwait, 1975–1979. London, 4/4/1997.

Green, Andrew, Assistant Political Agent in Abu Dhabi, 1970–1972. Riyadh, 30/12/1996.

Healey, Lord, Secretary of State for Defence, 1964–1970. House of Commons, 4/7/1995.

Helms, Richard, Director of the CIA, 1965–73, and Ambassador to Tehran, 1973–1976. Washington D.C., 2/6/1997.

Hurd, Lord, Political Secretary to the Prime Minister 1970–1974. House of Commons, London, 5/3/1997.

Kissinger, Henry, Assistant to US President for National Security Affairs 1969–1975. New York, 3/6/1997.

Meyer, Armin, US Ambassador to Tehran 1965–1969. Washington D.C., 16/4/1997.

Murphy, Richard, Director, Arabian Peninsula Affairs, US State Department 1969–1971. Washington D.C., 27/5/1997.

Parsons, Sir Anthony, British Political Agent in Bahrain 1965–1969. Devon, 10/6/1996.

Precht, Henry, US Counsellor in Tehran, 1972–1976, and Director, Iranian Affairs, 1978–1980. Washington D.C., 12/6/1997.

Ramsbotham, Sir Peter, British Ambassador to Tehran 1971–1974. London, 11/3/1997.

Rasa'i, Farajullah, Iranian Navy Commander 1965–1975. Virginia, 6/6/1997.

Rodman, Peter Warren, Member of NSC 1969–1977. Washington D.C., 15/5/1997.

Saunders, Harold, Senior Member of the NSC covering the Near East and South Asia, 1967–1974. Washington D.C., 23/5/1997.

Al-Qasimi, Shaikh Saqar bin Mohammad, Ruler of Ras al-Khaimah. Ras al-Khaimah, 7/4/1997.
Tillman, Seth, Consultant at the Senate Committee on Foreign Relations under Senator L. W. Fulbright 1964–1974. Georgetown University, Washington D.C., 10/6/1997.
Tripp, John Peter, Head of Near East Department, FCO, 1969–1970. London, 31/6/1997.
Tufanian, Hassan, Head of Iran's Military Industry Organisation during the early 1970s and Deputy Minister of War from 1970–1979. Virginia, 6/6/1997.
Van Dusen, Michael, Director for the House of Congress Sub-Committee on Europe and Middle East in 1977. Washington D.C., 22/5/1997.
Walker, Julian Fortay, Political Agent, Dubai, Trucial States 1971. London, 13/12/1996.
Wright, Sir Denis, British Ambassador to Tehran 1963–1971. Haddenham, Bucks. 9/5/1995, 7/6/1995, 9/6/1996.
Zahedi, Ardeshir, Iranian Foreign Minister 1967–1971. Montreux, 13/9/1996 and 18/11/1997.

Books and Articles

Abdullah, Mohammad Morsy. *The United Arab Emirates: A Modern History*, London: Croom Helm, 1978.
Alam, Assadollah. *The Shah and I*, London: I.B. Tauris, 1991.
Avery, Peter (ed.). *The Cambridge History of Iran, Vol. 7: From Nadir Shah to the Islamic Republic*, Cambridge: Cambridge University Press, 1991.
Ayoob, Mohammed. 'The Dynamics of Iran's Foreign Policy,' *Institute for Defence Studies and Analysis Journal*, Vol. 3, 1970, pp. 249–350.
Al-Baharna, Hussain. 'The Fact-Finding Mission of the United Nations Secretary-General and the Settlement of the Bahrain-Iran Dispute, May 1970,' *International and Comparative Law Quarterly*, Vol. 22, July 1973.
Balfour-Paul, Glen. *The End of Empire in the Middle East: Britain's Relinquishment of Power in her Three Arab Dependencies.*, Cambridge: Cambridge University Press, 1991.
Bill, James. *The Eagle and the Lion: The Tragedy of American-Iranian Relations*, London: Yale University Press, 1988.
Callaghan, James. *Time and Chance*, London: Collins, 1987.
Campbell, John C. 'The Superpowers in the Persian Gulf Region,' in Abbas Amirie, (ed.), *The Persian Gulf and Indian Ocean in International Politics*, Tehran: Institute for International Political and Economic Studies, 1975.
Carr, Christopher, D. 'US Arms Transfer to Iran: 1948–1972,' PhD thesis, London School of Economics, 1980.
Charney, Jonathan I. and L. M. Alexander (eds). *International Maritime Boundaries*, Vol.

II, Dordrecht, Boston and London: Martinus Nijhoff, 1993.
Chubin, Shahram. *The Role of Outside Powers* (Security in the Persian Gulf: 4), Aldershot: Gower (for ISIS), 1982.
Chubin, Shahram. 'Iran and the Persian Gulf: Iranian Policy and the Arab States, 1959–1967,' PhD thesis, Columbia University, 1969.
Chubin, Shahram and Sepehr Zabih. *The Foreign Relations of Iran: A Developing State in a Zone of Great Power Conflict*, Berkeley: University of California Press, 1974.
Crossman, Richard. *The Diaries of a Cabinet Minister, Selections*, ed. Anthony Howard, London: Cape, 1979.
Darby, Philip. *British Defence Policy East of Suez: 1947–1968*, London: Oxford University Press for The Royal Institute of International Affairs, 1993.
De Moraes Ruehsen, Moiara. 'The Advent of American Hegemony in the Persian Gulf, 1953–1956,' PhD thesis, John Hopkins University, 1992.
Destler, I. M. 'Can One Man Do?,' *Foreign Policy*, Vol. 5, Winter 1971–1972.
Gause, Gregory. 'British and American Policies in the Persian Gulf, 1968–1973,' *Review of International Studies*, Vol. 11, October 1985.
Hammer, Armand and Neil Layndon. *Witness to History*, London: Simon and Schuster, 1987.
Healey, Denis. *The Time of My Life*, London: Penguin, 1990.
Heard-Bey, Frauke. *From Trucial States to United Arab Emirates: A Society in Transition*, London: Longman, 1982.
Hurd, Douglas. *An End to Promises: Sketch of a Government 1970–1974*, London: Collins, 1979.
Jensen, Eric. 'The Secretary General's Use of Good Offices and the Question of Bahrain,' *Millennium: Journal of International Studies*. Vol. 14, No. 3, Winter 1985.
Kelly, J. B. *Arabia, the Gulf and the West: A Critical View of the Arabs and their Oil Policy*, London: Weidenfeld and Nicholson, 1980.
—— *Britain and the Persian Gulf 1797–1880*, Oxford: Oxford University Press, 1968.
Kissinger, Henry A. *A World Restored*, London: Victor Gollancz, 1973.
—— *The White House Years*, London: Weidenfeld and Nicolson, 1979.
—— 'Bureaucracy and Policy Making: the Effect of Insiders and Outsiders on the Policy Process,' in *Bureaucracy, Politics and Strategy*, Security Studies Paper No. 17, University of California, LA, 1968.
Klare, Michael T. *American Arms Supermarket*, Austin: University of Texas Press,1984.
Leacacos, John P. 'Kissinger's Apparat,' *Foreign Policy*, Vol. 5, Winter 1971–1972.
Litwak, Robert. *Détente and the Nixon Doctrine: American Foreign Policy and the Pursuit of Stability, 1969–1976*, Cambridge: Cambridge University Press, 1984.
Louis, William Roger. *The British Empire in the Middle East, 1945–1951: Arab National-*

ism, the United States, and Post-War Imperialism, Oxford: Oxford University Press, 1984.
Luce, Sir William. 'A Naval Force for The Gulf,' The Round Table, No. 326, October 1969.
—— 'Britain's Withdrawal From the Middle East and the Persian Gulf,' Royal United Service Institute Journal, Vol. 114, No. 653, March 1969.
—— 'Britain in the Persian Gulf,' The Round Table, No. 227, July 1967.
Mayhew, Christopher Paget. Britain's Role Tomorrow, London: Hutchinson, 1976.
Mirfenderski, Guive. 'The Ownership of the Tunb Islands: A Legal Analysis,' in Houshang Amir-Ahmadi (ed.), Small Islands Big Politics, London: Macmillan, 1966.
Mojtahedzadeh, Pirouz. 'Perspectives of the Territorial History of the Tonbs and Abu Musa,' in Amir-Ahamdi, Houshang (ed.), Small Islands Big Politics, London: Macmillan, 1966.
Nixon, Richard. In the Arena: A Memoir of Victory, Defeat and Renewal, London: Simon and Schuster, 1990.
—— The Memoirs of Richard Nixon, London: Sidgwick and Jackson, 1978.
Noyes, James H. The Clouded Lens, Persian Gulf Security and U.S. Policy, 2nd ed. Stanford: Hoover Institution Press, 1982.
Pahlavi, Mohammad Reza. Mission for My Country, London: Hutchinson, 1960.
Al-Qasimi, Muhammad. The Myth of Arab Piracy in the Gulf, London: Croom Helm, 1986.
Ramazani, Rouhollah K. International Straits of the World: The Persian Gulf and the Strait of Hormuz, Alphen ann der Rijn, Sijthoff & Noordhaff, 1979.
—— Iran's Foreign Policy, 1941–1973: A Study of Foreign Policy in Modernizing Nations, Charlottesville: University Press of Virginia, 1975.
—— The Persian Gulf: Iran's Role, Charlottesville: University Press of Virginia, 1972.
El Rayyes, Riad. Watha'ik al-Khaleej al-Arabi (Arab Gulf Documents), London: Riad El Rayyes, 1986.
Rodman, Peter. 'The NSC System: Why It's Here to Stay,' Foreign Service Journal, February 1992.
Sadeghi, Ali. 'United States and the Persian Gulf 1969–1978: Implementing the Nixon Doctrine,' PhD thesis, LSE, 1988.
Sampson, Anthony. The Seven Sisters: The Great Oil Companies and the World They Made, London: Hodder and Stoughton, 1975.
Schofield, Richard (ed.) Territorial Foundations of the Gulf States, London: UCL Press, 1994.
Sirriyeh, Hussein. U.S. Policy in the Gulf 1968–1977: Aftermath of British Withdrawal, London: Ithaca, 1984.
Smith, Hedrick. The Power Game: How Washington Works, London: Collins, 1988.
Standish, John F. Persia and the Gulf: Retrospect and Prospect, London: Curzon, 1998.
Stookey, Robert W. America and the Arab States: An Uneasy Encounter, New York, London: Wiley, 1975.

Taryam, Abdullah Omran. *The Establishment of the United Arab Emirates: 1905–1985*, London: Croom Helm, 1987.

Trevelyan, Humphrey. *The Middle East in Revolution*, London: Macmillan, 1970.

Verrier, Anthony. *Through the Looking Glass: British Foreign Policy in an Age of Illusion*, London: Cape, 1983.

Watt, D. C. 'The Decision to Withdraw from The Gulf,' *The Political Quarterly*, July-September, 1968.

Wilson, Harold. *The Labour Government 1964–1970: A Personal Record*, London: Weidenfeld and Nicolson, 1971.

Wright, Sir Denis. *The English Among the Persians*, London, Heinemann: 1977.

—— 'Ten Years in Iran, Some Highlights,' *Asian Affairs*, Vol. 78, Oct. 1991.

Yonah, Alexander and Allan Nanes (eds). *The United States and Iran: A Documentary History*, Frederick, MD: Athletic Books, 1980.

Young, R. 'Equitable Solution for Offshore Boundaries, The 1969 Saudi Arabia-Iran Agreement,' *The American Journal of International Law*, Vol. 64, 1979.

Index

Abu Dhabi: Buraimi oasis 5; and Federation of Gulf Emirates 30, 35, 89–90, 109; and Iran 91, 102; and Saudi Arabia 23

Abu Musa island: and Bahrain question 85–6, 87; British policy 45, 96, 97, 100; disputed sovereignty of 2, 9, 40, 45, 49, 78, 79–81, 88, 97, 98, 104, 112; 120–1, 127; Iranian takeover 98, 107–8, 112, 114, 121–4, 128; offshore oil 99; physical features 81–3; and Sharjah 116–19; strategic significance 81–4, 116

Acland, Sir Antony 50, 78, 86, 95, 100, 101, 123

Ad-Dali region 14

Aden 2, 7, 11, 12, 18, 19, 26, 27, 83, 101, 107, 125; British withdrawal from 14–17

Afghanistan 1, 84

Afshar, Amir Khosrow 33, 39, 41, 48, 72, 95, 101, 103, 104, 113, 120, 122

Aghassi, Hajj Mirza 2, 84

Ajman 99; dispute with Umm al-Qaiwain 100; and Federation of Gulf Emirates 30, 90

Alam, Asadollah: diary 67, 85–7, 91–2, 93, 96, 97–8, 99–100, 102, 107; foreign policy role 34–5, 36, 47, 53, 97–8, 99

Algeria 123

Amery, Julian 95

Amini, Ali 9

Amouzegar, Jamshid 45

Anglo-Iranian Oil Company 4, 5

Ansary, Houshang 72

al-Anwar 116, 117

al-Arabiyah island 37

Arab nationalism 4, 14, 40

Arab-Israeli conflict 28, 48, 65

Arab-Israeli war (1967) 17, 23, 30

Arabia 4, 12

Aram, Abbas 39, 42, 99

INDEX

ARAMCO (Arabian-American Oil Company) 34–5, 37, 42, 44
Arif, President 29
ARMISH (US Army Mission Headquarters) 68
ARMISH-MAAG 69
Arthur, Sir Geoffrey 52, 92, 120, 123
Atherton, Alfred 62, 69
Australia 94

Baghdad 29, 122
Baghdad Pact 6, 7 *see also* Central Treaty Organisation
Bahrain 5, 126, 127, 128; and Federation of Arab Emirates 30–1, 89, 90, 108; independence of 91, 109, 111, 122; Iranian claim to 1, 3, 9, 23, 26, 33–5, 36, 39–41, 42, 81 (resolution of 42–54, 55, 56, 78, 84, 85, 203, 104); and islands' dispute 85–8; plebiscite 40, 47, 49, 50, 51; and Saudi Arabia 32–3; social structure 36, 54; and United States 91–2 *see also* Britain (Gulf policy), Iran
Bakhtiar, General Teymour 9
Ball, George 18
Bandar Abbas 1, 70, 74, 112, 121
Bandar Gombrun *see* Bandar Abbas
Bani Forur island 83
Barger, Thomas 42, 44
Basidu 79
Bevin, Ernest 4, 11
Bishara, Abdullah 120
Britain: and Aden 2, 6–72, 11, 12, 14–17, 18, 19, 26, 27, 83, 101, 107, 125; defence policies and budgets 13, 14, 15–16, 16–17, 19, 21–2, 23–4; domestic politics 11–14, 16–17, 20–4, 27, 94–6; east of Suez policy 10, 12, 14, 16, 17, 18, 19, 21, 23, 24, 27, 94; and Federation of Arab Emirates 30–2; Gulf policy 2–6, 8–9, 10, 17, 19–20, 23–4, 30–2, 45, 47–8, 50–2, 55–6, 78, 79–81, 85–8, 91–105 *passim*, 116–21, 123–4 *passim*, 125–9 *passim*; and Iran (Persia) 1–2, 5–6, 8–9, 47–8, 50–3 *passim*, 80–1, 85–8 *passim*, 91–2, 93, 94, 95–6, 97–8, 99, 101–2, 102–3, 107, 110–12, 116, 117, 120–1; and Saudi Arabia 5, 101; and USA 5–6, 12, 13, 18, 16–19; 22–3; 27–8 *see also* Conservative Party, Labour Party
Brown, George 12, 17, 18, 21, 22, 23
Brussels 95
Bullard, Sir Julian 31
Bunche, Dr Ralph 52
Buraimi oasis 5
Bushehr 70, 74
Buttes-Clayco Company 119

Cairo 29
Callaghan, James 12, 13, 17, 20
Canada 13
Caribbean 11, 19
Caucasus mountains 84
Central Intelligence Organisation (CIA) 25, 63
Central Treaty Organisation (CENTO) 7, 30, 67, 81, 94, 96 *see also* Baghdad Pact
China 65
Churchill, Sir Winston 5
Clifford, Clark 61
Coles, John 100
Conservative Party 3, 11, 22, 37, 92, 94–6, 104
Continental Shelf Agreement 45
Crawford, Sir Stewart 90, 100
Crossman, Richard 21

Curzon, Lord George Nathaniel 81
Cyprus 4, 7, 16

Darby, Philip 12
al-Dawalibi, Maroof 41–2
Doha 46
Dubai 9, 23, 31, 35, 45, 88; and Federation of Arab Emirates 30, 35, 90, 91, 109; relations with Iran 91
Dulles, Alan 6

East European 25
East India Company 2
Eden, Sir Anthony 3
Egypt 2, 4, 6, 8, 46, 71, 93, 103, 104, 105, 114, 122, 123, 124, 128
Eilat 71
Eilts, Herman 34, 38, 41
Eisenhower, Dwight D. 6, 57, 61, 67, 93
Eley, Northcutt 99
Eqbal, Dr Manouchehr 44
Ethiopia 42
Ettela'at 49, 50, 54, 94, 98, 103, 111, 121
Europe 59
European Economic Community 18
'Exclusive Agreements' 2

Faisal, King of Saudi Arabia 32, 33–4, 38, 39, 41, 42, 44, 48, 55, 59, 109, 114
Far East 11, 12, 15, 18, 19, 21, 26, 58, 59
Farisi island 37
Fartash, Manuchehr 33
al-Fawzan, Yussif 32
Federation of Arab Emirates 36, 45, 46, 49; 88–91, 96, 104, 128; British proposals for 30–1; Gulf Emirates Conference 35; Provisional Council 88 *see also* Abu Dhabi, Dubai, Fujairah, United Arab Emirates
Feyerdoon oil field 37
Findley, Paul 72
Food and Agriculture Organisation (FAO) 36
Forur island 83
France 6, 71, 108
Fujairah: and Federation of Arab Emirates 30, 90
Fulbright, William 72

GENMISH (US Military Mission to the Imperial Iranian Gendarmerie) 68
Germany 23, 24
Godber, Joseph 122
Goodpaster, General Andrew 61
Green, Marshall 64
Guam 64
Guam statement 76

Halperin, Morton 61
Hassan, King of Morocco 40–1
Hay, Sir Rupert 30
Healey, Denis 12, 15, 16, 17, 19, 21, 23
Heath, Edward 92, 93, 94, 95, 96
Helms, Richard 63, 66
Henjam 83
Herald Tribune 73
Herat 84
Home, Sir Alec Douglas 95, 96, 101, 108, 122
Hong Kong 11
Hormuz islands 1, 2, 9, 23, 33, 37, 48, 57, 58, 84, 100, 108 *see also* Abu Musa, Iran, Tunbs
House of Commons 16, 17, 19, 108, 122
House of Representatives 72

INDEX

Hoveida, Amir Abbas 24, 27, 31, 54, 93, 95, 112, 121
Howard, Michael 14
Hurd, Douglas 92, 93, 95, 109

Ibn Saud 3
Imam Ghalib bin Ali 6
India 87
Indian Ocean 70, 83, 84
Indonesia 19
International Court of Justice (ICJ) 47
International Monetary Fund (IMF) 20

Iran: and Arab nationalism 29–31; armed forces 56, 69, 70–1, 73–4; arms purchases 68–70, 71–2, 73–6, 77; and Britain 1–2, 5–6, 8–9, 26–7, 47–8, 50–3 *passim*, 80–1, 85–8 *passim*, 91–2, 93, 94, 95–6, 97–8, 99, 101–2, 102–3, 107, 110–12, 116, 117, 120–1; claim to Bahrain 1, 3, 9, 23, 26, 32, 33–5, 36, 39–41, 42, 81 (resolution of 42–54, 55, 56, 78, 84, 85, 203, 104); defence policy and budgets 70–1, 74; and Egypt 103–4; and Federation of Arab Emirates 31, 87, 88, 114; Gulf interests and policy 1–2, 7–8, 31–2, 94, 95, 102–3, 104–5, 107; and Hormuz islands (Tunbs and Abu Musa) 32, 70–81, 84, 85–6, 96–8, 99, 107–8, 110–24; and Iraq 7, 30, 70–1, 83–4, 92, 123, 124, 128; and Morocco 40–1; and OPEC 106–7; and Saudi Arabia 8, 9, 34–5, 36, 37–45, 48–9, 55, 56, 66, 101, 123 (mid-Gulf oil dispute 34–5, 36–8, 42–5); SAVAK 9; and USA 5, 24–5, 25–6, 59 (grant aid 24, 68, 69; Nixon administration 58–9, 67–8, 76–7, 79); and USSR 25–6, 69, 70–1 *see also* Mohammad Reza Shah Pahlavi

Iran-Sharjah Memorandum of Understanding 119
Iranian Pan American Oil Company (IPAC) 34, 42
Iraq 4, 6, 23, 66, 83, 92, 104, 122; armed forces 73; and Iran 7, 30, 70–1, 83–4, 92, 123, 124, 128
Iraq Petroleum 4
Shatt al-Arab 7, 70–1, 83–4, 92, 128
Isfahan 70
Israeli 6, 20, 65, 73, 104
Italy 71

Japan 13, 23, 59, 70
Jask 74
Jeddah 42
Jenkins, Roy 20
Jensen, Eric 48, 52
Jiddah 59
Johnson, President Lyndon B. 18, 21, 22, 26; Johnson administration 13, 17, 18, 23, 42, 69, 73
Jordan 70, 123

Kamil, Hassan 90
Karim Khan Zand 2
Kayhan 27, 84, 111
Kelly, J. B. 111
Kennedy, John F. 61, 69
Khalatbari, Abbas Ali 117
al-Khalifah family of Bahrain 2
al-Khalifah, Shaikh Eisa, Emir of Bahrain 32, 33, 42, 47, 48, 49, 51
al-Khalifah, Mohammed bin Mubarak 23
al-Khalifah, Shaikh Khalifah bin Salman 48, 103
bin Khalifah, Mohammad 80

Kharg island 37, 68, 70, 74, 84
Khorramshahr 75
Khuzistan 3, 8
Kissinger, Henry 60, 61, 62, 63, 64, 65, 66, 67, 70, 122
Kuwait 2, 9, 15, 33, 41, 44, 45, 46, 48, 49, 92, 93, 98, 104, 128; attitude to British withdrawal 103; and federation 30, 35, 109; Iraq's claim to 7, 23; and islands' dispute 120, 122
Kuwait Petroleum 4

Labour Party (Britain) 3, 10, 11, 13, 16, 19, 20, 22, 24, 27, 92, 93, 94, 95, 96, 101, 103, 108, 109, 125, 126
Larak 83
League of Nations 3, 52, 81
Lebanon 123
Lengeh 2, 79, 80
Libya 4, 73, 106, 122, 123, 124
Luce, William 7, 101–2, 103, 108, 112, 113–15, 116, 117, 120, 123, 128

MAAG (American Assistance Advisory Group) 69, 71
al-Maktoum, Shaikh Rashid of Dubai 23, 35, 90, 91, 109
Malaysia 11, 18, 20, 94
Manama 42
Mansfield, Mike 71, 72
Masirah 16
Masoudi, Abbas 50, 54, 98
Maudling, Reginald 95
McGovern, George 72
McNamara, Robert 19, 24, 25
Mecca 9
Mediterranean sea 4, 11, 19
Meyer, Armin 39, 40, 41, 42, 46, 47, 49, 58

Mission For My Country (Mohammad Reza Shah Pahlavi) 66
Morocco 40, 41, 103
Moscow 6
Mossadegh, Mohammad 5
Murphy, Richard 65, 112, 122
Murray, Donald 111
Muscat 1

Nadir Shah 1
An Nahar 120
al-Nahyan, Shaikh Zayid bin Sultan, Shaikh of Abu Dhabi 23, 90, 91, 102, 109
Naser al-Din Shah 80
Nasser, Gamal Abdul 6, 8, 12, 44, 103, 104, 128
National Iranian Oil Company (NIOC) 36, 38, 44
National Security Act 60
Nawaf bin Abdul Aziz, Prince 109
New Delhi 50
New Delhi statement 78
New York 13, 61, 62, 67, 91, 98
New Zealand 94
Nixon, President Richard M.: foreign policy outlook 57–8, 59, 60–3, 76–7; Nixon doctrine 26, 63–5, 65–6, 79, 127; relationship with Shah 58–9, 76, 127
North Atlantic Treaty Organisation (NATO) 11, 12, 19, 65, 67
North Korea 34
Northern Tier 6, 81
An-Nur 92

Occidental (Oxy) oil concession 97–9
Oman 6, 16, 74, 83, 93, 108
'Operation Ajax' 5
Ottomans 2

Pahlavi, Mohammad Reza Shah: and 1953 coup d'etat 5; and arms purchases 24–5, 26, 67–8, 70–1; attitude to Bahrain 39–40, 40–1, 45, 46–8, 49–51, 78, 85; foreign policy outlook and role 7–9, 29, 35, 38, 42, 44–5, 52, 77, 83–5, 87, 91–2, 93, 94, 95, 96, 97, 98, 99–100, 103, 104, 111, 112, 113, 116–17, 119, 120, 121, 123, 126–7; and King Hassan of Morocco 40–1; and OPEC 106–7; relations with Nixon 58–9, 76, 127; US attitude to 25–6, 59, 66–7, 76–7; visits to Saudi Arabia 32–4, 36, 48–9, 55 *see also* Iran
Pahlavi, Reza Shah 3, 81, 103
Pakistan 6, 30, 83
Palestine 4
Pan-American Petroleum Corporation 37
Parsons, Sir Anthony 33, 42, 47
Perpetual Maritime Peace Treaty 2
Persia and the Persian Question (Curzon) 81
Persian Gulf 11
Peygham-e Emruz 112
Pharon, Rashad 33
Portugal 1

Qajar dynasty (Iran) 2
Qasim regime (Iraq) 7, 23
al-Qasimi, Shaikh Khalid bin Mohammed, Ruler of Sharjah 46, 86, 91, 99, 111, 115, 116, 117, 121
al-Qasimi, Shaikh Khalid bin Saqar, Crown Prince of Ras al-Khaimah 46, 108, 115
al-Qasimi, Shaikh Saqar bin Mohammed, Ruler of Ras al-Khaimah 86, 91, 110, 111, 113–15, 120, 123
Qatar 2, 15, 23, 36, 123; and Federation of Arab Emirates 30, 33, 35, 46, 88, 89–90, 91, 108, 109; independence 91, 111, 122
Qawasim 2, 79, 80, 81
Qeshm 1, 81, 83

Rafat, Wahid 89, 90
Ramazani, Rouhollah 123
Ramsbotham, Sir Peter 83, 116, 120
Rasa'i, Admiral Farajullah 71, 121
Ras al-Khaimah 2, 46, 79, 110; and Federation of Arab Emirates 30, 35, 90; and islands' dispute 81, 85, 88, 97, 98, 99, 100, 105, 108, 113–15, 116, 117, 119, 121, 123, 128
Al-Ra'y al-Amm 45
Riyadh 32, 33, 38, 41, 49
Roberts, Goronwy 30; visits to Gulf 19, 21, 26, 31, 39, 46
Rockwell, Stuart 59
Rodman, Senator Peter 66, 71, 72, 76
Rogers, William 62
Romania 25
Roosevelt, Franklin D. 61
Rostow, Walt 39, 61
Rusk, Dean 17, 18, 22, 25, 39, 40, 44, 47, 59

al-Sabah, Shaikh Sabah al-Ahmad 109, 120
Sadat, Anwar 103
Safavid dynasty 1
al-Sanhuri Pasha, Abdulrazaq 46, 89
al-Saqqaf, Omar 41, 102, 103
Saudi Arabia 23, 26, 30, 70, 87, 93, 95, 98, 103, 104, 109, 114, 122, 124, 126, 127, 128; armed forces 73, 77; and Bahrain 32, 33, 55; and Britain 5, 101; and Iran 8, 9, 34–5, 36, 37–45, 48–9, 55, 56, 66, 94, 101, 123; and US 57, 59
Saudi-Iranian Continental Shelf Agreement 37

Saudi-Iranian Maritime Boundary Agreement 37
Saunders, Harold 62, 65
Second World War 3, 4, 68, 70, 81, 125
Shah Abbas (Safavid ruler) 1
Shah Isma'il (Safavid ruler) 1
Sharjah 2, 15; and Federation of Gulf Emirates 30, 35; and Hormuz islands' dispute 80–1, 88, 116–19
Shatt al-Arab 7, 30, 71, 83, 92, 128
Shinwell, Emmanuel 16
Singapore 11, 18, 20, 94
Sirri island 2, 45, 80, 81, 83
Sisco, Joseph 62, 66
Al-Siyasah 41, 46
Sorensen, Theodore 69
South Arabian Federation 14
South Asia 22, 59, 62
South Yemen 123
South-East Asia 64
South-East Asia Treaty Organisation (SEATO) 64, 67
St Moritz 52
Stewart, Michael 15, 16, 87, 88, 94, 97
Strait of Hormuz 1, 40, 74, 78, 83, 84, 119 *see also* Abu Musa, Hormuz islands, Sirri, Tunbs
Suez Canal 20
Suez Canal Company 6
Suez crisis 4–5, 6
Sultan of Muscat 6
Sumaih, Abdullah 80
Sumaih, Hassan 80
Switzerland 48
Syria 8, 41, 122

Taif 44, 45
Taimourtache, Abdolhossein 81

Tehran 44, 45, 70
Teymour, Amir 37, 38
Thailand 64
al-Thani, Shaikh Ahmed, Ruler of Qatar 91, 102
al-Thani, Shaikh Khalifah bin Hamad, Crown Prince of Qatar 46, 88, 90
Guardian 120
Observer 33
Tillman, Seth 72
Toufanian, General Hassan: and Iranian arms purchases 70–1, 84
Treadwell, James 90
Tripp, Peter 87
Trucial Council 30
Trucial Development Office 31
Trucial Oman Scouts 31
Trucial States 30, 33, 35, 36
Truman, Harry 61
Tunb islands: and Bahrain question 85–6, 87; British proposals to Ras al-Khaimah 110–11, 113–15; disputed sovereignty of 9, 78, 40, 45, 78, 79–81, 88, 97, 98, 104, 112, 127; Iranian takeover plans 98, 107–8, 112, 114, 120, 121–4, 128, 129; physical features 81–3; strategic significance 81–4, 116
Turkey, Turks 6, 33

U Thant 50, 52, 53
Umm al-Qaiwain: and Federation of Gulf Arab Emirates 30, 90; dispute with Sharjah 98, 99, 100, 119
UNESCO 36
Union Oil of California 110
United Arab Emirates (UAE) 110, 122 *see also* Federation of Gulf Emirates
United Nations 12, 33, 34, 36, 56, 95, 120,

123, 127; Charter 51, 95; secretary-general and Bahrain 48, 50, 51–4; Security Council 33, 46, 47, 48, 51–4, 60, 123
United States 108, 112; arms sales (to Iran) 68–76, 77; relations with Britain 5–6, 12, 13, 16–19; 22–3; domestic politics 57–8, 61–3; Gulf policy 42, 59, 65–6, 76–7, 91; Nixon doctrine 26, 63–5, 65–6, 79, 127; relations with Iran 5, 24–5, 25–6, 59 (grant aid 24, 68, 69; Nixon administration 58–9, 67–8, 76–7, 79); National Security Advisor 39, 60, 61, 62, 64; National Security Council (NSC) 60, 61, 62, 64, 65, 66, 71; role in Middle East 5–6; USS Pueblo incident 34
USSR 6, 8, 52, 57, 58, 59, 65, 66, 67, 108, 113; and Iran 25–6, 69, 70–1; relations with Iraq 70

Van Dusen, Michael 72
Verrier, Anthony 6
Vietnam 11, 18, 23, 26, 27, 57, 59, 63, 65, 125

Walker, Julian 113, 115, 121, 122
Warnke, Paul 59
Washington 13, 18, 22, 26, 38, 42, 47, 49, 64, 67, 69, 70, 71, 72
Wilson, Harold 11, 12, 14, 16, 17, 18, 19, 20, 21, 22, 94, 125, 126
Winspeare Guicciardi, Vittorio 52–4
Wonckhaus 80
World Health Organisation 36
Wright, Sir Denis 24, 39, 40, 42, 45, 47, 50, 52, 78, 85–6, 87, 93, 95, 96, 97, 98, 99, 100, 107, 110, 111

Yamani, Ahmed Zaki 37, 38, 44–5
Yemen 8, 12, 122
Young, Richard 37

Zagros mountains 70
Zahedi, Ardeshir 33 41, 44, 49, 50, 52, 53, 72, 84, 85, 87, 91, 93, 94, 98, 101, 102, 103, 107, 108, 109, 112
Zand dynasty 2
Zelli, Manuchehr 54